From Ecstasy to Lunch

Samuel Avital

A caravan of visions, dreams, words, poems, situations, reflections, events, exercises, memories, lamentations, consolations and observations

Kol-Emeth Publishers
Boulder, Colorado

Other Books by Samuel Avital

Mime Workbook, 1975

Mimenspiel, German edition of Mime Workbook, 1985

Mime and Beyond: The Silent Outcry, 1985

The Conception Mandala: Creative Techniques for Inviting a Child into Your Life, 1992,
co-authored with Mark Olsen

The Silent Outcry: The Life and Times of Samuel Avital (DVD), 1992

The BodySpeak™ Manual, 2001

The Invisible Stairway: Kabbalistic Meditations on the Hebrew Letters, 2003

Haggadah shel Pessah, 1982, revised 2010

Copyright © 1958–2020 by Samuel Avital
Le Centre du Silence Mime School
Boulder, Colorado

All rights reserved. No part of this publication may be reproduced, distributed, or transmitted in any form or by any means, including photocopying, recording, or other electronic or mechanical methods, without author's express written consent

ISBN: 978-0-9861196-2-0

Cover design by Berger & Föhr

Published by
Kol-Emeth Publishers
Le Centre du Silence Mime School
Boulder, Colorado

www.bodyspeak.com
www.gokabbalahnow.com

DEDICATION

I dedicate this book
IN HOMMAGE AND WITH PROFOUND HONOR to…

All my beloved teachers, visible and invisible,
who took what was offered, and who gave what could not be taken.
The ones who inspire me to realize my sacred "Hidden Obvious"
and to wear the spiritual "impermeable" in any given situation,
in order to keep me sane in the midst of the madness
of "this world."

And especially, to celebrate the 49th Anniversary of
Le Centre du Silence Mime School. The school has sustained for its entire
history without any contribution or grant from any organization or
institution on this planet.

Our support comes only from our students who came from all over the world,
and who taught me how to survive forty-some years of what I term
my "American desert" and My Theatre of Sanity.

Samuel Avital, February 2020

TABLE OF CONTENTS

Dedication..3
Table of Contents..5
Preface..9
Acknowledgments......................................11
"If All Seas Were Ink"................................13
Introduction..15
Definitions of *From Ecstasy to Lunch*.................17
Biography of Samuel Avital.........................19

WORDS FROM FRIENDS 21
1. Samuel Avital, by Zohara Meyerhoff Hieronimus
2. Samuel Has Found a Way to Touch Eternity, by David Passig
3. Samuel Remained Faithful to His Roots, by Shalom Kalfon
4. Shemouel, by Moni Yakim

CHILDHOOD STORIES 31
1. My Story
2. My Grandfather
3. The Letters of Creation
4. In the Marketplace
5. The Dream of King Solomon
6. The Rock of Seven
7. The Sacred Silence
8. Saba Eliahu Ya'Akov Abitbol: Elul and Yamim Nora'im in Sefrou
9. One Night Alone in the House of Prayer
10. This Too Shall Pass
11. The No-Name Lo Shem
12. The Visit of Lo-Shem
13. The Assembly of the Lazy Ones
14. The Anusim (Hidden Jews) of Morocco

STORIES 71
1. A Fish Story
2. The Guest
3. The Gazelle of the Dawn
4. The Fragrance of the Rose
5. The Rabbi and the Alchemist
6. The Mouse and the Word
7. Sandstorm in the Desert
8. The Temple of Crystal
9. The Inner Revolution
10. He Came, He Worked, and Was Gone
11. The Antennae that Glowed
12. Old Man on a Hill
13. My Goat of Mount Sinai
14. The Two Dishes and the Insect
15. Send Your Bread Upon the Waters
16. The Secret of the Hidden Treasure
17. The Beginning Again
18. My Visit to Weimar

POEMS FROM PARIS 1959 – 1964............... 117
1. Goodbye
2. Morning
3. The Face
4. The Lake
5. The Mysterious Silhouette
6. The Place
7. The Room
8. The Wind
9. Why?

POEMS FROM NEW YORK AND BOULDER 135
1. A Breath of Love
2. A Song of Gratefulness
3. A Wave of Sadness
4. Above and Below
5. Ageless Echo
6. Between the Two Worlds
7. Divine One of My Heart
8. Holy Void
9. I Am Peaceful and Calm
10. I Am the Song
11. I Am Where I Am
12. I Live In Times Of…
13. Keep Me Hidden
14. Keep Me Sane in the Midst of Madness

15. Missing the Precious One
16. Morning Dew
17. My Tears Flood the Earth
18. Once Upon a "Time"…
19. Only Five Senses?
20. Sitting On My Rock
21. The Abandoned Temple
22. The Flame of the Heart
23. The High Chamber of Being
24. The Magical Treasure
25. The New Page of One Book
26. The Offering of Now
27. The Presence of the Flame
28. The Silent Tear
29. The Station of Love and Rest
30. The Veil of Silence
31. This Too Shall Pass
32. To The Beloved One
33. The Thee Beloved
34. Tonight I Cannot Sleep
35. Two Is One
36. Waves of Love
37. Welcome
38. While You Can…
39. Within the Silence
40. Words from a Cosmic Lover

ARTICLES AND TEACHINGS 213
1. Many Words, One Truth
2. The Age of Miracles is Now
3. Awareness, Silence, and Art
4. Conscious Innocence
5. The Condor and the Turtle
6. Cosmic Accordion
7. Declaration of Peace
8. Hands, Expressions of the Soul
9. Homage to Marcel Marceau
10. Human, Awake from Your Slumber
11. If I Am Because I Am
12. In the Beginning Was the Dot
13. The Journey from Thought to Action
14. Keep Me Sane in the Midst of Madness
15. Listening
16. Madness and Sanity on Broadway
17. New Artist – Tikkun Maker
18. The Other – Key for Peace!
19. The Puzzle of "The Hidden Obvious"
20. Spiritual Archaeology: Bodyspeak and the Hidden Obvious
21. The Spiritual Ratatouille of the "New Age"
22. Words, Web of Noise

FIFTY GATES TO PRACTICAL WISDOM: CREATIVE LIVING PRINCIPLES
.... 283

PRACTICAL EXERCISES 295
1. First Thought, Last Thought
2. Ten Gates of Wisdom
3. Use Your Time Wisely
4. 28 Daily Practices
5. 11 Principles for Teachers and Students
6. Learning from a Child and a Thief
7. 8 Gates to Become an Authentic Being

REFLECTIONS 311
1. Always the NOW
2. Love the Paradox
3. All Moments are Holy
4. The Silence Within
5. The Director of the Heart
6. Guidance from Within
7. Whispers of the Master Within
8. Guided by the Breath
9. The Great Flame
10. From the Center of Calm
11. In the Center of Silence
12. The Mother Whispers
13. Meeting the Divine Mother
14. The Riches of the Universe
15. Becoming
16. The Gift of Consciousness
17. It Is In Your Hand To Do It
18. The Flame of the Creator
19. One
20. As a Tree
21. The Dance of Being

22. A Circle Without A Center
23. In the Center of the Circle
24. A Vertical Line
25. My Bones Sing
26. Without Name
27. The Spirit of Love
28. Harmonious Will
29. The Fact that I Was Born
30. Friendship
31. Only Peace
32. Light
33. At This Quiet Place and Hour
34. The Song
35. No Heaven, No Earth
36. Beyond Appearances
37. Keep Me Sane in the Midst of Madness
38. With Eyes to See
39. May We Be Delivered
40. The Great Plan
41. You are the Path and the Destination
42. A Being of Light
43. Whisper to My Ear, Oh Beloved
44. I Am Confident About the Future
45. From My Heart

SACRED POEMS AND STORIES 323
1. Gratitude for the Gift of Life
2. Emet Mandala
3. Le Centre Du Silence Mandala
4. Shekhinat-Or
5. Singing Thy Name
6. The Horizon – Aleph
7. The Radiant Letters
8. Thus Saith the Aleph
9. Tree of Life Meditation
10. Waiting for the Messiah
11. The Song of Samuel, Son of Hannah

WHAT ARE THEY SAYING ABOUT SAMUEL AVITAL? 347
1. Marcel Marceau
2. Maximilien Decroux
3. David Passig
4. Melissa Michaels
5. Rav Zalman
6. Moni Yakim
7. Mark Olson

DEFINTUITIONS 351

LAST WORD 363
1. A Letter for These Times
2. Last Word

PREFACE

Because I consider myself a being of silence, spending most days in silence and speaking only when necessary, using words for this book seems almost embarrassing. But realizing that in "this world" we need this lower means of communication, I use the words for one intention only, to communicate that which is beyond words.

The content of this book is mostly words. The words are ones that capture the sense or event of certain moments in my life. These are thoughts and images from my time here, while passing through this world of duality and matter of the body. I find myself grateful for the knowledge given to me in this life by family, friends, teachers, students, and all the remarkable beings I encountered while being in "this world." This allows me to pass through this limited space and time, while understanding and living beyond the limitation of mere words.

Since we agree about communicating with words, at this time I ask you, my dear reader, to try to read beyond the word, the line, the poem, and the story, so that you may find that spiritual source that unites us all in this ephemeral human form, and the numerous ways to share the essential, rather than feeling ping-ponged between the opposites that we perceive in "this world."

Our being here at this time is very important, and I am confident, you will learn "something you did not know before," while traveling through the garden of "my" words and stories and practical wisdom. And if we breath together in unity and oneness, then I call that a good success of real human communication.

Why *From Ecstasy to Lunch*?

From Ecstasy to Lunch was an exercise I taught in my workshops in the 70's as a way to transform and transit from state to state—from sadness to joy, from warrior to coward, from coward to warrior, etc. When you are in a low state of energy, you shift to a higher state of energy. And if you are in a higher state of energy, extremely joyful, you should shift from that ecstasy into action—walking, doing, creating etc. This trains one to master their behavior and respond fully to the different states of consciousness we experience in life.

Mainly, From Ecstasy to Lunch was to shift from state to state, in order to experience *the transitional moment of shifting*. How do we shift effectively, quickly, and consciously from one state to another? This assists one in acting and performance, but also in life…. To shift states and not stay in the rut. So, I decided to call this book **From Ecstasy to Lunch**, because it is a journey—actually many journeys, from country to country, workshop to workshop, heaven to hell, and hell to heaven—all the different places in my journey. A kind of "exile" in "this world."

If you want, you can consider this book a caravan of visions, dreams, words, poems, situations, reflections, events, exercises, memories, lamentations, consolations and observations. It is an exploration of our travels in this life, and of what it means to be here. Most of the time, these experiences slip by us, leaving us unaware of the "mystery of our being." We miss it because it is so obvious, and under our very noses. I call this phenomenon "The Hidden Obvious" (see the article of that name inside the book), and it is a beautiful practical path to BECOME the mystery of being.

Like a performance, in this life journey we go from the state of laughter, to sadness, to wonder, to confusion, to mystery, to joy, etc. This is human condition—From this to that. From that to this. From the clouds to the rain. From winter to summer. From page to page, and every day is a new page in your book of life. So, this life is a constant shifting from that to this, and we are the time and space, passing over from here, constantly renewing itself every present moment.

From a dot* to a form, from the cell to the whole organism.
From complexity to simplicity, from simplicity to complexity.
From hijacked ego to essential self, from binding ego to the true free self,
From a chaotic state of being to the journey of the "the empty space" (חלל פנוי)

And so therefore, from your ecstasy to your lunch. Enjoy!

- Samuel
* See the article "In The Beginning was a dot…"

ACKNOWLEDGMENTS

Over the years, I accumulated many stories, poems and articles I had written, as I traveled to various places in the world and encountered different life experiences.

What triggered this book to see the light was when Neshama Bat-Li-Or (Alessandra Lior) gave me two volumes she printed with a collection of my poems, as a gift for my birthday in 2002. For some time, I wanted to publish that collection, and to call it *From Ecstasy To Lunch*. Over this last twenty years, more stories and other poems were added to make the collection complete. I thank you Neshama, for that gift, and your dedication of studying and being with me all these years.

For my friends and family that assisted and helped bring *From Ecstasy to Lunch* to light with their generous contributions, both spiritual and material, thank you for your contribution in bringing this book about.

May all these beautiful beings be blessed, and may all their families and friends be at peace with each other, may they cooperate toward that great state of **"being good and acting good,"** and may they find calm and serenity in the midst of activities in our perplexed times.

May the triple blessing from the Torah be with them always in prosperity and development of their spiritual lives both in **"This world"** and **"That World."**

I would like also to thank Devorah Henderson for her dedication and personal urgency for editing and revising these writings to be ready to publish at this time.

Samuel Avital

"IF ALL SEAS WERE INK"
In memory of my mother Hannah Robidah Zekri-Elbaz, Z"L.

When I was young, living in my mother's house, she used to tell me with great affection at certain times, "**If all the oceans of the world became ink and all the trees became pens, and the heaven and the earth became scrolls, I still could not describe the way I love you. Nothing will be sufficient to express my love to you.**"

That unique way of a mother expressing love to her child impressed and impacted my life concerning the power of genuine love. And since then, I cannot limit the power of love to a word only, but rather I feel that I must live it and express it infinitely, beyond the ability to describe.

I never forgot that expression and the good influence of my mother's love = Ahava—אַהֲבָה. I found her words so poetic and inspiring, and never knew the source of them, until one beautiful day in my deep study, remembering that unique sense of my mother's love, I read the following quote from Shir Hashirim Rabba, and from the Akdamot Poem we read during the Shavuot holiday.

> Rabbi Eliezer (Ben-Hurkanos) said:
> If all seas were ink, all reeds pens,
> and heaven and earth scrolls, and all men scribes,
> they would not suffice to write the Torah that I have learned,
> even though I abstracted from it no more
> than a man would take a dipping of his painting stick into the sea.
> Song of Songs Rabba 1: 3. #1.

רַבִּי אֱלִיעֶזֶר (בֶּן-הוֹרְקָנוֹס) אוֹמֵר: אִם יִהְיוּ כָּל-הַיַּמִּים דְּיוֹ וַאֲגַמִּים קַלְמוֹסִין,

וְשָׁמַיִם וָאָרֶץ מְגִלּוֹת, וְכָל בְּנֵי הָאָדָם לַבְלָרִין, אֵין מַסְפִּיקִין לִכְתֹּב דִּבְרֵי תּוֹרָה

שֶׁלָּמַדְתִּי, וְלֹא חִסַּרְתִּיהָ אֶלָּא כְּאָדָם שֶׁמַּטְבִּיל זְכָרוֹת שֶׁל מִכְחוֹל בַּיָּם.

שיר השירים רבא א. נ. א.

I was transfixed and filled with an immense sense of love for all mothers. My mother was profoundly connected to her spiritual essence. She descended from an illustrious lineage of great spiritual leaders, some 22 generations of Rabbis, Judges, Poets, Kabbalists, and Torah and Talmudic scholars, who contributed greatly to the community of Sefrou, Morocco, where I was born.

And today I say:
"If all the oceans of the world become ink and all the trees become pens and the heaven and the earth become scrolls," I cannot utter the profound wonder why most all nations on this earth are again rising to destroy the beauty of "ISRAEL" and its history and culture. No words, no thoughts, nothing, I repeat, nothing will be sufficient to express <u>my deep sadness, mixed with intense joy</u>, at the great world events, and the importance of the transition and great shift toward a new essential way of thinking, conscious and aware of the miraculous gift of life. The world looks to the time where every human being will cross that "magical threshold" to finally realize that there is <u>ONLY ONE ONENESS</u> in all creation and that the <u>CREATOR IS ONE and NOT TWO</u>. When humans realize that this is present everywhere in the stillness and the silence of every present moment of "this life," then at that time, death and disease shall be banished from the life of humans, in the new civilization to come.

April 15, 2003.
Boulder, Colorado

My Mother Hannah Robida Azekri Z"L

INTRODUCTION

Before I begin this attempt to say a few words about "myself" and my journeys in "this world," I would like to share with you why I decided at this time to publish my writing collection, entitled *From Ecstasy to Lunch*. We live in very interesting times now, when the voice of sanity needs to be heard on all fronts.

The first purpose of this publication is to share some highlights in my life journey, and also to celebrate the 49th anniversary of Le Centre du Silence Mime School, which I founded in 1971 in Boulder, Colorado, USA.

The second purpose is to give a small glimpse into the answer to a question that I was once asked by my students. The question was, "What makes human beings the way they are?"

The question is: What are the events in a person's life that shape their character? And how do we detect the mystery of our being and destiny? Ultimately, why are we the way we are? To this, I would add another very important question: How can we be a constant question mark, and maintain continual awareness and presence, to always be conscious of the process of becoming the answer?"

As I understand this now, I think that the events of one's life, the conscious and unconscious thoughts one carries, and one's inner environment—all of this guides our way of behavior and being. These truly do count in the long run. It matters how we use ourselves, and our creativity. And I think that, above all, one must come to accept oneself the way one is, and to "learn to swim in the ocean of life." One must learn how to learn by practicing honesty, the presence of the "inner peace," and daring to do and be what your inner true voice suggests to you to do right in this sacred present moment.

When read in a certain way, through these writings one can connect the threads of events, feelings, intentions and visions that allow me to be in this world of "La grande illusion," but not of it. The book is meant simply to be a glimpse or attempt in self-understanding, self-realization, and how to become nothing.

I hope that when you read these words, they will inspire you and maybe you will learn one or two things that can help you to make the switch from illusion to reality and from darkness to light. And I also hope that this will trigger that awakening, becoming conscious realized beings from the human slumber of "this passing life here."

So, let's begin our journey, now.

I repeat this again:
This book is dedicated in homage and with profound honor to all my beloved teachers, men and women on all planes of existence, who took what was offered, and who gave what could not be taken.

Samuel Avital,
Monday, February 10, 2020

DEFINITIONS of *From Ecstasy to Lunch*

From Ecstasy to Lunch: Trains the student in how to overcome extremes in one's states and emotions, in a theatrical situation, or in any life situation or event. Shifting from "**this**" to "**that**" in a conscious response, with balance and awareness.

From Ecstasy to Lunch: The power to SHIFT your attention from this to that, from thought to action, from this action to the next, while always being present. This makes you more mentally and physically agile. It becomes natural to shift easily from here to there, without awkwardness or accidents, when you learn to remain focused from moment to moment.

From Ecstasy to Lunch: The ability to return to the Artistic Zero (the neutral centered state) from any state at any moment.

BIOGRAPHY OF SAMUEL BEN-OR AVITAL

*"He teaches a Kabbalistic Tai-Chi in which God and Man
are fused in MIME."*
Reb Zalman Schachter-Shalomi, Boulder, Colorado

Samuel Ben-Or Avital was born in the small village of **Sefrou**, near **Fez**, in the Atlas Mountains of Morocco. He was educated in the home of a simple and remarkable family, which traces its lineage to **15th Century Spain** and before. This line carried with them, from father to son, in the **Sephardic tradition,** the ancient, beautiful and practical wisdom of the Hebrew Science of the **Kabbalah**.

At a young age, Samuel embarked on the first of many adventurous journeys, which led him to Israel and later to Paris, France, Europe and Scandinavia, and then to the United States. During his travels from East to West, Samuel encountered and explored different schools of knowledge, including Alchemical and Sufi traditions, which he absorbed, and later synthesized into his own organic and Cosmic Kabbalistic learning.

Over the years, he accumulated the knowledge of a few languages, which assisted him in living in the Western world. At the age of 14, Samuel traveled to Israel where he lived in a kibbutz and in Jerusalem, studying physics, agronomy, theology, arts and theatre.

His innate interest in the arts eventually drew him to Paris, where he studied dance and theatre at the Sorbonne. There, he discovered the world of mime in the teachings of the masters, Etienne Decroux and Marcel Marceau. Having met his art form, Avital threw himself into what he found to be the very essence of human expression. Decroux, Marcel Marceau, and others were all to have a profound influence on the formation of his own artistic expression. He soon began touring with the Mime Company of Maximilien Decroux and performing his own solo performances in Paris, France.

In 1964, Samuel joined his friend Moni Yakim in New York, performing with him in his Pantomime Theatre of New York and also in the off off-Broadway theatres, as well as teaching mime in the New York City schools. He has performed in many countries and shared his knowledge with all who have orbited in his vicinity. He has toured in North and South America, and Canada, and in 1969, he was invited to teach Mime and Movement Theatre as an Artist-in-Residence at SMU, Dallas, Texas.

In 1971, he established **Le Centre du Silence Mime School** in Boulder, Colorado. The following year, he created the **Boulder Mime Theatre** with his most dedicated students. The **BMT** performed during the next thirteen years in local, state and national engagements.

In 1974, Avital initiated the International Summer Mime Workspace, an annual intensive course attracting students worldwide. The same year, he published his *MIME WORKBOOK* followed by a second edition in 1977, a third printing in 1982, and *MIMENSPIEL* a German edition out of Frankfurt. Hohm Press in Prescott, Arizona, published his second book, *MIME & BEYOND: The Silent Outcry*, in **1985**. Inner Traditions, Rochester, VT, published *The Conception Mandala* by Samuel Avital and Mark Olsen. His video, *The Silent Outcry: The Life and Times of Samuel Avital*, was produced in **1992**. In 1985 Samuel was nominated for the Colorado Governor's Award for Excellence in the Arts.

His book, *The BodySpeak™ Manual*, was published in August 2001 by Author House. The recently revised and republished version is available now on Amazon.

Samuel's book *THE INVISIBLE STAIRWAY: Kabbalistic Meditations on the Hebrew Letters*, was privately published in 1982 in Hebrew and English, for possible limited distribution for close students and friends, and is now available in an English-only version on Amazon.

Over the years, Samuel developed his unique method of teaching, called *BodySpeak™ Moving Body and Mind.* He has also contributed numerous articles, interviews and essays in several languages to diverse publications throughout the U.S. and abroad. Currently, Avital lives in Boulder, Colorado, where he continues his artistic activities, and offers seminars, workshops and public talks on the sacred knowledge of Kabbalah.

Samuel Avital, at a Workshop Intro

WORDS FROM FRIENDS

Samuel Avital
by Zohara Meyerhoff Hieronimus

Samuel Has Found a Way to Touch Eternity
by David Passig

Samuel Remained Faithful to His Roots
by Shalom Kalfon

Shemouel
by Moni Yakim

Samuel Avital

SAMUEL AVITAL
by Zohara Meyeroff Hieronimus

Samuel Avital is a truly wise man. Combining his lifetime of practice as a Mime performer and teacher, and as a true and devoted lover of Torah, his offerings are like the holy dew of creation. Whether parable, wisdom teaching, or personal story, Avital's insights spark each person's mind and soul, in finding truth in their own lives and in the world around us.

Few are the truly enlightened who can combine wisdom, understanding and knowledge to reveal truth and beauty. Avital does just this, using words especially chosen for their task of showering gems of meaning for the reader.

As each person who has the privilege of coming into rapport with Samuel or his writings discovers: His love of life, good humor and impeccable talent of observation, whisper like the spirit into the heart and soul of every sincere seeker.

J. Zohara Meyerhoff Hieronimus DHL
Author of Kabbalistic Teachings of the Female Prophets (2008) and
Sanctuary of the Divine Presence (2012)

SAMUEL HAS FOUND AN ORIGINAL WAY TO DEEPLY TOUCH ETERNITY...
by Dr. David Passig

There are images in the life of a man that accompany him all his life. That is the image of Samuel for me. Samuel is the grandson, and I am the great great-grandson, of a great being that was the center of our lives—**Rabbi Eliahu Ya'akov Abitbol,** peace be with him. Among all my extended family, Samuel was the connecting link that was between me, my father and **my grandmother, Rachel,** peace be with her. (My grandmother Rachel is the sister of Samuel's father **R. Moshe Amram Abitbol,** may peace be with them).

I knew Samuel when I was in my early teens. Our paths met the first time when I immigrated to Israel and he came to visit us. The profound connection that was created then cannot be expressed with words. Today, it is a little clearer for me, the echoes that connect us.

Both of us drank from the same channels of great ancestors whose learning was their art of being. Although they traded in commerce to make a living, their heritage and tradition was invested within our souls, as great human beings with great faith and connection with the source of life. Of these was a man who was the father of my grandmother, the great sage **Eliahu Abitbol**. To my chagrin I did not know him, but I was privileged to know him through knowing Samuel.

Samuel is the one who followed the ways of our grandfather with his unique style of living and being. Samuel has found an authentic way to express Kabbalistic and cosmic ideas with the medium of the human body. With the soul's means, he has pierced many ways to the great wisdom.

He developed new ways to learn and teach the divine wisdom with an artistic style, and with a rich language that is close to every human heart at the close of the twentieth century and the new twenty-first century. Samuel has found an original way to deeply touch the eternity of our physical and spiritual existence in these times.

As a futurist in the beginning of the twenty-first century, I find myself trying to touch the same ideas and eternal visions, but through futuristic research. Samuel taught me that one must find unique ways to touch the eternity with our being. He transmitted to me the message from our ancestors, to not be afraid to express our uniqueness, even with the price of being ridiculed by people without expanded vision.

I am certain that our dear grandfather did the same in his time. We are confident that we will succeed in passing this message on to our offspring. Samuel's life work contribution will always stand within us as a flame of light and be for us all a good omen, a shining example, and a practical miracle within us.

Natanyah, Israel, January 2002. Tevet - 5762

Dr. David Passig is a futurist by vocation. He is a member of the staff of the University of Bar-Ilan in Israel. He is the author of the books "The FutureCode: Israel's Future Test" and "2048". He teaches in the Graduate Department of Communication Technologies, and is dedicated to futuristic research of the future human societies, developing new ways to envision various and possible futures. He heads the laboratory of Virtual Reality in the Bar-Ilan University and researches cognitive development with new advanced technologies.

SAMUEL REMAINED FAITHFUL TO HIS ROOTS
by Shalom Kalfon

About Shmuel we can say that he lives the verse 2:4 from the prophet Habakuk, "**The righteous shall live by his faith**" — "**וצדיק באמונתו יחיה**".

His faith in Hebrew is (אמונתו) **EIMUNATO** and his art is (אומנותו) **UMANUTO**. It's a play on words that fits his personality so well. Shmuel lives his faith as he lives his art, originality and faithfulness. His faith includes all the gamut of the Jewish Civilization in its colors and richness. His art includes all facets of art with emphasis on mime.

I have known him since childhood in Sefrou, Morocco, where we grew up together, and afterwards in Jerusalem where he started his interest in theatre and appeared with different groups. Shmuel was always gifted with great talent, seriousness and originality. I met him again in Paris, where he followed his vocation steadfastly by studying the art of mime with the great masters of his field.

I met him again in New York, where he was struggling to forge his personal style in his art. What distinguished him from other artists I know is his faithfulness to our heritage, to his roots. While advancing and progressing in his art, he also followed and deepened his studies in Judaism. He published essays in kabbalah in a very distinguished and refined literary Hebrew. His essays were published in the Hebrew weekly (הדואר) "Hadoar," edited and published in New York.

I had the privilege to be present in the opening class in Boulder, Colorado (USA), of one of his international seminars that he conducts yearly. On this occasion, I was surprised to listen to him reciting in Hebrew with such serenity (אלוהי נשמה) "Elohai Neshama" from our daily prayer book. We recite this prayer every morning, to thank The Creator of The Universe for his gift to us, the gift of our pure soul. In this prayer, we express our nothingness and our humility in the face of our short life in this vast universe. It expresses our faith and optimism in the worth of life itself….

Shmuel recited this prayer with such spiritual intensity that all his students, myself among them, were mesmerized, even though they did not understand Hebrew. They were captivated by the spiritual radiance that emanated from each and every word that he articulated, slowly, with his eyes closed.

Shmuel lives his art and his Jewishness with grace and pride. He kept his spiritual and cultural heritage and remained faithful to his roots. This is reflected in his many books, which are a spiritual inspiration to all his many readers, disciples and admirers.

In his books one will find his wisdom and his outlook on life. His theories enclose the richness and the wisdom from both civilizations in which he is so well rooted. His views are expressed with literary talent and with a deep knowledge of the philosophy of consciousness. He touches upon the problems of our confused and perplexed generation.

To know Shmuel and talk to him, one will learn about the richness of his life experiences and his achievements through consistency and suffering, without compromising his integrity as a Jew and as an artist. Throughout his life he remained a faithful friend and a genial and uniquely original human being.

Vancouver, B.C. Canada
Monday, Dec 16, 2002
יום שני י"א טבת, תשס"ג

Shalom Kalfon is a native of Sefrou, Morocco. He immigrated to Israel illegally at the time of British rule. He was a soldier in Israel's war of independence, lived in a Kibbutz, studied philosophy, literature & political science. An author & educator, he has served as a Rabbi and taught Hebrew at the University of Victoria.

He was VP of the Zionist Organization of Canada and VP of its charitable fund. He has served as a member of the Board of Governors of the Conservatory of Music and as a member of the Executive of the Canadian Zionist Federation and the United Jewish Appeal of Canada. He has published various books and essays in Hebrew, French and English. He is married to Rebecca and father to Edna, Itay and Vardit, and currently lives in Israel.

SHEMOUEL
by Moni Yakim (1975)

Occasionally, he comes out of his world of solitude, only to communicate and give the best of what he found within the depths of his soul. I was fortunate to meet Shemouel on such an occasion.

Restless, uneducated, undisciplined, stifling with boredom in a town where most people lay in their beds at 9:00 P.M., I was an outstanding member of a teen gang.

Bursting with the energy of youth, of frustration, angry, we roamed the streets, creating commotion, playing tricks that often led to minor crimes. This was my Jerusalem of 1951.

One evening, determined to take a good look at the sexy pieces in leotards, we set out to the youth center where a dance class took place. It was a disappointment. There were only two girls in the class, and they were dogs. With some not so refined gestures and sounds, we started out. I was suddenly encountered by the biggest pair of eyes I have ever seen, staring at me disapprovingly. My immediate instinct was to punch the bastard little man right between his cow eyes. But then he smiled, and that was the turning point in my life.

It was a ritual. Every Friday afternoon he came to my house. After gloating on my mother's cooking, comprising mainly of rice and bean soup, we went to his "house." It was a tiny little room with a small bed, a chair and a little desk. The walls were covered with drawings of Shemouel, for at that time he was also a student of painting.

This was the room in which I learned that there are things other than beating and stealing and that one can actually get his kicks just by sitting with Shemouel, listening to his words, daydreaming. He spoke of things foreign to me and gently, gradually, they became familiar: Paris, art, culture, mime. Mime above all. Mime was the dome under which the world was awaiting its discovery, and we would be the ones to discover it.

Enchantment, mystery, flight on the wings of strange and lofty ideas. Sensing creation, touching the Gods. This was the first chapel I had ever been in.

Consequently, I devoted more time preparing myself for the theatre and roamed the streets less. I joined classes in acting and dance and eventually we both took part in the founding of a theatre in Jerusalem.

Paris and Shemouel had to wait patiently until the completion of my long and miserable military service. Finally, the long-awaited day arrived and we took the first step towards the realization of our dreams.

We were in Paris, studying with Etienne Decroux, the creator of modern Mime and with Marcel Marceau, the greatest mime performer in the world

These were beautiful times. These were hard and trying days.

Living in a tiny room, at an old lady's apartment, our diet consisting exclusively of one can of sardines and one baguette per day — we were studying and living with mime, and we were elated. We practiced on the table, which was the largest available area in the room. It was our "stage." We took turns practicing on it.

There were discussions, there were arguments. Concepts began to form, ideas, opinions. We were together, yet we were alone. Shemouel needed his solitude. It was a means of survival to him. One thing was never in question — our love for Mime. We gave ourselves to it entirely. Years passed by.

We came to a cross-road and followed different paths. I toured Europe with Grillon's Mime Theatre (she was a long-time pupil of Decroux's) and Shemouel joined Maximilien's Decroux Mime Company.

Meanwhile, our dear Master, Etienne Decroux, was preparing to leave for New York, to open a Mime school there. I followed his steps about a year later to join his school and newly formed Mime company. Shemouel stayed in Paris with Maximilien's company.

A few years later, Decroux decided to return to France and I decided to open my own school and Mime company. I urged Shemouel to come and join us, which he did.

But this reunion was different from our partnership in the past. He joined the company yet he was elsewhere. He had developed his own ideas and philosophies, which I admired but which were very different from my own. Shemouel needed his solitude to make his plans, to structure his thoughts. He needed his own flock.

Shemouel is in Boulder, Colorado now, leading his Unique Mime Workspace, and I am in New York, leading my own Mime workshop and school. However, we are together. Shemouel of 1951, for the better or the worse, is what I am today.

If you seek some truth of direction in life or art, stay close to Shemouel for he might just then crawl out of his shell and give you of his soul.

Moni Yakim. Drama Faculty, Juilliard School. Author of the book *Creating a Character: A Physical Approach to Acting*. New York, February 1975.

CHILDHOOD STORIES

My Story

My Grandfather

The Letters of Creation

In the Marketplace

The Dream of King Solomon

The Rock of Seven

The Sacred Silence

Saba Eliahu Ya'Akov Abitbol: Elul and Yamim Nora'im in Sefrou

One Night Alone in the House of Prayer

This Too Shall Pass

The No-Name Lo Shem

The Visit of Lo-Shem

The Assembly of the Lazy Ones

The Anusim (Hidden Jews) of Morocco

MY STORY

My name is Samuel Ben-Or Avital. I was born on the 23rd of the Month of Teveth in the year of 5,692 in the Hebrew calendar (Jan 2, 1932), in a beautiful village in the Atlas Mountains in Morocco called Sefrou.

I grew up in a simple, remarkable and modest family called Abitbol, which traces its lineage to **15th Century Spain** and before, carrying from father to son, in an unbroken line, the ancient, beautiful and practical wisdom of the sacred knowledge of the **Kabbalah.** I was educated by my father and grandfather in this deep knowledge of the Kabbalah, as taught in the Sephardic tradition.

The years of my childhood were full of learning. This was during the Second World War, and as a child, I was sheltered from the news of the war by my parents. All I remember from those early times was that at night the electric bulbs were covered with towels, so the light would not be visible from the windows. I was unaware of the world situation then, but I still sensed the gravity of the years in various ways.

My childhood focus was on learning Torah in the school called "Em-Habbanim," which means "the mother of the children." My Grandmother, Rebecca Abitbol, worked with her women friends to raise money and also contributed her own resources to build the school. They wished that their grandchildren and all the children of Sefrou would learn the ways of the Torah and become wise.

I grew up with the Hebrew Language that I have come to love very much over the years. I am amazed by the beautiful and sacred letters, which are considered the blueprint of Creation. They contain within them the root, secrets and tools to all knowledge in the universe.

Also, with Hebrew I can express myself exactly and precisely, not only personally, but also with regard to concepts that may seem beyond my own comprehension. It provides the ability to understand the "mystery" of nature and reality beyond my small and limited three-dimensional way of being. I consider the Hebrew language not only a very valuable and esteemed treasure, but the source of great and profound inspiration in my life. It is a great tool expressing how to live a balanced and sane life, oriented for the benefit of all beings.

As I remember my childhood, I was busy learning and growing up in an extended and blessed family. I had the privilege to know most of the many members of my family, and my curiosity to learn was as natural as breathing. Mostly, I spoke less, and loved the inner silence of innocent childhood contemplation.

There is one story I remember very well which was told to me by my Grandfather, Eliyahu Ya'akov Abitbol, blessed be his memory, and which I know has shaped many aspects of my life. I call it **WORD ECONOMY.**

He told me that when we are born, we are given a certain number of words in our "**word bank**" to use in our lifetime. If one uses too many words, it is like overspending on wants instead of needs. When this is done, it empties our word bank account. The account becomes overdrawn and later we find that we have become mute, because we overused our word reservoir.

So, **when we use words properly and only when necessary, we practice word economy, and that is the real wealth.** Words, as we know, are only one of the ways to communicate. 99% of our real communication occurs in silence, stillness, and mostly through our body language. I highly recommend to practice **one day of silence a week** to achieve the ability to **speak less and do more** and **produce more and consume less** — practicing consistently and consciously this practical wisdom of **"Word Economy."**

In the practical and moderate religious life I grew up in, I found great comfort in discovering the many details about my family and about what it meant to be Jewish in Morocco. Every childhood discovery brought me a great sense of joy and happiness that I kept within myself without sharing it with anyone.

Although I was not told outright the situation of the world at that time, the intuitive childhood sense helped me to feel the gravity of the Jewish people in Europe. I was able to understand this through some of the practices I observed around me.

For instance, most of the children in Moroccan Jewish schools at that time, wore a black uniform with red threads or ribbons surrounding the edges. That uniform was, for me and many of my classmates, a sign of solidarity and mourning.

Although little was revealed to us, you cannot hide too much from intuitive Jewish children. We knew through various rumors, which we shared between ourselves, that we were living through another terrible time in our history. By our sheer existence, we were mourning our Jewish brothers and sisters who were burning in Germany at that very moment.

Without knowing the details of the war, our total dedication was to learning our beautiful Jewish tradition and to keeping the eternal and sacred flame shining and living within our little yearning hearts. And that will be the defiant spiritual answer to those who want to exterminate us throughout history.

As an innocent child, I was sure within my heart that since the enemies of Yisrael had not, in all of history, succeeded in wiping us from the face of the planet, that they would not succeed now. We, the Moroccan Jewish children, were the living spiritual answer. We answered by knowing who we were, by becoming the living flame of Yisrael with pride and joy of being, and by keeping the sacred covenant between our creator and ourselves throughout the history of our existence.

The Jewish communities in Morocco had inhabited North Africa since the times of King Solomon. For close to 3,000 years, the yearning of these communities was to return to the land of our ancestors. This was deeply written and carved in the everyday way of life.

The idea of waiting for the Mashiah was a daily prayer. The communities also kept a strong link to those still living in the holy land. They supported those Moghrabim (those from the West) who continued to keep a strong presence there over many years, ever since the destruction of the Second Temple, and the beginning of the tragic and dark exile in the lands of Yishmael. They waited for the deliverance and the end of the exile, which we call the GE'ULLA.

Suddenly, after the war, that ancient yearning was awakened like a dormant eagle of the holy Chariot (Merkaba), that suddenly spread its wings and rose to the sky. There was a great movement with the Jewish communities in Morocco, who sensed profoundly that this was the time to ascend to Israel. Many teenagers like myself began underground preparations for their journey to Israel.

However, in this area, moving between one city and another required a permit from the local authorities. Many disregarded that restriction. They began to move illegally toward Algiers, in order to gather there and take ships to Marseilles, France, and then to Israel.

Silently and discreetly, I also planned to smuggle myself and attempt my journey in spite of all the difficulties. One morning after awakening early, my father came as usual to take me with him to the Synagogue for the morning prayers. That day, I said to him, "I will come a little later." It was early in the morning. I took my little suitcase that had I prepared in secret well beforehand, and slipped out from my house to the bus station, which was just outside the walls of the village.

I took the bus to Fez and went to see some of my relatives who lived there to ask for more information how to proceed onward. At the time, I was not quite fifteen years old. But a few hours after I arrived, who entered the house, but my mother Hannah. She told me, "No, I am taking you back with me to Sefrou." That was the end of my first great adventure to ascend to the Land of Yisrael and end the exile of almost two thousand years.

Back to Sefrou. This time, I learned to be more discreet in my preparations. I began planning my next attempt in a more effective way in order to find a route to Algiers without my dear mother coming after me again.

This time I succeeded, but with a blessed surprise. As I was settling into my bus seat near the window, I looked through the big arched gate of the entrance to Sefrou, and here was my grandfather, walking with his cane, slowly approaching the bus. When he got closer, I opened the window and he smiled, blessed me, and gave me few gold and silver coins. He said to give these to the Tzedakah (charity) when I arrived in Jerusalem. My eyes were so wet and smiling, grateful to receive his blessings. I still wonder today how he knew about my secret plan to leave for Israel.

At that time, I was oblivious of many of the dangers of my long journey alone. But in spite of the dangers that might lay ahead, I felt within my heart a certainty that my journey would be bring me no harm and that I would be guided safely and protected until I arrived in Israel.

Arriving in Fez on the bus, I set out to find my way. I would take another bus to a city called Taza, and another bus to Oujda. Before taking the Oujda bus, I went to the market and bought an Arabic headdress, sunglasses, and an Arabic newspaper. I disguised myself so I could pass through without attracting any attention from the border police.

When I got on the Oujda bus, I was dressed in a white Jellabiya and the type of red hat known as a Fez. I noticed a few Jewish teenagers on the bus, and I knew that they were attempting the same thing I was, the sacred journey to our Holy land of Yisrael.

In the front of the bus, I noticed a few elderly people wearing the same traditional Jewish dress. They also noticed me, with a mysterious smile, as if they knew my game.

I remember being very nervous and scared, and constantly uttering and whispering the prayers I knew for good guidance to succeed in my journey. I knew I did not have any identity papers, and also that many teenagers like me had been caught and had disappeared into oblivion.

With this knowledge and the certainty of the prayer of my Grandfather, I just enjoyed the ride quietly without expecting any problems. But after a few kilometers, I saw the border check-point from afar. The French gendarmes began checking the bus and the people. I leaned back against the window holding up my Arabic newspaper, emphasizing my cover in order to remain invisible to the eyes of the policemen. I saw between the cracks of my newspaper that the Jewish teenagers had been taken out of the bus. My heart was beating so fast, I thought I was going to die. But at that exact moment, I heard the bus door slam shut, and the bus began to move toward Oujda.

After a short while, I finally put the newspaper down from in front of my face and realized I had been holding it upside down the whole time. I experienced a strange feeling of embarrassment. The elderly Jewish beings in the front of the bus smiled and waved with their discreet happy hands, signaling their joy that the policemen had not noticed me, and that I was safe, for now.

At that moment, I became very conscious that actually I did not have any identity papers at all. This was a frightening thought I carried with me until I arrived in Israel, where finally I received the ID of a new immigrant.

My heart was still beating with great thanks to my God-Protector who let me pass beneath the blind eyes of the policemen. Uttering my well-known prayers, I returned my discreet smile to the beautiful beings in the front of the bus.

Arriving in Oujda, the elderly Jewish beings guided me to meet the organizer at a synagogue. Here, they would prepare us to cross the border the next night. In the Synagogue there were many travelers there, both young and old. I sat down to rest from my frightening adventure, with my heart full with gratitude that I was still alive.

That night, after we were given a meal to eat, the guide who would take us across the border to Algiers gave us instructions. We would cross the border before dawn, journeying to the other side of the mountain. Then we would take the train to Algiers with another guide. I slept, imagining what would be coming next.

Before dawn, the guide came and took a group of about 15 of us, all teenagers like me. Out we went to cross the border to the other side of the mountain. He urged us not to make a sound and we began our ascent while it was still night. There were huge search-lights sweeping our path. We would lay down whenever they passed, until we succeeded to pass through. On the other side, another guide immediately took us, running away from the border. Now we were on Algerian soil. They drove us from there to the train station where we took the ride to the white City of Algiers.

In Algiers, we were placed in a tall multi-story house called Bab-el-wad, which means "the gate of the river." People were sleeping in the stairs. It was very crowded and not very clean. Elderly people, women, children, young people from all over Morocco who, like me, had succeeded to smuggle themselves, were piled like sardines, waiting to be called to take the next ship to Marseille, France.

I will not elaborate on this part of the story. Suffice to say that after some experiences in which I managed to stay alive, one day I was called to take the evening ship to Marseille. I counted the seconds and the hours and even forgot to eat because of that deep yearning to finally advance in my journey to the Land of my Ancestors, Israel.

Around midnight that night, the organizer assembled us downstairs and we took a few buses toward the port of Algiers. Like thieves, we were boarded on that old ship called Modika. I remember the name very well, because of the miraculous events I was to experience during that voyage to Marseille, France.

Remember, I had never seen the ocean in my life, let alone sailed on it in a ship. That was a first experience for me, and the verses of Psalm 104, which are most beloved for me, began to roll and dance strongly within my heart.

With all the meager belongings I had in a small suitcase, I stood aboard that ship and looked out at the great miracle called the ocean. That night was dark. I stood there, sensing the creation's beauty, feeling a strong sense of history running in my veins. In the background were the voices of passengers, children crying, mothers nursing their babies, all the sounds in the ship. That environment and the fresh night air mixed harmoniously with the balanced and awesome verses about the great ocean.

As I leaned on the deck, looking at the immensity of the sea, feeling the swelling and swaying of the ship, up and down and sideways, I sensed all this as the dance of my journey. I liked that movement of the ship, like a baby swaying in a crib.

That swaying continued for some time, the small night-time dance of the ship in the ocean. The motion was very hypnotizing and repetitive, helping me to organize my thoughts and contemplate once more about some essential questions of life. Who am I? Where am I going? What is the purpose and meaning of life? Why did I leave my family in Morocco? What is going on in this world?

As my eyes gently observed the movements of the water and the swaying of the ship, the ship's movements suddenly intensified. It rocked strongly right and left. As quickly as I opened my eyes, I was thrown to the other side of the deck, and I heard screams from the people who were still out enjoying the night. I ran to help some of them downstairs from the deck, where they could stay safely until the storm passed. I returned to the deck and strongly gripping the bar along the edge of the ship, I remembered the story of Yonah. I had a small book of the Psalms that my Grandfather had given me. I lifted up that little book in my hand. Pleading that the storm would end, I threw the book into the waters and continued to recite Psalm 104. After a few minutes, calm arrived and the ship steadied. I was very wet but happy.

I raised my voice and shouted my thanks to my Creator and noticed some elderly beings smiling from behind some stairs not far from where I was. Their faces were glowing and happy. I thought perhaps they were waiting to go downstairs after the storm. I stayed the rest of night, as if on guard, until the shining and beautiful colors of the dawn blessed the sky.

As the sun rose in its splendor, I saw people coming up to the deck. I looked for the three glowing elders of last night, and did not find them among the passengers. I tried looking for them again during the day. They were not there. Who were they? That remained a "mystery" for me to later discover.

After a few days of sailing quietly, we arrived at the city of Marseille, France, and we were taken to Camp David near the Camp d'Arenas. Many immigrants from Morocco were living there, waiting to take the journey to Israel.

I was placed among other young people in the small wooden houses at the camp, waiting for my turn to return to our homeland. Meanwhile they organized us, and gave us work to do, working in the kitchen and helping the elderly.

Finally, enough preparations had been made to go to Israel. I was chosen with other teenagers to join a group that would take the ship the very next day to Haifa, Israel. That night I could not sleep. That was a historic moment; I thought I was returning to the root of my ancestors after two thousand years in exile. I felt that in that moment I represented all the people of Israel yearning for so many years to return. Ascending to Israel is a great privilege, which even our great Teacher and Prophet, Moshe, was not given. He was permitted only to look, not to enter. And here I was, a child of the children of Israel, and I would be allowed to enter the land of my ancestors.

I did not sleep. I was living the destiny of my people, vividly feeling the suffering of the oppressive exile in Yishmael, the destruction of the first and second temples, the expulsion of my Jewish ancestry from Spain and Portugal. The way we lived in the little place called

Sefrou, my Jewish community, my teachers and friends, these were all so far away from me and I was sensing a sad separation from my beloved parents and my grandfather.

I was so emotional the next day. My heart was beating strongly with an ancient strange joy and happiness that I was part of this historical return to my source of being. I was busy in the ship, assisting the elderly and talking with them, praying with all my little heart for all of us. All of us were so happy to live that sacred moment of return, and our hearts were filled with a joy that cannot be described with words.

At the dawn of March 20th, 1949, we saw Haifa shining on the horizon and my heartbeat pounded with an immense joy. I saw the elderly and children crying and dancing, everyone spontaneously elevated by that sight.

At the port of Haifa, we were received in a great hall, each of us with our small suitcases in hand. They separated me along with a group of other teenagers and we were directed to another room where they sprayed us with DDT. I did not understand why they sprayed us with that white powder. I thought that was a welcome to the Land of Israel.

As we were approaching the Haifa dock, I stood on the ship, waiting to step into the beloved land I had dreamed of before I was born. I turned around to see the immensity of the ocean behind me, and realized the great distance that separated me from my family in Sefrou. I was seized with a great sadness, missing them and wondering if I would ever see them again. I wanted to jump from the ship and return to be with them, but it occurred to me that I didn't know how to swim. That moment I will never forget. I realized I must now be with this holy moment of arriving in the land of Israel, and apply the great Mitzva (good deed) to Be Here Now.

From there, I was taken with that same group of teenagers to a small Camp called Kiryat Shemouel not far from Haifa, where we were again prepared, given new clean clothes, and introduced to our new guide who would take us to the Kibbutz Ayelet Hashahar in the High Galilee.

After a year in the Kibbutz, where I wrote a play for our youth group and performed our journey from Morocco to Israel, I moved to Mikvei Yisrael near Tel Aviv. I studied agriculture in the Class of '32 for a few months. Then, I went to the army for a few years and afterwards, back to Jerusalem where I worked for several years in a glass factory and a glass laboratory in Romema.

In 1956, I traveled to the Festival d'Avignon in France as the Israeli representative for the International Theatre for World Youth. From there, I was off to Paris to study mime with Decroux and Marcel Marceau.

Because of financial difficulties, I returned to Israel to the glass factory, working for another year to save some money. That was 1957, the year of the Sinai war. In the summer of 1958 I was invited again to the Festival d'Avignon. This time after the Festival ended, I traveled to Paris with some friends I had met there.

In Paris I managed to find a place to live temporarily and began to study with Etienne Decroux, along with my friend Moni Yakin from Jerusalem. I stayed in Paris until 1964, when I returned to Israel to explore new possibilities and to find work in the Israeli Theatre.

From Israel, I came to the USA, responding to my friend Moni who now lived in New York City. I stayed with him in his apartment until I managed to get my own place in Manhattan.

I Lived in New York for a few years, performing first at the La Mama Theatre on Second Avenue, and at the small Theatre on Bleeker Street, and I taught some classes to my new students.

From there, I was invited to be a one-year Artist in Residence at SMU in Dallas Texas. At SMU, I taught Mime and Physical Theatre techniques and also produced a special play called "Resurrection," in which I worked with my students to explore chapter 37 of Ezekiel, "The Valley of the Dry Bones".

Following my time there, I was invited to perform and give a workshop in Denver, Colorado in 1971, at which point I had the opportunity to visit Boulder.

Boulder, Colorado looked like my home town, Sefrou, in Morocco. It was surrounded with beautiful mountains, and the pure air suited my being.

In Boulder I founded **Le Centre du Silence Mime School,** and spent 13 years directing the Boulder Mime Theatre, creating free public performances on Pearl Street mall. The school built a world reputation with the International Summer Mime Workshop. This workshop attracted students from all over the world to study the movement method I developed, which is called *Bodyspeak™*. **You can see more details about this and read articles at the website www.bodyspeak.com,** or read more in my book, *The BodySpeak™ Manual*.

In the last seven years, I also offered a special series called the **Gathering of the Sparks Kabbalah Seminars**, on the mystery of the Hebrew Letters. We explore the power of the letters to serve as keys, cracking the code of creation, and helping us understand our purpose of being here on earth at this time. See **www.gokabbalahnow.com.**

There are many more events, times, and places in my life, which I hope to write about in the future, and to describe some of the remarkable beings I had the merit to meet in certain unique situations. For now, the stories and poems here may give you some glimpses into some of the stations in my path in this life, until this moment of celebrating the 49th anniversary of the International Summer Mime Workshop in Boulder, Colorado, USA.

From Ecstasy to Lunch

Samuel Ben-Or Avital

MY GRANDFATHER

My Grandfather was slim, with a big, white, flowing beard and shining, piercing eyes. He was gentle and smiling. He lived downstairs from us and had a large courtyard nearby that he used as his workplace. Here, he made wine, and pursued other crafts which I learned from him. He did business with many merchants from the nearby mountains. Every holiday, they brought him goods such as sheep, goats, oil, honey, wine, good bread, and sugar.

In the midst of this practical daily life, the Zohar was never out of his hands. He uttered prayers continually in silence with a very mysterious smile on his face that I cherish in my memory. The Jewish and Arab sages honored him very much and asked his opinion in many cases. Because of his spiritual communications with them, he was known as a "peacemaker." Secretly, he supported young people's studies and contributed anonymously in many ways for the benefit of this small community.

His library contained many books and manuscripts by some of our ancestors, some of which were destroyed in the flood of 1950. That was the same year he went to Israel. I learned many practical and spiritual practices from this remarkable man that shaped me later in life. He is remembered as a "lamp of light and peace." He served the people he lived with in silence and humility, in his "invisible" way. May his soul be blessed.

He had a tremendous influence on my life. I was attracted to him because his words and stories made sense to me as a child. They were very wise and practical. I thought he knew everything.

I asked him many questions and his responses made me realize that I am also wise and creative, that wisdom is within us all.

He taught me by example the value of silence and of the words we speak. I learned from him what to say and how to be silent. I observed him speaking slowly. His words had weight. Words have power, and by observing, I learned not to answer quickly, but to wait, think, breathe and then speak. He used to say to me "Chew your words" before uttering them.

His presence was impressive—his white beard, his eyes radiant with the natural warmth, light and gentleness of his heart. When I was with him, there was no need for him to say that he loved me. He was a loving and living example for me, always present and attentive with his words, work and life.

I remember, while I was crushing grapes with my bare feet to make wine, he made me feel important, and would tell me stories as I stamped my small feet. I loved being with him. There was a genuine joy listening to him as he shared the analogy of making wine as a spiritual experience—as making the wine of life.

We human beings are the grapes. We are squeezed by life, by our thoughts and actions; our emotions are the juice, our sufferings and joys. We have to be squeezed in order to produce the "spirit," the wine of life. This analogy was one that helped me to understand the sufferings of life. It allows me now to say I am drunk with the wine of life, and mean something different than physical drunkenness. There with my grandfather, the process of making wine became the enchanting, unending quest of life itself.

Sometimes I just sat near him while he read from an impressive book with a golden frame, handmade and leather-bound, listening to his thoughts in silence. And every once in a while, he would raise his head from the book with some mysterious smile.

My Grandfather Eliyahu Ya'akov Abitbol, Z"L

THE LETTERS OF CREATION

Grandfather used to awaken at midnight to meditate and sing, and do various Tikkunim. His voice carried me through my sleep. I clearly heard his words that I knew so well. It became a habit for me to sing with him while going to sleep, and I hoped in my inmost heart one day to join him.

One day, while I was helping him with his wine making, I asked him why he awakened at night to sing. He replied, "My son, the life of this world is a passage, a corridor, and a preparation. The real life lies in the "other world."

For me, this was new. Seeing the puzzlement in my questioning eyes, he continued, "All the worlds are actually one." Illusion seduces us into thinking that this world, where man learns to be practical, is the real world. Here we encounter the tempter who lures us to follow the YETZER HARAH (the negative inclination), that leads to behavior that is inharmonious with Creation. The "other world" is where one recognizes the good in every living being and acts accordingly. So, the only time to see clearly and to sing praises of Creation and the beauties of nature is while the whole world is asleep.

I listened with eagerness as he continued, "There is a story in the holy Zohar in which Rav Hamnouna saba tells us of the Creation of the World". He opened his book of the Zohar and read from it, elaborating on the story as he read, to impress visually in my mind the impact of the holy letters.

Rav Hamnouna points out that the reason the Torah begins with the letter BEITH (in the word Bereshit), but the letters begin with the first letter of the alphabet, ALEPH, needs clarification. When the Creator wished to create this world, the letters were still embryonic; they had never been used, and therefore, they had no meaning. For two thousand years before the Creation, the One played with the letters. When the time came to create the world, the twenty-two letters descended from the Crown of God, each coming before Him with a specific plea. They came in reverse order beginning with TAV, pleading that the world be created through them, because they contained all His holy names that man can use.

BEITH, the last one who appeared before him, was chosen; therefore, the Torah begins with BERESHIT. But, the letter ALEPH remained in her place; she did not dare to ask that she be placed first in the creation. The Creator, blessed be his name, said to her, "Aleph, Aleph, why did you not come before me to plead like the other letters?" And Aleph replied, "Oh, Master of the Universe, when I saw that all the letters presented themselves before the throne to no avail, why should I present myself also? And when I saw that you had already chosen Beith, I could not ask you to give me an honor you had already bestowed." And the One, Blessed be his name, said, "ALEPH, ALEPH, though I have chosen the letter BEITH to help me in the Creation, you also will be honored, for you shall be the first letter of them all, and the Decalogue will begin with you, in the word ANOCHI."

While Grandfather's voice was vibrating with the story of the letters and their pleadings, I visualized all the letters as though they were living entities, speaking, moving and knowing the words they were forming. It was a direct experience in which I felt how the holy letters are a very dynamic form of expression. For many months and years, these images danced in me like a vibrant flame of eternal living. While musing in this way in my Grandfather's presence, I felt his smile, and this assured me that I understood.

Then, with a soft voice, he said, "The Creator also told the holy ALEPH that no man could describe her or grasp her, and that when man cannot describe something in the Creation, he will call the mystery ALEPH. Without ALEPH, there is neither life nor death."

This seemed a paradox to me, and I did not fully understand it. "I see you are having some difficulty understanding," he continued. "Just remember that all is in ALEPH, and without it there is nothing. When you grow in age and learning and begin to live in this world, you will understand. For now, forget about it all and just remember what I said. Also, now that I have shared this beautiful story with you, remember when you study the letters that you should be clean of any thought of this world.

Immerse yourself in the letters until you forget about time and the place where you are. This will surely teach you the importance of uttering the letters. Study the vowels well, and sing them always. Learn HOW to express yourself, HOW to say things, not WHAT to say. The intention is the most important of all. And now, we shall go to the prayer of ARVIT (evening prayer). The sun is almost gone in the West."

I had completely forgotten where I was, what time it was, and who was speaking to me. When he reminded me of the evening prayer, it was like a coming back to this world. I realized that we had been in some marvelous place of light. At the synagogue, I began to look at the words and letters differently than before. I felt a strange happiness engulf me.

That night again, I heard him awaken at midnight, and I enjoyed his voice until I fell asleep in that light. That night, I dreamed about a place I could not describe. First, I passed through a forest with beautiful trees, walking by myself and letting my body move as if following an invisible or inaudible voice. At the end of the forest was a valley that was very green. I walked into it and then stood in one place and reflected on the story of the letters. Suddenly, I saw a great door made of gold and silver ornaments. It was closed. Wishing very much to enter, I began to sing ALEPH many times until the door disappeared, and I found myself in a garden of marvels with beautiful trees of all kinds.

There was no one around. It was a quiet and harmonious place, and I sat near a tree, continuing to sing the letters. All at once the letters began to manifest in different forms of lights, lights in the forms of the letters, dancing so beautifully! ALEPH invited me to dance with her, and all the letters asked me to dance, to become like them.

I danced, but the fiery place became hot and I grew warm. I wished to stay there. Now, the letters began to form words that I could read clearly. They wrote my name, my name that has ALEPH in it. And after this sight, I saw my Grandfather coming from the light, saying, "My son, here I am. Remember, do not let any being describe you. You are a holy letter. Whatever you do in this world, it must be good. Act so that no one can say you are this or that, like the ALEPH."

After this brief message, I heard a voice calling my name. It was my father waking me for the morning prayer. I opened my eyes, smiling with intense happiness. My father said, "You were singing all night and saying many words I could not understand." I smiled and went with him to the morning prayer.

IN THE MARKETPLACE

At certain times in my childhood, I used to go with my Grandfather to the Jewish cemetery of our village. Many legends and stories were told of the sages buried inside some of the many caves in the high mountains nearby. These legends triggered my imagination.

During different holidays, many people came to these caves to pray and to ask for healing for the sick. I particularly remember one cavern known as "The Shrine of the Holy Unknown" where I went many times with my Grandfather. From quite young, I was always attracted to go into it, but was never allowed. They thought I would be afraid. I was not afraid. Actually, I wanted to go inside the cave alone.

I told my Grandfather this, and he said to me, "There is nothing to be afraid of, my son. One day you will be led there by a very wise man, a friend of mine, and he will teach you many things." I was confident that it would come to pass as he said.

Sometime before my seventh year, I was passing through the marketplace on my way home. I stopped in front of a shop that I loved, in a small, sweet-smelling street called "Attarin," that was filled with spice and perfume shops. One perfume attracted me more strongly than the others. I inhaled it, enjoying it deeply.

I had stood gazing at the shop and breathing in the special aroma for some time when suddenly a very beautiful man appeared. He put his hand on my young shoulder and asked, "What is the most beautiful perfume you wish to smell, my son?" Turning my head to look at him, I met a smile so loving that I trusted him immediately. I chose the oil of the Rose and pointed it out to him. He bought it for me and then told me, "Smell it, my son," which I did. While inhaling deeply of it, I was taken by the aroma, and when I turned back to thank him, he was not there.

I asked the perfume seller, "Sayeed Attar," as I called him, about the man. "Which man are you talking about?" he asked. I looked at the bottle of rose oil in my hand and looked back at him. He gave me a mysterious look. "Just go on home," he said. "Probably your Grandfather is waiting for you." So, I went home, thinking about this marvelous being who bought me the perfume.

I wished very strongly that this beautiful man would find me again. I prayed to see him once more. I never spoke to anyone about this incident, but kept it in my heart. It was my "secret."

THE DREAM OF KING SOLOMON

One day in school, we studied the dream of King Shlomo (King Solomon). And, I remember that this study really set me afire. So, after school, as was my custom, I went to the garden where Saba, my grandfather, could usually be found manufacturing his goods—his salt, his wine, his woodwork, or reading while things were cooking.

It was always such a beautiful scene to me, to find him there in the sun, reading from the Zohar. It was something magical and comforting. And this day, I approached him and burst out with, "Today we studied about King Shlomo and his dream! That he dreamt and was asked to choose what he wanted—fame, wisdom, or wealth? And, he said, 'I only want wisdom.' And, because he asked for wisdom and not for fame and fortune, he was given all of them!"

From this, I thought to myself that if you choose the essence of life, you get them all. But, in my innocence, I was also anxious for something like that to happen to me. So, I said to Saba, "Why should King Shlomo alone have such dreams? What about me? I also want wisdom, and I have no such dreams." And, he looked at me with his lips curling into a smile ever so slightly, and finally answered, "Who said only Shlomo? You also could have such a dream. What did Shlomo do? You know his decision? What did he choose?" I said, "He chose wisdom." "So, you too can choose wisdom. When you go to sleep at night and they ask you, 'What do you want?' You will know what to answer. It is not just Shlomo, it is you, too."

Exuberantly, I thought, "Oh my, now I have a purpose for going to sleep at night!" And, when night came, I closed my eyes very tightly and repeated, "My answer is wisdom. I want wisdom—That is all!" So, when the dream would come, I would be ready. And, that is how I learned how to sleep and dream consciously.

THE ROCK OF SEVEN

When a person died, it was a custom for the children to walk to the community cemetery behind the coffin. One day, the children of my school had gone to a burial, and after all the other children left to walk home, I stayed to wander around the cemetery. I was looking for the tomb of one of my ancestors. While walking, I lost the sense of time and space. Forgetting that I was looking for a specific tomb, I found myself near a huge tree. I sat under it, leaned against its tall trunk and fell asleep.

Suddenly, I heard a roar. I opened my eyes slowly and saw a large cat, a mix between a mountain cat and a lion, there in front of me. I sat there transfixed, rooted to the spot, ready to be eaten. The lion-cat sat there, also frozen, gazing at me. My insides began to tremble. My lips started speaking the psalms with great supplication, and suddenly, as I watched, the lion-cat transformed itself. I rubbed my eyes to see more clearly, and there in front of me appeared the man from the marketplace, smiling, and saying, "Why are you sitting there glued to that tree?"

I couldn't utter any sound or word. Giving me time to return to my senses, he offered me his hand. I took it, and he said, "Come now, I am not a lion-cat. You don't need to be afraid of me like that," and together we walked off into the forest.

Although I didn't know where I was walking with this strange and beautiful man, I felt very good in my heart, and calm. We sat on a mighty rock not far from there and looked out at the deep green valley, immersed in the beauty of the horizon.

After a silence, he said, "You are soon going to be seven years old." While he spoke, I opened my rose oil bottle and smelled it a little. He saw this and said, "Yes, you should remember the smell of the holy rose. It will give you much strength." He spoke to me as if I were his child, an equal, which amazed me.

I wondered to myself why I felt such trust for this beautiful being, and he spoke aloud in reply, "I am not a stranger, my son, I am your protector and teacher. You should remember whenever you need me to call me, and I will appear to you, to offer help and teach you what you need to learn at that time. It is good that you have kept your tongue quiet since you saw me in the marketplace."

"Your grandfather is a friend of mine and he will also teach you many beautiful things. I know you love him very dearly. Do not be afraid to ask him anything you wish to know, but remember the "Golden Bit" for your mouth. I will direct you in many ways unknown to people here, so you should banish fear from yourself forever. For now, just remember the number seven. You will remember it in any case since every Shabbat is the seventh day, which you celebrate in your house as a very harmonious day. That will help you remember this seven, and the rose oil will make you smell good."

THE SACRED SILENCE

For days I thought about these two events, the marketplace and the **Rock of Seven**, and I even saw this man in my dreams at night. I had not asked his name, and even though I didn't know what to call him, I thought that perhaps later on I would have a name for him.

Many things occupied my mind in those days: my studies in school, my sessions with grandfather, and other activities. I found myself becoming more silent and more observant of life around me, concentrating on the calligraphy of the Hebrew letters, and learning the psalms by heart.

When I sat with my Grandfather, I noticed a mysterious smile on his face as though he was in on the "secret," as if he knew what was going on within me. As though reading my thoughts, he would say, "It is good, Samuel, that you begin to enter this Sacred Silence at such a young age. It will be helpful for you later in your life." I began to sense that he had a hand in all this, but in a very discreet way.

One day, Grandfather asked me to come help him make wine. I remember his majestic silhouette sitting in the warm sun at the entrance to the winery. He was wearing white, the Zohar in his hands, waiting for me to come.

"Ah, there you are, my Samuel," he said. "So, let us work." There was one big area filled with grapes. We took off our shoes and squeezed the grapes with our feet, like dancing, singing psalms, reciting in melody, until the grape juice reached our knees. Then, we left the winery and he sent me to our house nearby for the evening prayer, reminding me to come later that evening to see him. Full of joy, I awaited the moment when I could be with him again, knowing it meant meaningful stories and some new initiations in the holy tradition of the Kabbalah.

That night, he spoke about silence and living in the worlds that are invisible to the human eye. Then he told me about birth.

"When we are born," he said, "we are given a specific amount of words to use in this life. If we use them properly, we will have plenty. If not, we find out later that we do not have any more words in our Cosmic Bank. So, my beloved one, be economical with the words you utter, for they are counted."

With that mysterious smile that always sent me to another realm of beauty and calm, he finished, saying, "Let this thought be in your heart, and meditate on it, and finish learning your psalms by heart." He kissed me goodnight, and I went upstairs to sleep.

When my father saw me returning, he said, "There is a luminous light around you when you come from seeing grandfather. You must "drink his words" with your thirst." Then, smiling, he left me to my evening prayer and meditation.

From Ecstasy to Lunch

My father was a very silent man. Never in my life did I hear him speak except when it was necessary. Immersed in his mental recitations, he was always uttering prayers. When working, his actions were precise; he always did no more and no less than what was needed. I was much impressed by his unique, silent presence. He seemed content in joy and sorrow, always ready to come to the aid of anyone in need. Sometimes, it seemed to me that he was also in on the making of what was happening to me in the realm of "Invisibility."

I kept many things in my heart and thought no one knew the details of the "strange events." I already had a great love for my "invisible teacher" because in his presence, I felt very happy and content. I was always asking him to come again and take me places.

I composed some poems in his honor and kept them with me, thinking that perhaps I could tell him about them. Here is a poem I still remember that I wrote at that time. Loosely translated from the Hebrew, it goes like this:

> "Oh Invisible One
> that found me in the marketplace,
> and with the Rose Oil that you gave me,
> like the fragrance of the Garden of Eden,
> in my heart you dwell,
> and through my eyes you see,
> and through my ears you hear.
> In this Silence so holy, so sacred,
> you opened the door of quiet to me,
> and to myself, to teach me,
> in this Gilgul, this circulation of the soul,
> how to go around and go around a circle of LIGHT,
> you said that,
> you protect me in all ways.
> Without knowing your name,
> Oh, the one without name, (Lo-Shem),
> maybe I will open up to give you a name I can call you by.
> Be always with me.
> Oh Invisible One,
> dwell always in my heart,
> and show me the marvels of the creation.
> Through your teaching, I may one day dwell among realized beings,
> and bring love and peace wherever I walk.
> Be my holy pillar,
> beloved one without name,
> without form.

Shalom peace of my heart is the witness
of this handwriting.
Bless me again with your presence."

SABA ELIAHU YA'AKOV ABITBOL
ELUL AND YAMIM NORA'IM IN SEFROU

In Sefrou and other communities, Saba R. Eliahu Ya'Akov Abitbol, Z"L was both known and unknown on many levels.

Saba was known to receive guests from all over the world. Rabbis, Dayanim, business people, and Kabbalists knew that they would find a benevolent host and a place to stay while doing their work, writing or giving drashot, collecting money for the poor, etc. His house was open for all the spiritual, the visionaries and the poor.

We lived in a street called 285 Rue du Serpent, El-Bestna, because the street was so narrow and winding, like a serpent, with house entrances lining the sides of it. Our three-floor house was the first in that street, not far from the main river running through Sefrou called Ouad Aggai.

Saba Eliahu lived on the ground floor, my own family lived on the first floor, and other families like the Elbaz family lived there also.

The door to our house was heavy wood and copper and was sealed every night for protection. My family lived in a big, long, triangular room where I lived with my 3 brothers and 3 sisters. Everyone had a place to sleep and the room transformed itself all the time according to the events of life. At night we would all sleep in various places - mine was on an elevation near the window, from which I saw the Minaret and heard the Muezzin call for prayer every morning.

My father R. Moshe Amram Abitbol Z"L also slept nearby and had a bookshelf where he kept many priceless books and other family valuables. I loved to look at his treasured books, keeping his promise with me that someday I would be able to know and understand their contents. My father was a very humble man who spoke little. Like my grandfather, he spoke only when it was necessary. I grew up to understand this as a given, and I learned by osmosis from their behavior. That is probably where the love of silence and deep contemplation, and my tendency toward the art of Mime came from.

Our house entrance was on the left side of the street. My grandfather's work area, his garden and his perfumed soap manufacturing and wine making areas were there. This was the place of many experiences I had with my grandfather. After school I used to go there first, even before going to my house, and I would help him with whatever he was doing. Sometimes I would find him reading the Sefer Hazohar while sitting on a padded rock when it was sunny. I would just sit and be with him, looking at him and asking a question if I dared, but mostly being. And I waited until he spoke with me, or smiled, or asked me to do something.

This was the place where many stories and experiences were invested in me during my childhood there in Sefrou, that village that is now called "Lost Paradise". Part of my family were descendants of the Megorashim from Castile (exiled from Spain after the expulsion of 1492), and one of the characteristics I was imbedded with, because of them, is the good quality of discretion, almost secrecy. Some of my ancestors were Kabbalists of renown and even "miracle makers", and knew from intuition that it is better to be silent than to speak small talk or just babble. I was very observant in that precious childhood environment, and I absorbed and learned many lessons that later would serve me greatly in my life.

Saba would rise after midnight some nights to pray and do the Tikkun Hatzot, the restoration of Midnight, a kabbalistic practice to assist the creator in restoring the world and ourselves. The prayer was for healing, and to focus on new visions for the community, increasing the awareness that the Shekhinah, the divine presence, is in exile with us while we wait for the Messiah.

There was also another practice called Ta'Anit Dibbour, meaning fasting from words, and we practiced it as a spiritual discipline, to collect ourselves and be of service to those in need.

During the month of Elul, the spiritual practice intensifies and then comes to a peak at Rosh Hashanah and Yom Kippur. These are the days we call Yamim Nora'im, the Days of Awe. Every night of Elul we woke up at midnight and practiced the Selihot prayers, forgiving and asking forgiveness. This is the month where we do a spiritual inventory, checking our thoughts and deeds. We sort out our deeds to see whether they have been for the good or the bad, and then ask forgiveness for any wrongs we have done during the year.

I would wake up and go downstairs to my grandfather's place, where a good number of people would assemble and pray. We moved our bodies back and forth, in standing meditations and blessings, and I observed discreetly certain elderly people wiping tears from their cheeks. I would steal a quick look and then turn back to my book of prayer to continue the Selihot.

This event happened in all of Sefrou's synagogues and houses, but mainly in the synagogues. And although our house was not far from the Mellah (the Closed Jewish quarters), around midnight, from my window I could hear the voice of an elderly man saying loudly: "Awake from your slumber, human beings. Awake to give account of your deeds. Awake and repent, awake and ask forgiveness. This is the time to do the Tikkun, restoration. Awake from your slumber, inhabitants of "the Little Jerusalem." (Sefrou was known in Morocco as "The Little Jerusalem" because it produced many Rabbis and Kabbalists and for its important role in the history of the Jewish people since the time of the expulsion from Spain.)

I sat by my grandfather and observed and also prayed silently. I noticed that there was a certain innocence in their behavior, something that today I call "conscious innocence", a deep knowing who they were, why they were there, and what they were doing.

After a whole night of song, contemplation and meditations, when the dawn gave its first light, all the participants of the Selihot would be served hot tea or coffee or juice, and then a good breakfast. They would leave the house and would come again the next day, for the whole month of Elul, until Rosh Hashanah and Yom Kippor, when we would meet at the synagogue.

From Ecstasy to Lunch

The night of Rosh Hashanah, the Synagogue was full. The aura of a great event was in the air. My heart beat very fast and I would cry for no reason from the songs and the prayers. I sat by my father and grandfather and saw in stolen looks that they were crying also. The Hazzan, in the Teva (The central stand where the Shaliah Tzibbour, the messenger of the people, reads the Torah and guides the people to prayer), was standing with great reverence. He raised his voice and all the congregation responded.

Now the Sacred Arc was opened and a sharp and terrible silence enveloped everyone. The Shaliah Tzibbour raised the Shofar, and everyone prepared to listen. I heard some short breaths around me and saw a discreet look from my grandfather and father, observing me with my big, open and questioning eyes. The Shofar was blown and there was not one movement in all the space, all was still; only that sound was heard, the ultimate way of listening, not even a fly disturbing the air. It was like an ancient echo I knew, or my soul recognized. My ears listened deeply to it. Everyone was standing as if the Creation of the world was happening right at that sacred moment. I held my breath and I sensed a cool liquid caressing my face and the hands of my grandfather and father on my little head, holding me so I would not burst with the experience.

Finally, the sound exploded out from the people with such a force, and a song filled the whole place. All my 248 organs and all my 465 veins trembled and were uplifted, raised with the whole voice of the community. I was one with the whole creation. Two hands held my head and my inner sound also burst out from me along with the others, yearning and begging for forgiveness and that we would merit having our names written in the Book of life on Yom Kippur.

That night I dreamt of the sacred Hebrew letters, flying like brilliant white birds from the opening of the Shofar, in an endless way, flying and filling all spaces and times with their being. I told my grandfather that dream and he just smiled and whispered something not audible to my ears. But as a young boy then, I understood his communication without words.

Yom Kippur night, we went to the Synagogue barefoot, ready for the great cleansing of all our bad deeds and to focus and ask that our names be written in the Book of LIFE. That night, even more people filled the place. There was that same incredible intensity of being, but even stronger than the night of Rosh Hashanah.

When the sacred Arc was opened that night, the beautiful voice of the Shaliah Tsibbour was so profound and so yearning, while uttering the great KOL NIDREI (a declaration that was composed in Spain to allow the merranos and those who were forced to choose between accepting another religion or the Auto da Fe, to pray with us. It was a declaration of inclusiveness; Even the criminals can come and pray with us, because we are all humans). I trembled again from the awesome moment. The words and their deep meaning reverberated in me deeply and the response of the congregation was overwhelming to me as a young boy, and also to the many others who were there.

The sound of the Shofar intensified even more that night. Its sound transfixed all of us in that marble-walled Synagogue of Sefrou. It sent chills through me, knowing that all over the world my people were assembled and focusing on the event of forgiveness and restoring the world.

The echo of KOL NIDREI is still with me today. Whenever I sense a tension somewhere, I recall that moment and I find ease or a solution. The environment of my childhood marked many qualities in my being and had such a strong effect on me that I feel grateful now that I am able to utter what I remember.

Saba, my grandfather, was a benevolent human being who did many things very discreetly. He had a beautiful voice and when he sang, everyone listened. I was told a story by my brother Raphael, that when my grandfather was a young boy, he used to go late at night to the synagogue and sing the Bakkashot or Piyutim so well that the people who listened thought that there must be an angel in the Synagogue that night.

One night, the legendary Kabbalist and Spiritual leader of Sefrou at that time, Rabbi Raphael Moshe Elbaz, who was known as RAMA and was an ancestor from the side of my mother, woke up one night and heard a voice like a nightingale arising from the Synagogue. That synagogue, which was called after his name, was not far from his house, and he was so curious he thought the Prophet Eliahu was calling him.

So he went to the Synagogue and entered slowly and he still heard this voice beautifully expressing a great yearning. He approached the voice and asked this young boy, "Who are you my young man?" And my grandfather answered "I am Eliahu." And RAMA asked again "Who are you?" And he replied "I am Eliahu."

Now RAMA was puzzled. Was a dream or a Kabalistic vision upon him? He realized finally that the boy was indeed real. My grandfather was simply revealing his identity, that he was Eliahu Ya'akov Abitbol, a descendant of RAMA's own teacher and initiator, who appointed him to the head of the community, the Great Rabbi Amor Abitbol, Z"L.

The Great RAMA was very moved that this boy's voice had awakened him. He put his hand on his head and blessed him with these words: "May you uplift the spirit of everyone you meet, and may your seeds be brilliant in the wisdom of the Kabbalah." He continued, "You may come to the Synagogue anytime to sing the praises of the Creator, so the Shekhinah will hear and uphold and sustain us in this long bitter exile."

Saba was a "central pillar of support," as one of my teachers in Sefrou called him in one of his books. Indeed, he was a central pillar in my life, from whom I learned by osmosis so many things. And because of this, I knew since a young age that I am protected. And some events in my life have proven this to be true. I have encountered situations of life and death that, somehow, I overcame with ease and with not much upheaval.

This story was told to me by my brother Raphael Avital (Abitbol).

Thursday, Sept 5, 2002,
28 Elul 5763 - Rosh Hashanah.
Boulder, Colorado, USA

ONE NIGHT ALONE IN THE HOUSE OF PRAYER

The synagogue where my family prayed was small. It had wooden benches near the walls, and small windows opening onto the narrow streets outside. In the middle was the Teva (the Ark of the Law), in which the Shaliah Tsibbour (the leader of the prayer) stood. Many large glass oil lamps hung from the ceiling, burning in memoriam for the souls of the departed. The dim light made it dark inside, but it was very warm. The saying goes, "Do not look at the flask, but what it contains." The warmth of the synagogue was like the heart yearning to meet its Creator.

One evening after the prayer, I stayed on my small wooden bench studying the letters and meditating on the saying by Rabbi Tarfon in *The Ethics of the Fathers* (Pirke-Avoth):

"The day is short and the work is great. The workers are lazy and the reward is great. And the Master is urgent."

I repeated this many times to myself, trying to understand this holy urgency that Rabbi Tarfon speaks about. I was also searching for some clue in the letters so I could decipher the saying myself. While repeating the phrase, I gazed for some time at the flame in one of the big glass lamps above. As I gazed, the flame grew bigger and bigger. My eyes became wet and I fervently continued to delve into this saying.

The colors of the flame began to illumine the whole place and I saw clearly what a flame is and how it is formed. As the light spread over my whole being, enveloping me, I continued to repeat the saying mentally. The more I uttered the words with Kavvana, intention, the more a myriad of splendid colors, all spherical, developed, until I too, was in the spheres of light, in a very conscious state.

Now I saw a crown of light and a very bright light on the horizon. Letters began to fly and dance out of it through the air. I made sure I was still on my wooden bench. I felt a smile enveloping all of me, as the dancing flame, the letters of the saying, performed the life that they contained, right in front of my eyes.

I could see how the DAY is short and the lazy workers are barely moving to work. The whole human condition was acted out in flames and colors. It seemed to me that I saw the whole world in the letters. Now, the urgent Master, wearing the crown of Light, appeared in all the splendor of his being. It was indeed a celestial view of the drama of existence. I began to sing the saying and the more I sang, the more everything became clear. I thought the whole world was watching this with me. And then came the voices!

Voices seemed to come from within me, so many voices! I was both speaking to myself and answering myself. Definite faces I had never seen appeared clearly before me. Were they Celestial beings? Sages from another time? Tzaddikim? Prophets of old? "Who are you?" I asked, "I am just a little child in meditation, please tell me who you are!" And the flames continued to dance that magnificent dance of the heavens.

"We are the souls of your brethren who are now being burned at the stake. With our sacrifice, the sons of Israel will be saved," they said. Suddenly from this mass of beings arose a mighty voice: "Listen, little one. Listen, and absorb into yourself what you see, and afterwards go and tell your brothers and sisters what you have seen."

This drama was still being performed with the flaming letters. Were the letters living beings? I began to understand the urgency of the "Great Good Work" that we are here to do on earth. Now I began to pray. Words of prayer flowed from my trembling mouth to ease the suffering of my brothers and sisters. Suddenly, all became silent, calm, and awesomely frightening.

I opened my eyes to find the "Shammash" (the guardian of the synagogue) shaking me. "Wake up, wake up. It is morning. How did you get into the synagogue? I open it every morning. They probably left you here yesterday without noticing you."

I looked at him, and within a few seconds, I understood what was going on. I did not answer. I felt very good and proceeded to the morning prayer as if nothing had happened. A few moments later, Grandfather came. The Shammash told him I had slept in the synagogue all night. Again, I noticed a smile on the lips of the old man as he glanced at me.

After the prayers ended, he came to me and asked, "What did you see?" I told him with much fervor about the dancing flames of the celestial spheres. He smiled and said, "Keep this in your heart. Now explain to me the meaning of the saying of Rabbi Tarfon."

We spoke together on the way to the classroom, where he left me with the teacher. I watched him as he walked away and blessed him because he had not scolded me. What an understanding heart his Soul contained!

And so, I remember well this saying:

רַבִּי טַרְפוֹן אוֹמֵר הַיּוֹם קָצֵר, וְהַמְּלָאכָה מְרוּבָּה.
וְהַפּוֹעֲלִים עֲצֵלִים. וְהַשָּׂכָר הַרְבֵּה. וּבַעַל הַבַּיִת דּוֹחֵק:
פרקי אבות פרק ב. טו.

"The **day** is short and the work is great.
The **workers** are lazy and the **reward** is much.
And the **master is urgent**."
Rabbi Tarfon – Sayings of the Fathers 2.20

THIS TOO SHALL PASS
GAM ZEH YA'AVOR

I was too young to know what was happening in the world during World War II. I spent my time with Grandfather or with my studies. One day, I noticed that the lights in our house were dim and the shutters closed so no light would escape. In school, we were told that our brethren in Europe were being exterminated burned, killed and mutilated. All the children wore black clothing as a sign of mourning. I learned that we, the Jewish people, had been in exile for many years, ever since we had been expelled from our homeland, Israel.

In our studies, we learned about many sages who died "Al-Kiddush Hashem" (to sanctify the holy name). In my lonely, meditative moments in the synagogue, I felt as though something in me had died, as though I was that one burning to sanctify the holy name. I always chose to join in the communal prayer to save my people in Europe, praying fervently. I often awakened in the middle of the night to ask the Creator to remember us and not to extinguish the flame of light in us. Salty tears coursed down my young face as I prayed.

I remained in this state constantly during the war. I often went to the forest in the mountains alone to sit on the "Rock of Seven" to wait for the beautiful man, the Invisible One, to come to illumine my being, to tell me more of what was going on in this world. I composed short mental invocations to call him. I would cry desperately, hugging my knees to concentrate more, praying with all my heart.

One day while praying in this way, I suddenly heard a noise. Turning to see what it was, I was struck by a liquid luminous light. Now he materialized in a beautiful robe of gold, smiling his radiant smile. He held my head with his hand and said, "Be not sad, my young one. I read your thoughts about what is happening to your brethren and came to comfort you at this hour. Raise your eyes to the heavens, look! The body may perish, but not the spirit.

"Although you are young to know exactly what is going on, you sense the sorrow and the tragic historic events of this time with your soul. Indeed, you were born at a very hard time of human evolution in order to imprint these events in your soul, so that when the time comes to express yourself, you will be ready to see, learn, experience and condense the essence of human suffering."

He sat with me for some moments in silence and said, "Learn your letters well and continue to pray to ease all human suffering. It is indeed you who is passing through this dark time. Just remember, all things pass. Only the spirit lasts. You will live to see justice and peace reign among all humans. Be happy, my young one, be happy."

I rubbed my eyes to see him better and he vanished from my physical sight. I sat quietly for awhile and then stood up, stretched, and walked back to the village. Grandfather asked why my eyes were so red. I replied that I was praying alone in the forest for our brethren.

"Yes, my son," he said, "indeed, you feel the suffering of others in your guts. We are all one in Him who created us to follow his law, and this too shall pass. So go with peace back to your studies."

After this event, I tried to think of a name to give this beautiful invisible being. I tried to compose a name that would aptly describe him from the letters. But how could I describe this "invisible" man with a name so others could understand without judgment? This thought occupied my mind for many months. I was dissatisfied with every name I came up with.

I watched my dreams to see if some sign or hint would appear but to no avail. Finally, I let it drop, recalling that nothing comes by force. I decided to let nature take its course, confident that the name would come in time.

From then on, I went about things in an ordinary way, no longer tormenting my young self, just observing, experiencing and learning.

THE NO-NAME LO SHEM

During those young years, curiosity filled me continually. The plate of my consciousness was a pure sheet of gold metal, ready to be written on with new wisdom.

I often sat on "my rock" gazing at nature, going to "places of learning" in other planes of awareness. I sat receiving the "holy influx" (Shefa) that came to me in those quiet moments of meditation, holding the thought as if it were something tangible.

The focus of all my thoughts and meditations at this time was the Name. This radiant being of light who came to teach me and to remind me of the essence of life and all creation, the one who visited me at rock of seven—what name should I give to him? Finally, I decided simply to ask his name the next time he came.

One day, while being with this focus, I felt a warmth surround me, one I had felt many times before and had come to know. There he stood, more luminous than ever. This time he had a "crown" of splendor on his head. We both remained silent for some moments as if bathing in a holy light. He spoke and said, "I know you have been occupied with this thought of the name. Why do you wish to know my name?"

"Look carefully at your own name that your Grandfather gave you, and play with the letters. I assure you that you will be astonished by the "answer." Here, let us do this together. What is your name?"

"Shemouel."

"Look at the letters. Sheen, Mem, Vav, Aleph, Lammed. Now play with them, form them while meditating, and I will stay here until you find it."

I tried to do what he asked very fast, mentally, and soon I came on the letter combination (Tseruf) of Lammed, Aleph, Sheen, Mem, and Vav.

The last letter Vav dropped off as if it had disappeared, and I received the name **Lo-Shem**, meaning **NO NAME**. At that a mysterious smile glowed upon my face. At that moment, smiling too, he asked, "Well? What do you say now, my beautiful one?" And when I looked again, he was gone. I walked straight home from the "Rock" with the thought in mind to see Grandfather. I found him reading the weekly portion of the Zohar which was about our father, Jacob. I sat down and he said, "Did you study this in school this week?" I said "yes," and he had me read it again.

It was the struggle of Yaakov with the angel. In the story, Yaakov did not let the angel go until after he had asked his name. The angel replied, "Why do you ask my name?" And he blessed Jacob there. (Genesis 30:31)

Jacob was then able to give the name **PENIEL** to the place because he saw Him "face to face." In my young mind, I tried to compare this with my own experience with Lo Shem.

Grandfather asked, "Are you dreaming? Do you understand? Our father Yaakov was blessed after this experience. Some day you will find out the great meaning of "Peniel." For now, just retain the story and all will be revealed to you in time." He added, "Do you remember that the same thing happened to our beloved teacher Moshe?"

"Yes," I said, "When Moshe asked God, 'When they ask me what his name is, what shall I say to them?' And God said to Moshe, "Tell them **I AM** sent you." (Exodus 3:13-14)

"Well," he said, "Do you connect?" I nodded my head, thanked him for his attention, entered that dreamy state once again, and left. Later that night Grandfather told me the story of my birth, and the story of my name, SHEMOUEL, that was given to me by him. "As you know, my son," he said, "we are in exile, and the only thing that holds us together all these years is the Shabbat and the study of the Torah."

We apply the teachings in practical ways in our daily lives, and this makes the connection from our past to this present. "When you were being born right here in this room, there in that place," and he pointed out the right spot, "I was reading my regular "**TIKKUN CHATZOT**" (A Kabbalistic practice done from Midnight until the morning).

"Around dawn, the radiating horizon of the Holy Soul, I was reading the prayer in the story of Samuel, prayed by his mother Hannah. At that moment at the words of praise of Hannah, your Gilgul (Soul) incarnated. As you know, during the first seven days in this dense world we do not give a name to the new born. In this way, we remember that the Holy One, Blessed Be His Name, has no name.

This holy "EIN SOF" (the infinite, without limits) is above all names. You have probably learned about this already. Only on the eighth day, in the presence of Eliahu Hanavi (Eliahu the prophet), do we give the child a name." I was listening eagerly, eyes and ears open, as in the saying, "I am open, I see, I hear."

He continued with his beautiful smile, "And so, on the eighth day, after the circumcision ceremony, I was the one to give you a name. All the eyes in the family turned towards me to hear me utter the name, and I said, 'And his name among Israel will be Shemouel.' After everyone rejoiced on the naming of the child, they wanted to know the reason for this name. I satisfied their curiosity by telling them about the Light of the dawn of the horizon and the story of Hannah's prayer.

Then I added the last connective link, pointing out that both the mother of the prophet Samuel and this newborn Samuel are named Hannah. Then, everyone was indeed very happy. This is how we apply the teachings to our everyday life in a very practical way."

With this story, it became clear to me why everyone in the family and later at school called me "Shemouel Hanavi," Samuel the prophet. This nickname had embarrassed me many times, but now that I understood it, I no longer felt embarrassed. "And so, my son," Grandfather continued, "remember that the Holy One has no name. No mortal may dare to give Him a name. As soon as a name is given to Him, he is not that. Some day you will grasp the beautiful meaning of your name. Then you will know what this Initiation—name is about. May the Light of the Zohar be with you, my son."

All this had a profound effect on me deep in my soul. I meditated and understood that just as our Father Ya'akov had been given a name for the angel, I had also found the name of my radiant being of Light. I called him LO-SHEM = No-Name. From then on, I was filled with joy.

THE VISIT OF LO-SHEM

As many days passed at this time of my young life, my dreams grew more and more meaningful to me. As I wrote, the letters slowly, beautifully and very clearly, each letter communicated secrets to me. I only spoke about this with my Grandfather and my Father and only when it was necessary.

I was very silent in my young years; thus, the habit of speaking only when necessary was built at a young age. Seeing this very thing manifested in my Father's life was encouraging, too. One day, I went to "my rock" as usual to reflect on what I was learning. The day was beautifully clear and the area was filled with a vibrant life.

I sat on my Rock in the position for studying I had learned, and just listened to the sounds of nature around me. Then, the familiar sensing of the presence of Lo-Shem sent a warm breeze all through me. As the friend of my heart, he shined now in that bright, bright light! Feeling that I perceived his gaze, he smiled and said, "Peace be with you my beloved one. By now you must feel that I shine as a Guardian all around you. By now, you know that I direct your steps from the "invisibility" so that you absorb the essence of life now, when you are young. And it will become a good habit for you."

"In this way, you shall find guidance coming from within yourself later and be able to offer it to others when the time comes." He extended his hand towards me and touched me on my head. I felt a unique warmth all over my little body, sweet and peaceful. "Remember, my dear one," he reminded me, "never let anyone describe you. Develop your talents so they can serve you in times of need. You will pass through many dangerous things, but I will be with you to suggest how to act in those moments.

My suggestions will come into your own vessel as specific intuitive signs. If you act at those times with this guidance, you will find a way. If, not, if you hesitate, then no answer or way will do you any good. From now on, begin to listen to that voice. Don't believe it blindly, but test it yourself. The experience will be your certainty. The night you "dreamt" about the letters, I was directing the vibrations of your consciousness so you could UNDERSTAND them.

This is only a means, not an end. With this understanding, you will learn not so much WHAT to say but rather HOW to speak. Before speaking to anyone, ask your heart how to speak in the wink of an eye. Follow that inner voice and you will succeed. I know that the letters occupy you completely now, but do not forget the practicalities of this life. Take care of your body.

When you eat, always give thanks. Know that actually you are all humanity, and know that therefore you are eating for all the hungry ones as well. Nourish this thought all the time and it will become a habit. I will make sure that you follow the voice. Whatever you do, do every action with good intention, and help will come from me when needed." When I blinked my eyes, he was gone.

From Ecstasy to Lunch

I came back slowly to this world and walked home. On the way, I ran into my Grandfather walking home, too. I took his hand and we walked home together. It was a Friday afternoon and Grandfather said to me, "Are you ready to receive the Shabbat Queen?" With elation, my heart filled with the sanctity of the Shabbat.

THE ASSEMBLY OF THE LAZY ONES

There was a group of Kabbalists in our village that I called "the assembly of the lazy ones." Their work was very beautiful in many ways, being practical and very spiritual simultaneously. They were always ready to aid anyone who needed them, with food, clothing, etc. But they acted in a very discreet "invisible" way, so that those who received would not feel embarrassed. It was called "Gemilut Hasadim," which means benevolence to others.

They spent most of the night studying the Zohar. They danced with the bride and the bridegroom at every wedding, whether rich or poor, and made the new couples happy with their gifts. If some person was too poor to marry, these "lazy ones" took care of their financial difficulty discreetly. They were the ones to make peace between husbands and wives, or parents and their children. They always had a good word for the widow and the orphan.

They used their skill and knowledge to perfection when someone died, knowing exactly what to do, and acting as always with great discretion, tact, and simplicity. They would help a dying person by preparing him or her for the new realms, giving guidance about passing through these planes, thus allowing the person to leave the body peacefully. Miraculously, they were always available at the very moment one needed them.

I suspected intuitively that my Grandfather was among this assembly of servants. I learned much from them in my childhood. No one knew where the money came from to support all these concerns. Probably, donors in the community anonymously supported them. All their work was done in silence, serving all in need. It was beautiful for me to learn about giving by watching such beautiful human beings acting for the good of the other, may their memory be blessed.

I remember vividly as a child, I served them in a simple way by being their "Errand Boy." My grandfather, blessed be his soul, would send me on simple errands, to deliver a package or envelope to someone in the community, and I obeyed with no hesitation. I just responded to honor him without asking questions.

One of the events I remember now is of my mother preparing meals for Shabbat. Some Fridays she would prepare much more food than our family needed. Then she would send me with the whole bowl of stew, telling me where to go, to place it on the doorstep of a particular family. She urged me to do it quickly, and to immediately return home, so no one saw me. And so, I simply obeyed her, acting quickly without being seen.

I innocently suspected that my she did this with the instructions of my Grand Father, to do that mitzvah (good deed) very discreetly.

The way I see it now, interestingly speaking, I can see how my mother, blessed be her memory, was practicing what the "Great Eagle," Maimonides, suggested to us in his teachings—that the best way of giving Tzedakah, Charity, is that the giver and the receiver do not know each other.

Later in life I began to understand that I was a "Shaliach Mitzvah" a messenger, a tool, to do a good deed. But I was at first unaware of what kind of work these Lazy Ones were doing. I just obeyed, and finally I detected their sacred work and technique to assist the poor and the unfortunate. I learned directly through experience how to help others very discreetly without speaking about it to anyone, just acting silently with no publicity.

This was a beautiful childhood lesson that stayed with me all my life.

THE ANUSIM (HIDDEN JEWS) OF MOROCCO

My grandfather, Eliahu Ya'akov Abitbol Z"L, once took me on a journey to the city of Fez, some 20 kilometers from Sefrou, my home village.

Without any preparation or warning, one day he simply took me to the bus outside the gates of the village and we traveled to city. And from there, the silent journey began by foot to the Medina, the ancient Muslim quarters of Fez.

We passed through a series of narrow streets where many merchants shouted of the low prices of their wares, hoping to attract buyers. The smells of the spices filled the streets with those memorable exotic perfumes.

Holding the hand of my grandfather, and silently walking through the maze of the Kasbah into this aromatic space was very mesmerizing and exciting for me, not knowing the destiny of our adventure, or why we were there.

After a while, we arrived at a small store, a sort of hole in the wall. Outside of it, they sold the Moroccan kufta, a typical food of ground beef on skewers. It was grilled on a hot charcoal fire right there, with that tasty natural Moroccan bread, and with slightly fried and juicy green peppers, to satisfy any hungry traveler with delight.

I stood there, smelling that kufta, thinking "why did my grandfather stop here?" My grandfather greeted the merchant by placing his right hand on his heart. I did the same.

The merchant prepared a small piece of bread and inserted the kufta in it, added some spices and offered it to me, smiling and saying "Eat it. It is good." Now, since I knew that this was a Muslim environment, and doubting within me if this food was Kosher, I lifted up my head to my grandfather, as if asking this doubting question in my pleading eyes

My grandfather looked at me with a benevolent and kind smile, confirming with his head movement up and down, affirming that it was ok to eat it. As the Muslim merchant and my grandfather exchanged a few silent looks, I understood that they had known each other from before this encounter.

After I ate that tasty meal, my grandfather followed the merchant inside the store, and together we descended into a dark spiral stairway below the store.

My surprise was so strong. It was amazing, unbelievable for me to see before my eyes a beautiful synagogue, almost like ours in Sefrou, with a beautifully decorated Arc for the Holy Torah, the big memorial oil glasses hanging from the ceiling, and few men sitting quietly, ready to begin the afternoon prayer of Minchah.

They were eight people there, waiting to complete the Minyan (the 10 persons needed to pray). With my grandfather and the merchant, we were 10, plus myself, experiencing and absorbing the holiness of this place—a real synagogue, deep inside the Muslim market.

Why had my grandfather brought me here? And why at this particular time? It was during the Second World War, probably in 1939. I prayed the Minchah with them, as we do in Sefrou, and as soon as it was over, we ascended up to the store front, and left after a few silent greetings between my grandfather and the merchant. The merchant particularly smiled openly to me, as if he was silently pleading with his eyes to remember this "special journey." I felt he was communicating some "mysterious story" to me that I needed to keep in my heart and to know and remember.

I was wondering what a Jewish Synagogue was doing inside that store, hiding in the heart of the Medina in the Muslim quarters. I noticed also that the names of the men were Mussa, Ibrahim and Saliman and Dawood, the Arabized names derived from their Hebrew origin of Moshe, Abraham, David and Salomon.

Those were the questions scratching my mind as I returned to Sefrou, gently holding the hand of my grandfather. Finally, we arrived back at Sefrou, and the familiar environment I am used to.

The smile of my grandfather puzzled me more, and I knew he was communicating in silence some historical secret that I needed to know in my childhood and that later in my life I would understand.

This journey was done in total silence and not a word was ever uttered to me by my grandfather about that experience.

He allowed me to **enter and feel the experience inside the story**. He did not communicate with explanation or comments, only with strange and kind smiles, eye movements, head movements, and discreet hand pressures—as if he was directly transmitting this understanding to me. But what is the "mysterious Story" that he was sharing?

That was a great wonder to me for many years of my life.

Afterword:
At first, I hesitated to write this story, for personal reasons and because of the paradox of it—how can I convey a silent teaching experience with words? However, I think the history beneath this mysterious journey of my youth is worth the challenge of expressing.

My grandfather took me on this journey, without uttering a single word to me. I guessed later that he wanted to instill the experience within me by being there.

The experience caused me to wonder strongly about the strange ways of the Jewish people living in the Medina of Fez, hiding their Jewish tradition below their storefronts, and praying in secret.

It was only later in life that I learned about the fate of the Jewish people that were forced to convert to Islam during exile in Morocco and other Muslim countries, but who still practiced the Torah and the Jewish tradition in secret, silently and very discreetly.

This is why the store that we visited appeared Muslim on the outside, and Jewish on the inside. This hidden Jewish community was practicing our tradition in secret, and continuing to relate between themselves in marriage, celebrating the Jewish holidays in hiding, still there after so many years. Probably there are many other hidden Jewish Congregations such as that one throughout Morocco, Tunis and Algeria.

Growing up, I knew less about these hidden Jews and was more familiar with the story of the expulsion of the Jewish people in 1492 from Spain and Portugal. Some of my ancestors were among them. They were called "Megorashim," the expelled ones, who came to Morocco after that traumatic and tragic experience. It is very notable that the expulsion happened exactly on Tisha B'Av, the ninth of the month of Av, the exact same date when the two Hebrew Temples were destroyed, first by the Babylonians and then by the Romans.

I experienced this "Story" directly, rather than hearing it with words, and that is probably why I still remember it so vividly today. Later, what I saw was confirmed for me by various stories I read concerning the Jewish people who were forced into Islam and Christianity, yet continue to practice the laws of Judaism in hiding to this very day.

STORIES

A Fish Story

The Guest

The Gazelle of the Dawn

The Fragrance of the Rose

The Rabbi and the Alchemist

The Mouse and the Word

Sandstorm in the Desert

The Temple of Crystal

The Inner Revolution

He Came, He Worked, and Was Gone

The Antennae that Glowed

Old Man on a Hill

My Goat of Mount Sinai

The Two Dishes and the Insect

Send Your Bread Upon the Waters

The Secret of the Hidden Treasure

The Beginning Again

My Visit to Weimar

A FISH STORY

Once, there was a fish who lived in the great ocean, and because the water was transparent, and always conveniently out of the way of his nose when he moved along, he didn't know he was in the ocean.

Well, one day the fish did a very dangerous thing for a fish. He began to think, "Surely I am a most remarkable being, since I can move around like this in the middle of empty space."

Then the fish became confused because of thinking about moving and swimming, and he suddenly had an anxiety paroxysm, and thought that he had forgotten how.

At that moment he looked down and saw the yawning chasm of the ocean depths, and he was terrified that he would drop.

Then he thought, "If I could catch hold of my tail in my mouth, I could hold myself up." And so he curled himself up and snapped at his tail. Unfortunately, his spine wasn't quite supple enough, so he missed.

As he went on trying to catch hold of his tail, the yawning black abyss below became ever more terrible, and he was brought to the edge of a total nervous breakdown. The fish was about to give up when the ocean, which had been watching with mixed feelings of pity and amusement, said, "What are you doing?"

"Oh," said the fish, "I'm terrified of falling into the deep dark abyss, and I'm trying to catch hold of my tail in my mouth to hold myself up." So the ocean said, "Well, you've been trying that for a long time now, and you still haven't fallen down. How come?"

"Oh, of course, I haven't fallen down yet," said the fish, "Because, because—I'm swimming!"

"Well," came the reply, "I am the Great Ocean, in which you live and move and are able to be a fish, and I have given all of myself to you in which to swim, and I support you all the time you swim. But here, instead of exploring the length, breadth, depth, and height of my expanse, you are wasting your time pursuing your own end."

From then on, the fish put his own end behind him (where it belonged) and set out to explore the Great Ocean.

THE GUEST

We have all experienced the wonderful warmth of being a guest in someone's home. Equally, we know the deep satisfaction of having been a host or a hostess, offering our hospitality to another. There is a genuine give and take when a visitor is welcomed into the home, an exchange that has been imbued with great meaning and significance in all cultures down through the ages.

Consider for a moment the house you live in as your host, and you, yourself, as a guest residing within. The house provides you with shelter, warmth and a place to live in. In return, you maintain it, keeping it clean and orderly. You, the guest, are actively contributing to the life of the host. In fact, you are the very life within that house.

What about your own body, the "Temple of the Soul"? Is it not also a house, a dwelling for a most important guest? The house that shelters us, made of stone or brick or wood, is obviously not conscious or aware of our presence within its walls. But we are endowed with the gift of consciousness and self-awareness, and so we should be aware of the guest residing within us — living in the eternal moment of now.

We may sense the presence of a "still small voice" — in Hebrew Kol Demama Dakka (קול דממה דקה) — sometimes referred to as the Inner Self or the Master Guide Within. We may even have begun to develop a relationship with this presence. But are we using the consciousness we have been given to truly know the Inner Guest?

In Hebrew, the word for guest is Ore'ach (אורח), which also means visitor, path, the way, the traveler on the path. In Aramaic, the word is Ouspiz (אושפיז), meaning visitor or the "holy" or honored guest.

The idea of the honored guest has been carried with us since ancient times as part of our human heritage. In the Hebrew tradition, there is a saying, "He who has fed a stranger may have fed an angel." We see an example of this in the Bible, when three guests appear to Abraham and receive from him unquestioning service and assistance. Abraham learns from these "messengers" that he and his wife will have a son, even though they are both old and Sarah has been barren for many years.

The story of Abraham symbolizes the high stature of the guest as a divine messenger. Surely every guest brings a "message" and should be received with the same reverence that Abraham had for his visitors. We learn the quality of hospitality from Abraham our ancestor.

Let us now consider the less obvious meanings of the Hebrew and Aramaic words for "guest," such as "the path," "the way," "the traveler on the path."

In the spiritual writings of the world such as the Zohar, the sages lived their lives as examples, pointing the way for others to follow. They were wanderers, shepherds, and "travelers on the path," like moving focal points — spiritual reference points of living paradox.

What then about the Guide Within, the "ONE" that dwells in our bodily temple, formed by cellular bricks of light? It, too, is a guest, a messenger from the Cosmic, deserving of our highest respect. The guest that resides within each of us is a part of the great Cosmic Soul.

This inner guest also represents the path or the way. It is by keeping our inner ear tuned to the silent self, our inner eye focused on the invisible guide, that we are directed on our proper course.

Like the great avatars whose lives have inspired us, the Master Within is also a traveler. This traveler comes to us from afar, entering the body with the first breath. It carries nothing in the way of material gifts, but brings to us the richness of a knowledge more vast than we can imagine, a knowledge that is drawn from every corner of the universe.

How do we attune ourselves to the holy presence within us? First, we must learn to be like nature — ready, grounded, still, and silent — for it is in the stillness and silence that the Master Within reveals himself, and only to the one who is waiting and ready to receive with an open heart.

It may take some time for us to reach this state of receptivity. In preparation, we must keep a watchful eye on all that enters our "house" and all that radiates out from it, so that ours will be a temple worthy of the presence of the Inner Guest.

Each thought that knocks at the door of the mind should be examined and only the purest allowed to enter. Likewise, each word that we utter, each word that tickles the tongue to be said, should pass through three holy gates — truth, necessity, and kindness. Our actions, too, must be constructive and harmonious, so that we may prove ourselves to ourselves as deserving of the Master Within.

In thus preparing ourselves for attunement with the Inner Self, we are reminded that this guest resides in all other beings as well. There may be many "houses," but only one "guest," and many bodies, but the same ONE Soul expressing itself in a myriad of special ways, like the many petals of our beloved rose or the many rays of the one Sun, the source of light of our solar system.

When two houses, two beings, face one another, they may recognize the same guest looking out through the "windows of the soul." In this constant reflection, the Inner Self is ever manifesting. That is why we are instructed in the ancient texts to "welcome everyone with joy." For as the Midrash states, "To welcome a fellow human is to welcome the Shekhinah (שכינה — Divine presence)," that sacred Divine spark that animates the physical form of all beings. In our tradition, this is called, "The Sacred Meeting."

What better encouragement could we hope for, what greater security, than to know that the all-embracing Consciousness of the Cosmic is everywhere and in everything? We need only direct our personal small questioning mind to this great fountain of wisdom, in order to draw from its infinite consciousness the message that we need at any given time.

To do this, requires that we expand our personal "little self" view to include the Guest residing in all beings and in all things. With a heart that knows how to wait, we must gradually extend our boundaries far beyond the physical, mental, and emotional definitions of the self. Only in this way can we partake of the whole.

But, a word of caution from our brethren, the Sufis! "Don't make friends with an elephant trainer unless there is space in your living room for an elephant!" And they remind us, "Trust in God, but tie your camel first."

We experience disharmony only when we cut ourselves off from the perfect connectedness of all creation. This is obvious to the true and honest student. The Guest residing within us and around us is our constant reminder of our rightful place in the cosmic scheme, ever affirming our true sense of belonging and purpose. It is by being attuned to our Greater Self — through proper word and proper action — that all health and harmony are restored.

When we stop to reflect and consider, we see that the Guest is the very life within us, just as we are the life within our material homes of brick and stone and wood. The guest keeps the eternal flame of LIFE burning in our house, radiant and resplendent. We behold the same LIGHT shining within every other house. It is the fire of LOVE, a jeweled lamp in the window of every dwelling to welcome the weary traveler. It is the fire waiting to be acted upon with the blessings of the essence of being of our hearts. The Life, Light and Love of the Guest, always guides us on our journey and reminds us that our real home is the whole universe.

And we simply call the Guest, THE BREATH.

THE GAZELLE OF THE DAWN

In a green valley, beside a tree and in front of me, is a beautiful hill full of blooming flowers. Now, before the sunrise, the dew caresses the plants all around, and on the horizon appear the antlers of a being unknown to me. Rising on the horizon, a beautiful gazelle, with bright eyes like the sun rising. The reflection of the sun's rays seem to pass through the gazelle to me. I watch as she walks toward the tree and me, my heart full with the joy of this meeting. She approaches with her gentle walk and stops a few feet in front of me, facing me with clear and steady eyes.

In her mouth is a flower she has picked up from the field. She bends and places the flower in my lap. I sit in total stillness, recognizing in her action a grace or a blessing. My eyes are wet with a high emotion, looking at her and nourishing the constant thought of thanks and gratefulness.

Then, she walks on her way back toward the horizon. And as she walks away, my eyes do not leave her steps. I count seven times that she stands in the field and turns her head to look at me again. And the seventh time, at the top of the hill, in that infinite line of the horizon, she turns her head with the majesty known only to Mother Nature. Then, she disappears into the void.

This was the meeting of two beings in tune with nature, the gazelle and me, Blessing the Creation with our presence while the sunrise witnessed this union.

THE FRAGRANCE OF THE ROSE

During a trip to Israel, I had the opportunity to visit the Old City of Jerusalem. One afternoon, after visiting some of the holy places, I passed through the market, alive with its fragrant and pungent smells. One particular store caught the attention of my nose. It was the perfume seller's — a shop filled with oils, perfumes and incense from all corners of the world. I decided to stop in and purchase a small bottle of rose oil, a scent with which I have a particular affinity.

It was a small shop, a tiny shop in fact, with barely enough space for the seller and the customer. I made my request. The seller, in showing me a little bottle, said that this was a particularly high-quality oil of roses made especially for him by someone in a far distant land. Though the price was high, I immediately took out my wallet to pay him.

As the shopkeeper was preparing my change, I felt the presence of someone entering the shop. I turned, and was transfixed by two eyes and a smile on a radiant face. The man greeted me by name. He was a distinguished looking man with silver hair and a well-trimmed gray beard. He wore a simple Western-style suit with a noticeably elegant tie.

Though slightly taken aback at being addressed by name by someone with whom I had never made an acquaintance, his calm voice and peaceful manner gave me confidence. He asked about my work and my trip to Israel. He seemed to know everything about me. Then he said, "I see you have finally come for the rose oil." I acknowledged this fact and then asked him how he knew all this. His answer was a beautiful smile and illuminating eyes. At that moment, I understood. I determined that indeed, I would like to spend some time with this man.

As if answering my thought, he said, "Let's walk. I have something to tell you." We walked in silence. I don't know for how long. We passed the city walls and walked to the foot of a mountain. There he wished to show me a hidden sanctuary which was held sacred in our tradition.

We walked up the mountain, the rays of the setting sun at our backs. When we reached the summit, we found an old structure, partially in ruins. It looked rather like an archaeological site. We descended seven stairs, barely discernible in the midst of the broken stones.

We found ourselves before a camouflaged door and my guide knocked three times. The door opened. We entered. A great silence enveloped me such as I have never felt before. In front of me were a table and two chairs. In the middle of the table rested a small lamp, which mysteriously illuminated the entire room.

My guide motioned me to sit, and he sat opposite me. After a moment of complete stillness, he smiled his benevolent smile and said, "In this quiet and peaceful place, I would like to impart to you some words which you must carry on," and for the first time, he addressed me as "Brother."

He said, "You know well, my brother, that when people speak to one another they rarely speak of that which is most essential. People talk to each other, generally, about the most unimportant and unnecessary things, just using words randomly. You know that to use words properly is one of the real principles of our work and is a mystical value of silence.

"So, what I'm going to tell you is very important. You have found from your own observations that the cause of disharmony, disease, and war in this world stems from the sense of separateness, a sense that has caused many casualties to humanity. As we enter, now, into a new cycle of activity, a turning point in our history, a new sphere of thought, of development, of higher achievement in human consciousness, we must counteract this illusion of separateness by generating, more strongly than ever, a positive attitude and unity among people, in spite of all the negativities that vibrate around us.

"This means that while these negative vibrational thoughts are being broadcast, affecting everyone, we must do all in our capacity to balance them with positive thoughts. You know that, in our time, the forces of light and the forces of darkness have come into a very dangerous friction. It is difficult for the average being to distinguish between the negative signs and the positive ones, because man has strayed from his own nature—he is out of attunement with all that is, and has forgotten the source of his own being, which is light. Instead, he focuses on the material forces—he focuses on "having," rather than "being".

"This occurs because the spiritual aspect of man has been, and is being, utterly denied by the temptation of the material forces. It is sad to notice this state of affairs, and if we will awaken to renew and re-contact the vital spiritual force within us, much of the disharmony in this world will literally disappear."

"Therefore, what we think and vibrate now, on any level, will occur. The ignorance and temptation of the illusion of appearances is what makes one fail and become attracted to only the material aspects in this life."

"Knowing that the forces of darkness in this world are in the majority, we who are working on the inner path of sanity should enforce and increase this inner work and our peace within, in order to balance this state. The relationship between the children of light and the children of darkness is known to take its course in each age and generation. Wherever one is placed in the world today, one feels this strong tendency toward destruction. This has a purpose. It occurs in order to bring about the whole picture of harmony within our own immediate living and awaken within us the sense of fullness and unity. While there is destruction, we balance it with constructive thought and action."

"Maintaining this state of balance between the spiritual forces and the material forces, the invisible and the visible aspects of ourselves, is not simple work. It is easy, however, for the one who wills it and the one who realizes that the purpose of life on earth is to radiate the light of the spiritual forces. In these transitional times, it is asked of all who still retain the unity and balance within them, to increase hope and to transcend these opposites, creating a better world to live in."

"These efforts must be taken by everyone personally and consciously. In this way, we can banish ignorance and the denial of the real self, and deserve to carry on the flame of light."

"The essence of all this, actually, is hope. I say, do not despair, my brother. Do not despair even if you see around you the world crumbling; change happens gradually. Remember that little prayer that you learned in your childhood, "Keep me sane in the midst of madness." Reflect on it every second. Today, we walk sanely and peacefully among the imbalance and perplexities around us. All the negativities from the media, and other sources, seem to come in order to instill fear and condition the human masses to yield to the obscure wills of governments and other groups motivated by greed and selfishness. Their purpose is to weaken the human will so they can control it and bend it to their own selfish ends."

"For those who know, this is a difficult transition offering us the opportunity to balance the opposites in our own living and to reach higher states of consciousness by recognizing the spiritual aspect of our being and overcoming the so-called 'fear,' not allowing ourselves to be contaminated with the tactics of verbal terrorism."

"The basis of all the trouble in this world is the personal denial of the spiritual self, expressed through talking about that which is unimportant, using words merely to impress one another, and believing in this instilled fear. In other words, we abuse the energies of our being, rather than use them to build the constructive lives and attitudes that we need in order to be creative and become the light that we are."

"If one expects catastrophe to happen, it will happen. In many ways, these expectations are generated all over the world unconsciously. Due to this ignorance and fear, people believe in it and there is an expectation of catastrophe. Sadly enough, this is vibrated and nourished all over, and one must be on guard to counteract it."

"So, our work is to increase our good efforts and expect *benestrophes* rather than catastrophes. (Bene is Latin for "good;" strophe means "to turn." Thus, to turn everything for the good). We can say that as we focus our imagination constantly on generating benestrophic events in the future, so it will be—by our positive attitude in action. By overcoming the negative with the positive, by filling the darkness with light, by finding balance and peace within, one can indeed remain sane, happy, and calm, while sailing his ship amidst madness and turbulent waters."

"To be serene and content while surrounded by noise, pollution, hatred, and violence is a great act of courage today. This courage is the sign of knowledge in action, guided by the inner self. While the outer temptations and illusions attract the ego, the soul personality balances the being with its positive qualities by simply being in tune with nature and leading us from darkness to light, thus immunizing us against the ubiquitous confusion."

"This is said from a deep living concern for the humanity that we love. Everything is in the hands, thoughts, and hearts of those who care. Those who are now being trained on the path—any path that leads to light—must increase hope, conscious effort, benevolence, sharing, and goodness in spite of everything. To bring about this balance and sanity in the world is the work that is awaiting us, and this is indeed, holy in the sense of wholeness."

"So, I repeat, in spite of all negativities, disease, and suffering on earth, be calm, so that you can balance the energies around you. Radiate your spiritual light and express your serenity and peacefulness to all. Share your thoughts and hopes with those who need them, and encourage goodness. Be gentle and happy. In this time of transition, one must be a balanced being in order to walk safely upon the road of excellence."

"May the spiritual light of the One being who unites us in our thoughts and actions guide us toward that which is our destiny and our work—to spread light and harmony and Peace Profound. Be well, brother."

When I realized that he had finished, I could not help asking him why he had told me all this. He said that upon my return to the United States I might offer these words as an encouragement to those who would be willing to listen.

We sat for a moment in deep silence. Then he said to me, "Did you like the fragrance of the rose oil?"

"Ah," I replied, opened the bottle, closed my eyes, and inhaled deeply, savoring every second of the extended inhalation. I exhaled with a sigh and opened my eyes to see the shopkeeper handing me my change. He smiled kindly and said, "Thank you. Take care of yourself, Brother."

June 1983

THE RABBI AND THE ALCHEMIST

Once there was an Alchemist, very learned and wise. While working in his laboratory, he reached a phase of his work that was difficult to decipher. He searched through his books of old, and consulted other alchemists, but was not satisfied. Then a thought came to him—he would go to see a Rabbi who was known to several alchemists as a luminary in Kabbalah.

With reverence, he entered the abode of the Rabbi, saluted him with peace and said, "Rabbi, in many years of study, theory and practice in the art of Alchemy, I have perfected my techniques to a degree that has been satisfactory to me. At this time, I am working on the last phase of the process that finally produces the Elixir of Life. However, there is a mysterious section in the book of instruction, which deals with the final preparation, and I have difficulty understanding it. Would you please assist me with your wisdom?"

The Rabbi, caressing his beard, smiled gently to him and said, "My son, you do not need now to confuse yourself further. That formula is very clear to us and I will gladly reveal it to you because of your genuineness, sincerity and perseverance."

The Alchemist thought that the Rabbi must be one of the invisible living Masters on this planet, and he was eager to hear.

The Rabbi continued, "You can take the roots of humility, collect them together before dawn with some leaves of patience and the hope that grows all over the land. Add some twigs from the Torah, also found in the earth. Find the seven thirteen-petaled ROSES of wisdom and, when all is collected, use your mortar of penitence and grind to a state of fine powder. Try to use much affection of Love and add also the waters of fear. This must be cooked in the oven (Tannour) of thanksgiving and over the hot fire of suffering and purification.

"When this process is fully accomplished and cooked well in the heart of the essence, pass it through the sieve of truth and faith. Then fast two full days in the desert of the self, waiting for the third day's glowing horizon. Wait until the dawn star appears and, at that very moment, drink the influx of God's Light through the Elixir, and let the fluids of the rivers of Life flow in your veins and thus be illuminated in Him that blessed you with the holy dew.

"This is the formula that is known to us. It may seem invisible to some, but to the wise, this is the way and this is the REAL Elixir of Life. Peace be with you, my son. Take the Shalom of the Heart and give it to all you see and hear."

THE MOUSE AND THE WORD

There was a little mouse who was hungry to Know. He didn't know what exactly, but he was determined. He thought the knowledge he sought must be high up on the shelf in the Big Book. So, he began to climb and was met by many obstacles.

At last, he reached the top. He was very excited. But the Big Book he found was jammed in between many other books and he was too little to move it.

To another, the situation might have been hopeless, but the little mouse was clever and his teeth were sharp. Up to the top of the Big Book he climbed and began to eat. Soon, he had eaten right down to the middle.

The owner of the Big Book began searching for a definition. He pulled the Big Book from the shelf but the word he sought was gone. He slammed the Big Book down on the arm of his chair, and the little mouse, observing, almost jumped out of his skin at the noise.

The little mouse smiled for he had found the Word and his stomach was full. It remained for him now to digest the Word in silence. And as for Man, he calls the whole situation a Mystery.

SANDSTORM IN THE DESERT
ARAD, ISRAEL

In 1962 I traveled from Paris, the City of Lights, where I studied Mime with Etienne Decroux and Marcel Marceau, to Israel to visit family. I journeyed to visit my sister Ruhamah, who was living at the site of the building of a new city in the desert of Israel, named Arad.

A number of young couples from various places in Israel had volunteered for this national project – to build a new and modern city in the desert. I stayed with my sister and her husband in one of the small tin huts that these volunteers lived in. I remember the dusty gold sand on the windows in the midst of the white and beautiful desert. They were the pioneers, who left their comfortable places in the cities to realize the national dream of building a new city. I noticed that most of the women were fully pregnant, bringing forth a new generation to grow up in the pure air of the desert.

One day I went out for a walk, to contemplate the beauty of nature and isolate myself from the noise of this world. I enjoyed the fresh air of the warm day, simply being in a moment of serenity with nature's abundance there.

It seems that I went far away from the dusty barracks as I enjoyed the open space and listened to that unique silence of the desert. The desert seemed to whisper to me the hidden secrets and the primordial history of this ancient site. Images of the history of our ancestors played like a small film in my head, imagining their passage from the desert to the promised land of Yisrael. It felt as if I was vividly living and experiencing that great exodus from Egypt.

While I was deeply absorbed in this imagery, feeling as if I was between here and there, without warning I began to see and feel the birth of a great sandstorm coming towards me. The sand began to surround me, and I was in the center of it, totally still, watching the sand circulating around me.

I sat quiet in the middle of the sandstorm, hugging my knees with the posture of an embryo. I knew that the storm does not last forever, and this too shall pass. So, I just waited patiently, and completely still, witnessing this miracle performed before me with great splendor by the majestic desert. I was like a dot in the middle of a living and undulating circle of sand. It was so awesome to be within it, with calm and poise.

And then, suddenly but slowly, the sand began to fall on me with golden particles, covering my little body embryo, almost burying me alive. And here I was, sitting still in the midst of it, waiting until it was over. "Am I alive or dead?", I wondered. I whispered the meditation that says that the creator renews the creation every minute always. Unaware that I was almost buried in the sand, still like a rock in my same position, I was I actually enjoying my unique situation immensely.

When the sand came to a halt, I began to stand up very slowly, my eyes still closed, with the intention of trying to remove myself from the accumulated sand all around my body. After I managed to stand, shaking myself like a tree shedding its leaves, I opened my eyes to reorient and try to see the barracks of Arad. There were no barracks in sight. They had disappeared, and I found myself experiencing that desert silence, so quiet and calming to my whole being.

That situation reminded me of an event that I had experienced while serving in the Israeli army in the early 1950s, the early years of the state of Israel. We were in evening training with a group of ten soldiers. Everyone had to call out their number to the commander to confirm we were all present. After some time, I no longer heard the voice of any soldier repeating their number. It was night and I thought I had lost touch with my friends. Again, I just sat in that place, quiet and waiting for the dawn to appear, when perhaps I could find a way to return to the camp.

I was in that state, feeling lost by myself, waiting for a "miracle." After a few hours, I suddenly heard voices screaming and calling my name. Instinctually I responded back with all my strength "Hinneni! Hinneni! Here I am! Here I am!" Some of my friends arrived quickly and took me back to the camp. They told me I was in enemy territory and was lucky I had not been killed or kidnapped.

After remembering this event, while still shaking off the sand that covered me, and searching for the barracks that had disappeared, I saw from afar figures of human beings running toward me. I ran like a deer to meet them, but it was like the mirage of an oasis, imagined while I tried to find the barracks.

So, I continued running nowhere until after some time, I begin to view the barracks from afar. I continued my run, thinking my sister must be worried about my disappearance. Reaching the barracks, I knocked on every door I reached, realizing I did not know which barrack my sister was in. Finally, I knocked on the door of one hut, my sister opened the door, and I went in.

Apparently, most of the inhabitants of the barracks had closed themselves within until the storm passed. My sister was surprised and happy that I had survived.

This event instilled in me a greater understanding of patience, perseverance and using stillness to experience my deep essential self, and it served me as great inspiration in my artistic performances.

Translation from Hebrew
Boulder, Colorado. July 4, 2012

THE TEMPLE OF CRYSTAL

Today, while in my daily reflections, I noticed that I was particularly still. I felt as if I was not of this world. I observed very closely what I saw and experienced, and in that mighty silence, I saw that I was with another presence, another being. When I looked more closely, I noticed that she was a woman of great beauty and light.

I did not ask her name or why we were now walking on a green field in a beautiful valley, with mountains on the horizon, and without a word between us, just walking as though we had a common destination.

We stopped near an oak tree and gazed at one another for some time, and then we were transformed into two white doves flying away in space.

High above the mountains, having a magnificent view of earth and the whole universe, a part of me knew that I was dreaming while I was awake, knew this to be somehow an experience of great importance for both of us. I knew that I was being transported to some destination simply by the gaze into the eye of the beloved.

After some time, if there was time there at all, I thought to land in a place that I had visualized many times. I wished to see and experience the energy of that place.

As soon as I thought this, I noticed the flapping of my wings responding to my thought, and I began a descent to a snow-white mountain of great beauty. I felt a great calm and silence which felt as if it radiated from within the cells of my body.

We landed smoothly on a flat area, and while looking around, I noticed that the weather was surprisingly pleasant in spite of the snow and ice. It felt warm. Little by little I found myself wishing to wear a new body, one made of light, as I think I really am. And soon after that, we, the two white doves, began a new transformation, into new bodies with hands and legs, heads and hearts, until these new bodies became complete in their formation.

Now I had the time to look more closely at my companion, and I saw the most beautiful and meaningful smile I have ever experienced in that other body. And as we gazed at each other, there was a new and mutual recognition of our deepest essence.

Conscious now of this new insight, we walked and suddenly saw in the distance a glowing light, a luminosity. We walked toward it, and our smiles increased as though we were creating this luminosity simply by thinking it, and an immense joy overcame me as she touched my right hand.

Our bodies were both in the form of light, and conscious of this change, we began to see clearly this place before us, which was called the Temple of Crystal. It had a beautiful form, made in crystals of all colors and shapes. The door was decorated with small particles of light, crystals of great beauty.

From Ecstasy to Lunch

We stood before that door, and it opened slowly. When we entered, I heard a familiar sound, and in that sound, I understood the purpose of this temple. We looked at one another and smiled again without speaking.

In the center of this place, there was a big pool of blue water, and for a second, I thought that it was crystal water, icy and solid, but when we walked through it, it was somehow both solid and fluid. We crossed the waters to the other side of the temple.

A beautiful being of light greeted us with a language that also seemed very familiar to me. He guided us to another beautiful room with very comfortable furniture and offered us two glasses of a green liquid. He asked us to drink for our health.

As soon as we finished drinking that elixir of light, we saw ourselves in the company of thirty-six beings sitting at a triangular table of marble. While being there, we saw on the surface of the table the whole history of the creation, and the formation of humanity and its purpose. Time was of no importance here. This was a kind of learning without words, only by experiencing and remembering.

The observant part within me urged me to be patient and not ask anything at all, JUST BE. We were now told to take a breath, and as we did, we found ourselves outside the temple at the same place where we had landed as doves.

Upon each of our chests was a crystal of great beauty. I touched mine and there was light on her chest crystal. She touched hers, and mine glowed. I understood that this was a form of communication that I would explore and know about only in time of need.

Now the echo of the white wings of the two doves came to my attention, and it was time to return to the ordinary world of matter. But this time, we kept the bodies of light as we began to hover in space and travel again. However, I wished to take back my body of cells so that I might perform the work of light as an ordinary being.

While in space, we saw the earth from above, beautiful and shining, and noticed some areas below that were darker than the rest of the earth's surface. This sight made me feel human again, the reminder that there are two sides of light and shadow, and that the role of light is to dispel darkness. As soon as I thought this, the places of darkness became brighter and lighter.

When we looked at one another, we communicated that whenever we needed one another, we would simply hold our crystal and it would light the other's. In that way, we would know that we were calling one another and could unite again and work as one, and this would assist in removing all difficulties around us wherever we were. And we knew we must use the creative force of light for the benefit of all concerned.

At that moment we parted. And when I became aware of this usual body I inhabit now, I found myself at the very place where I began this journey and realized that I was in my sanctuary here on earth.

My face was wet with tears, water flowing through me as I realized I was "crying." Yes, it was that which we call crying, but not crying for some self-concern. I did not even wish to analyze it further. It simply was.

I wished to see my companion once again, wished it, closed my eyes, and I saw her again smiling and holding her crystal. I understood at that moment that the crystal was one and the same in both our breasts. I opened my eyes and was again in my cellular body.

Now, as I began to feel my body, it was a new sensation, very new, as though I had a new body, new organs, new cells, and all this vessel had become new and fresh for a new work given to me through the thirty-six Crystal beings of the Temple of Light.

I sat in the kitchen, drinking the tea I had just prepared. I noticed the beauty of the taste of the tea. I realized how focused and clear my attention was. I felt light and love all around me, everywhere. Who had made the journey to the temple of Crystal? Could it have been me? For I was somehow a different being—I was new, I was free.

THE INNER REVOLUTION

There are those of us who are trained to keenly observe the phenomena of life around us. These are mystics, who are in tune with the forces and laws of the universe, and who are both analytical and reverent toward all life. Such people are increasingly aware of the corruption and decadence of our society; Yet, we try to see beyond such appearances, and to intensify our vigilant work to better ourselves and bring about beneficial influences to all living things.

These observations and reflections must be acted upon daily in our lives, so that the manifestations of our actions will become visible. Thus, we prepare the ground for change. And we are willing to accept that change with our whole being, and with understanding and compassion.

We are entering an era of wonder and great changes. We are already seeing this affect many people all over the planet Earth. Only the blind and selfish, which ignore the hunger, war, and upheaval of nations and individuals in all walks of life, are content with the world as it is today.

Despite the negative thoughts and actions vibrating around the sphere of Earth, we must keep the light shining and visualize only that which is good for all concerned. In spite of the illusion of appearances, we must keep the flame alive. We kindle it with the murmurs of our hearts, by serving with the best of our talents and skills.

The strength to serve comes from within and must be maintained with all our love and understanding. By so doing, our strength increases and is manifested with more power for the service of all.

This inner power exists in every human being. The mystic is no different from others. He is simply trained to nurture an attitude of reflection and vigilant study of the laws of the cosmos. Knowing that the laws are impersonal and are at work in all things, he becomes more and more successful in his labor of love.

He knows that the source of being is one, and that invisible threads of love and light connect all things for a specific purpose in this lifetime. He understands many of the paradoxes, which puzzle everyone who is not observant of life. Thus is born the deep conviction in the efficacy of his work.

The mystic knows that the inner revolution is caused by one's own thoughts, and he increases his efforts even when results do not come quickly. He waits patiently and learns how to learn. These are the qualities that make him so ordinary and simple in his way of living.

From observation and experience, the mystic learns that our planet is surrounded by clouds of mankind's negative thoughts and actions accumulated over years of hatred, greed, selfishness, and unwillingness to share in many fields of life. This fog of darkness must be cleared by positive thoughts emanating from him and the many others who are involved in the same work.

The mystic joins the great number of like minds to heal the aura of the planet through his quiet work. He mentally and spiritually activates the rays of light to scatter the clouds of doubt and selfishness, first of all from his own heart. For the primary purpose of the inner revolution is to cause a change in the character of the person who aspires honestly to live in harmony here on Earth.

The first step in initiating the inner revolution is simply to begin listening inwardly and to examine the quality of thoughts in the mind. This must be done regularly to cause any effect at all. Observing one's thoughts can reveal what we are made of. Little by little, thoughts come forth that urge us to heal that which is inharmonious. By listening more deeply, the steps toward restoration and healing come to our aid. By acting in this way, we assist the inner forces to manifest as we visualize them.

This simple process enables us to penetrate the depths of our beings. We must be willing to change so as to enjoy this beautiful transformation, which can open before us a door of infinite possibilities.

This process begins with the determination to cultivate self-honesty, and to act selflessly, with love, in all thoughts and deeds. An attitude of harmlessness is of great necessity to assist this change. In time, the results of constant effort will manifest in self-evolution and a new urge to serve others in ways suggested by our inner guide.

Perseverance and simplicity are the keys to this sacred work — the discovery of the inner jewel residing in our heart. This is the Flame of our being, the Light from the source of our becoming. By having a firm conviction, an open heart and mind, our way will be clear and sane. But we must work diligently and not expect results quickly. By changing ourselves, we can change others by the example of our being, without preaching or proselytizing. Simply by being true to self, we radiate that inner light to all who come around us.

Those among us who are aware of the immense psychic and mental pollution of the Earth are ready enough to do something about it. The mental vibrations occupying the hearts of the ignorant have caused enough crime and war and now must be elevated by everyone concerned with the welfare of humanity.

In his book, *Shambalah, Oasis of Light*, Andrew Tomas says, "What is most essential in order to neutralize the frightful aura of the Earth, brought about by the accumulation of the most vile instincts of humanity? Synchronized meditations on Peace and Brotherhood, if only for a few minutes on certain days, could accomplish miracles if directed to the whole globe. Already, this task is assumed in part by some esoteric bodies and religions, but every human being aspiring to Peace, Brotherhood, and harmony could participate in this noble effort."

One need not be affiliated with any religion to participate in this task, to dedicate a few moments in dwelling on peace and harmony to balance the atmosphere around the planet.

The awareness of this inner revolution can bring one to this work selflessly for that purpose, but one must cultivate the silence within in order to be effective.

I found on the walls of the library of the Chateau du Silence in France, during a retreat there, this inscription contributed by a Sufi brother: "If the word that you are about to say is not more beautiful than silence, do not say it." This golden rule guides us to cultivate the silence within so as to listen deeply, speak less, and do more in humility and reverence.

This attitude is what we need in order to join the assembly of minds and hearts united in this beneficial task. It comes as a result of the invested effort in changing one's self and contributing to the wellbeing of all from the light within.

This inner revolution on the personal level can bring about the manifestation of humanity's evolution. With the radiation of one's light toward all, one adds to the healing and restoration of the planet that we cherish. This is very necessary for the continuation of human civilization. We also help bring about the leap to the next level of realization of Cosmic Consciousness, and serve the spiritual Masters in their Great Work.

May these words agree with your innermost aspirations and further the work toward that noble goal of being in all and with all.

***Shambalah, Oasis of Light**, by Andrew Tomas (French version), p. 219. Editions Robert Laffont, Paris. (Quotation translated by the author)

HE CAME, HE WORKED, AND WAS GONE

There was a valley surrounded by high mountains on all sides. Between the walls of the mountains was a little village run by one man who was very tyrant-like. This one man dominated the people of the village spiritually and materially.

In fact, they were like automatons, although inside they were very much alive, and they resented their condition. But, alas, there was nothing they could do except wait. And they were waiting.

One day, seemingly from nowhere, a man appeared in the village—a man from the outside. Since he was fresh, an independent spirit, all the people flocked to him.

"You are new," they said. "You must save us!"

"Oh?" he replied, looking carefully at them one by one. "What can I do?"

"There is a man here," they cried, "who interferes in our lives, in our wills. We are like slaves. But you—you are from the outside. You seem to have a strong will. You can deal with him. You must help us."

"Direct me to him," said the new man with no excess of word or movement.

They gave him directions to a certain shop and explained that they would follow closely behind, but that they could not go in with him.

When they got to the little shop, the new man walked in without hesitation. And there he saw a man sitting at a low table with a large wooden bowl in front of him, mixing something carefully with a great and heavy spoon. His face was blue and green. His hair, silver and shining, hung to his shoulders in flowing curves.

"He seems powerful," thought the new man to himself as he approached softly. A few feet from him, the powerful one lowered his head and seemed to the new man to be avoiding his eyes. The new man stood his ground, directing his gaze and his thoughts steadfastly towards the seated figure. After a time, the silver-haired man slowly lifted his head to meet the gaze. The movement was done with much presence and with a certain knowing. In that one gesture, he looked very majestic and powerful indeed, but not demonic.

The new man watched in a kind of awe as the man's head slowly lifted; it seemed to take an eternity. When the eyes of the two met, there was a great light, and the beams of the new man were steady and parallel and never wavered. In an instant of contact, the man with the blue-green face turned into flame. From the depths of the blinding light in front of him, the new man heard a voice: "It is my work," it said. And then there were only ashes.

And the ashes spoke: "It is OUR work, brother."

Suddenly there was a great uproar, and all the people of the village were at his feet.

"We saw!" they cried. "Beams from your eyes burned him. He saw the light. It is a miracle!"

Already, myths and stories began circulating among the people of the village. "Teach us. Stay with us. Lead us. You have saved us. You have conquered him. You have saved us," they all shouted, elated at the occurrence.

The new man opened his mouth to speak. There was immediate silence. "No," he said. "You are free." He snapped his fingers and was gone.

From the invisible sphere he watched the people of the little village. They were raising their hands to the sky crying, shouting, and laughing. Soon they were dancing and rejoicing. Circles formed, heaviness lifted, and a new dawn was born in the little village.

THE ANTENNAE THAT GLOWED

"Go to the ant, lazy one; Observe and study her ways, and be wise" Proverbs 6.6

There was once, somewhere on this planet, a small remote village inhabited by intelligent ants. On the top of their heads they had a certain kind of antennae, but these were not connected to their hearts. They thought themselves to be very intelligent, and everything they needed for living was within the confines of their own village. And so, they were entirely self-sufficient, happy with what they were, their work, their hopes, their sorrows, thinking that they Knew.

One day, a stranger ant came to the gate of the village. He-she was a relative of another ant family. When he-she knocked at the gate, the doorkeeper asked, "Who is there?"

"I am an ant, an ant like you," said the visiting ant.

"An ant like me? Do you have antennae like our race?"

The doorkeeper peeped out the door and what he saw seemed to be a reflection of himself, except that instead of having black antennae, the strange he-she ant's antennae glowed.

The guard was bewildered. It seemed to be an ant like himself, but he was not sure. He went to ask the elders of the village at the parliament of the ants. They met for seven days and seven nights, but since they lived closed off in their own tiny world, they could not accept the possibility of there being other kinds of ants. After much deliberation and discussion, they came to the decision not to admit the strange he-she ant because he-she was not exactly like them.

When the doorkeeper returned to his post and approached the gate, he smelled something strange. Peeking through the door he saw the other ant near the entrance, but he-she was not moving. The guard finally opened the door and discovered the strange he-she ant had died.

After the guard had notified the great parliament, the whole village gave an impressive funeral for the he-she ant with the glowing antennae. They realized only after the death of the he-she ant that they had only black antennae over their heads, while even after death the strange he-she ant's antennae still glowed brilliantly.

The parliament of the ants then decided to add a new law to their statutes: They must not judge by appearances, because inside they were all the same.

But how can we humans be expected to learn anything from such tiny, insignificant beings? We have no antennae at all, neither black nor glowing. And perhaps, it is that very difference that accounts for our greatness.

OLD MAN ON A HILL

The ocean, shining the deepest blue, stretches as far as the eye can see, and as wide as the imagination can grasp. Its surface shimmers in the sunlight. Its mysterious contents remain hidden except to the most daring mind that could dream on what its unknown depths might hold.

The sand glows yellow and golden in the reflection of the sun's rays. The gold and the blue blend to create exquisite dots of light and color. But, who is here to view this great wonder? On a green hill, overlooking this expanse of ocean, an old man sits under a tree, silently and patiently watching the horizon.

He looks to his left, toward the glowing light in the east, where a prince, his body of shimmering gold, begins to run and leap toward the center of the horizon. He jumps with graceful ease and his arms reach out in anticipation.

In the west, another light forms and a princess emerges, sparkling like crystal. Her hair blends with her garment in a waterfall of shining, transparent folds. She runs toward the center of the horizon, her every movement embodying the joy of expectation.

As the old man observes the converging figures, the space between them disappears very slowly. Although, both figures are running, the distance that separates them decreases ever so slowly.

The man's sense of time disappears; his breathing grows calm and even, until it synchronizes perfectly with the sound of the waves as they inhale and exhale, tumbling over one another in an endless watery succession.

The old man suddenly becomes aware that the figures are almost at their meeting point. Just as he reaches the height of an in-breath, they merge, spiraling upward like a heavenly fountain. Then, for an instant all becomes light. He holds his breath and at the moment the first tiny stream of air begins to slip through his teeth as he begins to exhale, the entire sky begins to rain crystal diamonds, each one creating a spectrum of color in the sunlight. The sparks fall silently toward the sea and hang for a brief moment above the water as if to prolong their presence in the sunshine, and then vanish without causing the slightest movement on the surface of the water.

The figures are gone. The sun shines undisturbed on the ocean and the sand; a soft breeze blows on the green hill.

The old man slowly exhales; he feels as though many years have gone by, but he notices that the sun still hangs in precisely the same spot in the sky. He wonders—were the figures real or only in his imagination? Were they dream figures, or celestial beings of another dimension?

The green hill still stands, round and soft in the sunshine. And the old man—perhaps he was only a dream of himself.

And you, friend. Who are you? What are you in all of this, as the waves still roll onto the golden shore?

MY GOAT OF MOUNT SINAI

During a Spiritual Gathering on Mount Sinai in 1984, I met some very interesting beings who had assembled together for discreet spiritual work. Our intention was to project focused thoughts of peace to "this world," which seems to be functioning like a "drunk at the edge of the roof."

One night in the desert, I offered a contemplative Mime performance. We arranged the stage in a half circle, surrounding it with brown paper bags, filled with sand and illumined from within by bright candles. This was the "**stage**" lighting for what I would later call my "**Silent Desert Performance**."

It was interesting to note that I was running a very high fever that night. But, with the good help of my friends, I prepared the desert setting for the performance. Once the performance began, my fever was gone. I was able to perform mime pieces, such as "Jacob and the Angel, "Black & White," and others.

After the performance, the fever returned, and I ran to my tent to rest and prepare for the ascent of Mount Sinai that everyone would make that evening.

Around twelve midnight, we assembled and prepared for the journey up the mountain. Equipped with water in hand and with light feet, we began the ascent in the dark with guides and lighted lamps.

Slowly and silently, I walked. There were just a few people by my side. After awhile, I realized I was walking by myself up the path. I stopped now and then to sip water. My thoughts and words were focused on reciting and whispering words from the Psalms as I walked up the mountain.

After a few hours of walking, I realized that I was enjoying every step. It was as if Moshe was helping me to continue the walk upward, many of the others having ascended ahead of me at a faster pace.

I found myself becoming physically "weak," "tired," and walking very slowly, very slowly, when suddenly, two soldiers who were accompanying us noticed my difficulty in walking and approached me to help. Each took hold of an arm and assisted me up the mountain. I was unconscious during that time and completely trusted them.

After a while, the soldiers disappeared, and I found myself again walking alone with more vigor than before, ascending to the top. I sensed the echo of the dawn, and continued to whisper the Psalms with every breath and step, hearing my breath and the sound of my feet walking.

I began to see the light of the dawn on the horizon at the top of the mountain. I was aware of an inner power in my body, urging me to continue to walk until I reached the top. People were already reciting their prayers. I sat down to rest and look at the great marvel of the dawn rising, mesmerized by the beauty of the mountains and the surrounding hills.

Now and then, an immense eagle would soar past, bringing with him more eagles to join the majestic flight—the flight of the dawn. Realizing, "I am here" at the top of Mount Sinai, I became fully aware of the sacred moment of being "here" and "there." It was physically very cold, but mentally and spiritually I was warm. I was connecting myself to Moses and the People of Israel who were waiting down at the bottom of the mountain to answer him. They would make that unimaginable and "illogical" shift of human thinking by responding, "We will do and we will hear." They would agree to do what was commanded before hearing it. Doing before hearing, something that seems illogical to the ordinary way of thinking.

For a while, I imagined the whole scene of Moses in the mountains fasting 40 days and 40 nights, and reflected that, down at the foot of the mountain, the Israelites were forcing Aaron to make them a Golden Calf.

As I mused, the warm sun enveloped all my being. The eagles still circled as if guarding us from an unknown danger.

After this "quiet time of reflection at the top," we walked down the mountain a short while, to enjoy a tasty breakfast with good spices, hot cayenne and exquisite Bedouin coffee. We were then ready for the descent.

The group began the descent a short while later, each person following the ones before them on the path. Once again, I found myself alone, looking downward to figure out the best path down the mountainside. Standing at the edge of a huge rock, observing the majesty of the scenery, I observed the ways others had gone. At that very moment, a beautiful mountain goat appeared from nowhere. He was looking my direction and made a dynamic movement with his head, as if to say, "Follow me," and pointed me in the direction to go down the mountain.

Amused at the goat's precise way of communication, I replicated the same movement, as if to say that I accepted his guidance. And now, the goat began to walk slowly down the mountain, and I followed him diligently. When he stopped, I stopped, and took that moment to consider my situation and to take another conscious breath.

Again, the goat made the same dynamic movement with his head, and I responded by doing the same. This time he began to run, and I was running madly after him down the mountain, jumping over rocks, left and right, kind of like a little dance, maybe a goat dance? I was literally unaware of my movements. I felt as if my body took over with its own intelligence—strong and light. I jumped down the mountain exactly like my guide, the goat, was doing, without allowing my thoughts to interfere.

It took exactly 26 minutes for the goat and myself to arrive at the foot of the mountain. The others were sitting there and resting. My guide and ally, the goat, stopped, and did his precise dynamic movement three times, as if to say, "Now you are safe." Standing there in the morning air, with his impressive stillness, he seemed to be saying shalom. I repeated the three dynamic movements to my guide, expressing gratitude, and then went and sat with the others to rest after the relatively short descent.

As soon as I arrived among the people, rest took control of my body, and out of the corner of my eye, I saw the goat jumping a few times in the air, saluting me, and then he disappeared back from where he came.

Now, my friends told me that they saw me jump and it was almost as if I was flying down the mountain. I gently said, "I had a guide who took me on the shortcut, my guide, the goat of Mount Sinai."

Boulder, Colorado. April 1984

THE TWO DISHES AND THE INSECT

Ami and Adi were sitting down with their plates before them, about to eat and give thanks. Ami saw a little poisonous insect on Adi's dish, so he took the dish and threw it away, to Adi's amazement and surprise. He then gave his own plate to his companion.

"Why are you doing that?" asked Adi.

"I am not hungry," Ami replied.

SEND YOUR BREAD UPON THE WATERS

שַׁלַּח לַחְמְךָ עַל־פְּנֵי הַמָּיִם כִּי־בְרֹב הַיָּמִים תִּמְצָאֶנּוּ: קהלת פרק יא. א.

"Cast your bread upon the waters, for you shall find it after many days."
Ecclesiastes 11.1

Once upon a time there was a wealthy businessman who was very simple. He read the Torah every day and believed everything it said. One day, he read the words of King Solomon: Cast your bread upon the waters, for you shall find it after many days.

Because the man was very simple, he took these words literally. Every day he brought one hundred loaves of freshly baked bread, carried it to the beach, and threw it into the sea. It didn't take long for the fish to tell each other about this wonderful man, and every day when he came, hundreds of fish were waiting to eat bountifully. There was enough bread to feed many, many fish.

At last, this pious man grew old and was about to die. He called his son to his bedside, saying, "My son, before I die, I wish to tell you the secret that has kept me successful, happy, and blessed by good fortune and peace for so many years of my long life. Every day I do as King Solomon instructs, I cast bread upon the waters of the sea. When I die, you go and do the same, and do not miss a day. Do this work joyously and you will lead a blessed and peaceful existence as I have done."

Soon after this, the old man died. Every day the son took one hundred loaves of bread to the sea and cast it upon the waters. Every day hundreds of happy fish feasted upon his loaves, and it made him very happy. Now the son was not a very wise businessman, as his father had been, and little by little his fortune dwindled away until finally there was nothing left, and the business had to be sold, and the poor man barely had enough to eat for himself. Then, he spent his days begging at the doors of bakers and rich men, asking not for money, but for loaves of bread, and every day he collected one hundred loaves, and cast them upon the waters.

One day, as he stood on the shore watching the fish eat the bread, a huge fish swam up and swallowed him whole. It carried him in its belly to a great house, deep in the abyss of the sea, and vomited him up. Then it spoke to him as follows: "Man, we know of your work, feeding my people, every day, and this work has been brought to the attention of Leviathan himself, King of the Sea. He wishes to thank you personally, and I shall take you to him. He will offer you a reward, and you may choose anything in the world you wish to possess. But listen to my advice, O Man: Ask for nothing. Tell Leviathan you want only one thing, for him to spit in your mouth, and you will receive a gift more precious than anything you might ask for." When the man was taken to stand before the king of the vast deep, Leviathan gazed at him silently out of one eye for a long time. Then, he opened his great mouth and spoke.

"The voice of Solomon came to your father, and his understanding of the words of that wise king brought blessings upon many of his fellow creatures. You too, have taken good heed of the words, "Cast your bread upon the waters, for you shall find it after many days." Now, we wish to thank and reward you for your great daily work of caring for your fellow creatures. Choose any reward you like; it shall be yours immediately." The tiny man looked up at the great fish and said, "I ask no reward but this, that Leviathan spit in my mouth!"

Then he opened his mouth, and received the spit of the monster of the deep. With that, he was swallowed up once again and vomited out on the same beach from which he usually fed the fish. He lay in the sand for a long time, only partially conscious, amazed by all that had happened to him. At last, he was aroused a little by some strange shrill voices speaking near where he lay. The man peeked out of one eye and saw two pigeons walking toward him on the sand, talking together.

"Do you think he is dead or just sleeping?" one pigeon asked the other. "I don't know," replied the other. "Let us go peck him first on the leg, and if he doesn't move we will know he is dead, and then we can peck his eyes out and eat them."

When the man realized he could understand every word of this conversation, he was amazed. This was the gift of the fish, the ability to understand the languages of all living creatures! He almost jumped up laughing, but he decided to have a little fun with the birds, and he lay still.

One pigeon pecked his leg, but he didn't move a muscle. He let it peck its way all the way up to his chin, and then with one swift movement he grabbed and held onto it very tightly so it could not get away. "Now, I have you my little friend," he said.

"Ah, ah," cried the bird. "I am a creature of the air, and I cannot live without my freedom. Let me go!"

"Why should I let you go?" asked the man. "You were going to peck out my eyes."

"If you let me go," cried the bird, "I will tell you something that will be of great benefit to you."

"What could you possibly tell me that would be of use to me?" asked the man.

"We know what you have done for our brothers, the fish," said the pigeon. "If you dig in the sand directly below the spot where you now lie, you will find a great treasure. Now, let me go!"

"How do I know you are telling the truth?" asked the man.

"Dig in the sand with your free hand where my sister is standing, and you will find a great treasure," she answered. "But please, do not hold me too tightly with your other hand!"

So the man dug a little with his free hand, and soon he found money and jewels buried in the sand.

"Take care," warned the bird, "that you take only a little of the treasure at a time. Otherwise people will wonder how you became rich so quickly, and there will be trouble. And take care that you remember always to cast bread on the waters every day."

The man thanked the little bird, and then he let her go. He took a little of the treasure home every day, as the bird had advised, and soon he became a rich and happy man. Every day he followed the words of King Solomon as he understood them, and cast one hundred loaves of bread into the sea. And he lived in peace all of his days

My father told me this story when I came from Paris, France to Israel to visit him and be with my family. (1964, 5724)

My Father, Moshe Amram Abitbol Z"L

THE SECRET OF THE HIDDEN TREASURE

**"I was a hidden treasure, and I longed to be known,
so I created the world that I might be known."** Ancient Proverb

In the following visualizations, the secret of becoming One is hidden. Visualize for a moment this planet we inhabit, circulating harmoniously in its orbit. See what it contains and contemplate the power by which it keeps turning: See the peoples and their cultures that strive for life, the mountains and oceans that surround it, the treasures of metal and liquid inside its belly — gold, oil, and others — matter full of spirit. What is this secret?

Think of this liquid we call oil hidden inside the rocks. This black gold, as it is called, can make nations rich or poor. Industries turn these riches into energy that serves us. No industry can change the character of one nation or another, but from the energy treasures that are found inside of this earth comes the will of that nation.

Any nation strives to be prosperous and useful to its people through the use of these treasures, but our secret is not in the matter itself. It is not **in** the matter that **it** can be found.

Visualize the man that works in the mines or sits at his desk or drives a bus. You do not know him personally; you have never met him, and even if you meet him, you will not recognize him. Even when you look in his face, you will not see anything out of the ordinary. He is not in the front pages of the news. He is not a criminal, he is not a thief, he is not a public speaker and he is not of any political party. He does not belong to anyone, and yet, within him is the secret ONE.

He is a gray man, one without a name, who does not strive to be famous. He is not one who is looking for honors and awards.

You can see him flying a plane over his land. You can see him rowing a boat in the rivers or surfing in the oceans. You can meet him everywhere — in the busy streets and supermarkets, wherever man can be. He digs wells to find water. He guards his territory.

You need not lift your eyes to the heavens too far! You need not take your eye from this reading. Send your inner eye to see your neighbor in the public bus or train, to see the man or woman you meet casually walking along your way. He, too, is busy walking, living, or digging a hole.

Daily life keeps him busy with himself. At first, you will not recognize him. He will appear unimportant and insignificant, this gray man lacking in splendor and greatness. He is usual and invisible.

He does not like wars, but when he is called to defend his country, he is ready to fulfill his duty. With his simplicity, he does wonders. He does not like the extreme, but when his conscience talks to him, he listens and responds accordingly. He does not worship symbolic flags, but honors the land in which he lives and serves. His reasoning is simple and his honesty is worth gold. He is not too proud with his deeds. His actions are guided by the voice of conscience and these add up to great achievements.

Sometimes he is young, and sometimes old, but in his soul, there is a mysterious nostalgic yearning for what was, and for the possibilities of what could be. There is a memory of great days that demands imitation and continuation. His thoughts form a chain connecting him with his maker. He remembers the essence and ponders the infinite possibility of creating for the benefit of others. He yearns to have a simple life full of these small things that add up to great attainments.

He is here, living before you at this very moment. When he listens to that voice of conscience, he is always ready to respond with his murmuring soul. If you call him, he will reply with great love. He will shine his brightness upon you, and the world will wonder again at this magnificent work of the invisible.

Within this being, is the great treasure, the shining One, the forgotten One, the One that is laughed at and ridiculed by the ignorant. This treasure may be covered with so much dust of cynicism and indifference that it is unrecognizable, but it exists.

We need not go far to find him or to hear his voice. We need not search for him in caves or in the dogmas of religions. He is living and breathing, he is moving and vibrating right here, now. He may be reading and thinking over these words. He is inside you, present in your own beloved heart. Greet him with all thy might.

From that bright place in your heart, you can find at this very precious moment, the secret of being and becoming One with your maker. He reveals himself only when the heart yearns for this holy meeting. Thus, One meets One and becomes a greater One.

THE BEGINNING AGAIN

Once upon a time, after a great cataclysm that almost obliterated life on this planet, a small group of peasants, who were very old, were the only survivors of the global disaster. They were struggling to survive by farming the blighted earth. But the earth was so damaged that their efforts to cultivate a few food crops were in vain.

Finally, in desperation, one aged man, wiser and more courageous than the rest, proposed to go out into the world in search of food. The other villagers were too frightened, discouraged, and weakened by illness and hunger to accompany him, so he decided to set out alone.

He found a path into the large, dark forest that stood on the edge of the village fields. As he entered the forest's shadowy depths, he began to feel uneasy, and with good cause. No sooner had he reached a point where he could no longer see the village fields behind him, then a host of strange and fearsome creatures began to attack him. An upright writhing serpent crept up behind him, a hairy crawling beast without a name threatened his ankles, a sharp-taloned flying thing with great flapping wings descended from the sky upon him.

Despite his terror and infirmities, for he was very old, the man fended off the terrifying apparitions as best he could, knowing he had to continue on his quest for food.

Suddenly he heard a sound like none he had ever heard before—a haunting wail of utter misery, the thin and pitiful cry of an abandoned child. He could not possibly ignore it. He stepped off the path and made his way through the trees and underbrush, following the reedy cry, as if entranced.

Pushing aside a leafy branch, he stepped into a small clearing. He saw before him the ruins of an ancient temple, its stone walls covered with moss, its cracked columns grown round with vines. The cries seemed to come from within the temple, so he mounted the worn stone steps and entered through a low, arched doorway.

Once his eyes had adjusted to the dim light inside, he saw a small figure huddled in front of a simple altar. It was moaning softly, rocking back and forth, its head bent upon its knees and half hidden by its encircling arms.

He crossed the uneven marble floor and knelt in front of the strange little being. Reaching out a weathered hand, he lifted its head so that he could look at its face.

But what was this? The being had no face; its head was featureless, a smooth white oval, without eye or mouth or nose or ear, as blank and seamless as an egg.

He drew back, horrified, staring at this human form that looked sightlessly towards him for a moment and then quickly covered its terrible blank face with its hands, as if anguished by the revelation of its deformity.

The old man remained motionless, battling his impulse to flee from this travesty of humankind. Frightened and bewildered as he was, he sensed that the creature was suffering almost beyond belief. Tears came to his eyes and he felt his heart expand. Instinctively he reached out to the poor miserable creature and embraced it. It collapsed against him, its shoulders shaking with sobs.

Steeling himself against the horror of that blank visage, he cradled its head gently in his hands and turned it up towards him. Gazing intently at its eyeless face, as if to will a response into existence, he caressed the featureless oval. Its skin was soft and flawless, like that of a baby.

He felt an odd sensation growing in his hands. They were warm, so warm that they tingled. They seemed to move without his willing them to do so. Quickly they began to mold the little creature's smooth resilient flesh, making an indentation for eyes, shaping a nose, a mouth, ears. His hands moved now more rapidly and deftly until a fully human face, which seemed to have been waiting for a touch such as his to take form, looked back at him.

For a long moment, he and the newborn person gazed into each other's eyes. And then the person, whose fresh and perfect features reminded him of everyone who had ever been dear to him in the past and who might become so in the future, smiled. With this benevolent and grateful smile, which the old man matched with a joyous smile of his own, the two joined hands and walked out together into the waiting world.

KADDISH AND TIKKUN IN BUCHENWALD
MY VISIT TO WEIMAR. NOVEMBER 2000

> "We do not see things as they are; we see things as we are."
> — the Talmud

On my visit to Weimar on Sunday, November 19 to Friday November 24, 2000, I offered a special workshop to the Theatre students in the National Theatre—the same place where the constitution of the Nazi party was established. My whole being, flesh and bones shivered and trembled when I was told this information by one of the students.

I took some notes both in Hebrew and English during my stay in Weimar, and when I returned to Boulder, Colorado, I shelved them and did not want to look at them because they were full of sadness and heavy memories.

This was until June 4, 2009, when the President of the United States visited the Buchenwald death camp, accompanied by Elie Wiesel, who was liberated from the camp on April 11, 1945.

I watched the whole documented visit on Sunday, June 7, on Israeli National TV, and the memory of my visit arose in my mind. I decided at that moment to finally open my sealed notebook to record my notes as I wrote them then, without any editing whatsoever.

My open notes from Weimar visit on November 19 - 24, 2000:

Sunday Nov 19, 2000

I taught in Weimar the day before visiting the Buchenwald Death Camp, located just few miles from Weimar.

My voice was so silent, as if the ability of speech was taken from me. A cold that made my voice not audible surprised me, as soon as my feet stepped on this cold earth of Weimar.

The eighteen theater students present tonight in my first Workshop introduction were very attentive and listened to my words deeply, something also necessary because of the quality of my weak voice. This attitude gave me hope that they would learn some of the 10 components of BodySpeak. This is a body work method that I developed over the years in America, that was specifically designed for theatre and arts students, in order to improve their artistic expression in their careers.

During this workshop, I knew that on the morning of Wednesday November 22, I would visit the Death Camp Buchenwald, with my workshop host Anna Karoline - and just the thought of this shivered me and shook all my being.

I brought with me the Jewish Sephardic Siddur of Prayers to practice what I called the "BUCHENWALD TIKKUN".

I did not know that this concentration camp was near the city of Weimar until Anna told me, and suggested we travel the short distance there together on the public bus.

I welcomed the suggestion, and from that moment on, I began to feel strange both physically and spiritually, as if a heavy stone was weighing inside my heart, and I made a great effort to do the workshop, hiding my deep and painful emotions within me.

Strange images visited my inner view that terrified me all day, I could not understand these new feelings. And actually, I did not want to understand them, but to just feel the intensity of these feelings, sensing these frightening images in their fullness.

Tuesday, Nov 21, 2000

During the workshop, I lived in an upstairs artist's studio. Tonight, I opened the TV and saw a program on the Holocaust, and a discussion afterwards by people who were in Buchenwald and other camps - authors, artists and writers from Germany and other countries.

The whole two-hour program was in German, and Anne translated the contents to me, while holding my wet handkerchief to dry my flowing tears, from the images and the words of the participants.

Tomorrow, Wednesday, November 22, we will visit the Camp and I will utter and read the "Buchenwald Tikkun," a Restoration and special prayer for my people who perished in that cursed and cold earth.

Wednesday, Nov 22, 2000

It was very painful for me to sleep last night, because of the vivid images of burning bodies that flooded my inner screen. My eyes were in pain when those terrifying images visited me.

This morning we departed from the Weimar Bus station and it was painful for me to take the bus to the Death Camp nearby. It was a kind of an acute and penetrating pain stronger than I could have imagined, a sense of guilt of being alive at that suspended moment I was living.

At the entrance gate of the camp, there was a tower and a white clock on the top, fixed at the hour of 3:15. My host told me that that the clock was stopped by a bullet during the liberation of the Camp in April 1945 by the American GI's. That day was very cold and very gray; the sky seemed to agree with my state of being, and I felt every moment deeply.

I wore my heavy black coat, which protected me from the cold, and a black hat also, as a sign of mourning for my people that perished there.

At the gate was written a few words in German, and I asked Anna to explain the meaning to me, it was: "TO EACH HIS OWN".

I stayed in that camp three full hours under the cold and the gray skies, walking between blocks surrounded by heavy wood marks, with black stones inside the blocks. My thoughts and many vivid images raced through me, as if I saw the people that were there at that time.

I saw a group of teenagers visiting the camp, with guides that told them about the history and the events that took place in that place.

Later in the Memorial Museum, we saw films about the Camp—a brief history and how it was liberated, showing the atrocities and tortures that occurred inside this cursed place.

KADDISH and TIKKUN in Buchenwald.

Alone in a corner of the Crematorium
I stood still, my eyes closed at the
Visions and images that appeared
in my inner screen to haunt my spirit.

I saw visibly the faces of my people
with open and terrified eyes
chanting with loud voices our declaration of Oneness:
screaming: "Shema Yisrael, Adonai Eloheinu, Adonai Ehad"
"Hear oh Israel, the Creator is One and his name is One."

A great question mark
hovers above their heads,
the light of the SHEKHINAH (Divine Presence)
was shining above their silent graves.

I was both visible and invisible,
my heart beats hard and strong,
And I screamed EL MALE RA'HAMIM – Oh Creator, full of mercy,
The Shekhina trembled with the shaking lights of the world.

I stayed four days in Weimar,
and they showed me the hotel balcony
Where that cursed man spoke; all my being was
electrified while standing still near that balcony.

At the voice of madness and evil
broke the sacred vessels of my people,
I was transported between the images
of horror during my "quiet" visit in Weimar.

I addressed the young Theatre students
in that Weimar Theatre
as if I am invisibly doing,
the Tikkun restoration in their hearts.

They were all receptive and welcoming,
Every word I uttered I sensed
very strange as I looked in their faces,
Innocent faces.

I screamed in total silence
and stillness, the unuttered, the
Sacred Holy Kaddish,
to restore the souls of my beloved people.

A Kaddish that broke through the gates of heaven
and made the earth tremble,
The wind whistled swiftly and carried the souls
on the wings of the Shekhina before
the throne of the Creator, the Merciful one,
And the angels of the heavens screamed in silence,
Like me standing there, alone and uniting with them,
Lost in this mad world in deep prayers for the restoration of my people.

And the words of the Prophet Ezekiel 37. 3
appeared in my consciousness saying:
"Can these bones live"?
וַיֹּאמֶר אֵלַי בֶּן אָדָם הֲתִחְיֶינָה הָעֲצָמוֹת הָאֵלֶּה וָאֹמַר אֲדֹנָי יְהוִה אַתָּה יָדָעְתָּ

Will the world ever learn?
from these atrocities that happened
to my people in this cursed land on earth?

May the words and meditations
Of my heart and mouth
Break through the gates of prayer
And restore their souls forever, Amen.

In the Crematorium Room
I lean on the corner of the Crematorium Room
I close my eyes and I see, I sense, and I smell,
the ashes still fresh bones, crying.
El Nekamot Adonai, El nekamot Hofiah.

I open my eyes, and I see myself,
Leaning on the EDGE of the threshold
of Life and Death.
Am I here or where? What a question!

I lean on the grey wall of the Crematorium Room,
and I listen to longing strong voices
uttering KOL NIDRE.

I look at their eyes, singing silently,
and they were empty.
Full with a great ocean of fire, water
and air of a NEW Creation.

I was not alone there,
Many eyes looking at me,
Pleading and longing, with a haunting
Silence, which shook all my being from its root.
"Remember us! Remember us!"
I open my eyes and I am a visitor of the future,
I close my eyes and I see Millions of profound eyes
Staring at me, "Who are you? "Stranger"? "Visitor"?
We know the source of your Neshamah, your soul.

My voice was silenced, no words,
No movement, no respiration.
Only one single candle, the light of the Shekhina, the divine presence,
wearing a black and white garment,
walking toward the horizon.

I open my eyes and see those who
call themselves humans, tied in so many chains,
traps of meaningless words and empty ideas of delusions,
Insulting the intelligence, dignity of being,
daring to pretend to be called humans.

I close my eyes and I am terrified
By the visions of dark forests of cement,
an architecture without soul,
Forms of alienation, and Madness called Sanity.

I open my eyes again,
And vividly smell the human ashes,
Fifty years later, they are still glued to the walls
of the crematorium room.

I walk out of the room of death
to the dark grey sky of the cursed Buchenwald,
and the trees wet with fresh rain and crying
as if to cool my heart on fire.

I walk slowly my thousand and one steps,
totally oblivious of my immediate surroundings,
as if being within a new world of pretentious reality.

I exit the cursed camp and visit the museum,
and looking at the guest book an inscription
That brought me to this place, and time
of November 2000, Buchenwald, Germany.

That inscription said:
"Thank you, Hitler for your great work,
We will finish it soon"
Signed with heavy and dark swastikas.

"Welcome to Planet Earth, Samuel.
Walk, live and activate your Tikkun".
A voice said:
"And join Rabbi Shimon Bar Yohai, who said:
"Where there is destruction, we build;
and where there is suffering, we heal."

From Ecstasy to Lunch

One great candle was extinguished,
the world was dark. One candle was lit,
a new world was born, with a new great and bright light,
to break through the darkness of humans on this earth.

As the Great Hebrew Prophet said:
"…And those who walk in darkness, shall see the Great Light".

Weimar. Wed, November 22, 2000 3:15 PM

Samuel Avital

POEMS FROM PARIS
1959 – 1964

Goodbye

Morning

The Face

The Lake

The Mysterious Silhouette

The Place

The Room

The Wind

Why?

GOODBYE

Time will be given
To pass,
And ink will cease
To flow
On while paper
And pen will return
To its case.

Time to leave.
I shall fold my thoughts,
My ideals,
And my dreams
In my suitcase.

Prisoner of Thanks owed
To white paper
And to pen…
With Love,
Written and manuscript.

Paris, November 12th, 1959
English adaptation from French by Kriss Fleury

MORNING — Dedicated to my brother Raphael

Cloudy sky,
Brightness in the horizon,
A white horizon
Which promises.

Solitary house,
Up there, a chimney
Announces to the sky
The new morning.

Meeting in space,
Branches murmur,
Whispering happily,
The new-born day.

A gray face,
Stands between the branches,
The house and its chimney,
As a pensive statue.

The expression is remote,
Firm, angry,
Sadness mixed with joy
In his eyes.

The man is thinking;
His face, sculpted;
His thought, distant;
Near the horizon.

The man is dreaming,
Features expressing majesty,
The eye observes
The early morning glow.

Paris, May 22nd, 1960
English adaptation from French by Kriss Fleury

THE FACE

Black eyes,
Sad face,
Boy's head,
Curled hair;
He walks slowly,
Triste, Triste, Sad, Sad

Gold is he,
Gold is his soul,
Gold outside
Gold inside,
Gold is his face.

A happy woman
Passes by slowly,
Her look meets
The boy's eyes.

"What is it? So sad
Young man.
Why do your eyes
Tell of sorrow,
And so black is
Their expression?

"A street lamp glows,
It seems that its light
Shines.
Open your eyes
And see the brightness;
Around you perhaps,
The glitter of your star
Has risen.

"A plentiful meal
Is waiting for you
Somewhere, Someone
Thinks of you
Somewhere.

"Awake, boy,
From your deep sleep,
From your dream,
From your sadness."

Samuel Avital

And the long boy,
With black eyes
On his face
A frozen expression,
Tight lips
And far-away look,
Not a moan nor a word
Has he has pronounced.

Only his eyes,
The large,
The black,
The lengthened eyes,
Look at her face,
The beautiful, the radiant face;
The quiet look,
The entire look,
Says…
Talks…
Expectation, hope.

Oh! Your Silhouette, Woman,
Going your way,
If on your road
You meet eyes,
Black, sad eyes,
I shall call you
From the remoteness of my soul
Which aspires
To happiness and to love.

Paris, December 3rd, 1959. English adaptation by Kriss Fleury

THE LAKE

A quiet lake
Lives among the trees,
At sunset
The place is for lovers.

The forest is like ropes
Its head reaches the sky
With the wind,
Its leaves move into space.

This is war, a fight,
The swan demanding
Against the female,
In the pure waters of the lake.

He approaches a little,
She approaches a little;
This seems a love encounter,
A show which rejoices the heart.

The beauty of their long necks,
The purity of their whiteness,
Come and go, draw near,
But the meeting is cruel.

One would think
That it is a courtship,
But her soul he wanted;
And he jumps toward her
With frenzy.

Silence, stillness,
No sign of life.
When he rises to the surface,
His wings announce
Destruction.

He darts forth, with beating wings,
And with his neck he persists,
Reciprocal strangulation,
Jerky motion, and in his heart
The joy of the fight.

Samuel Avital

Again silence,
Again stillness,
Calm of the death.
No male,
No female,
On the water.

And in this calm,
The whisper of the branches
And the murmur of the water,
In the air
And between the trees.

In the wink of an eye,
Leaps master swan,
Shaking his wings,
Rocking his neck in the wind,
Victorious.
She is swallowed by the bottom of the lake.

Sorry show
Which disturbs the on-looking eye.
She is gone
Just as men go.

Around this sight,
This cruel sight,
Many human eyes
Have seen, in silence,
And with calm,
The struggle of the sexes.

Paris, May 15th, 1960.
English adaptation by Kriss Fleury

THE MYSTERIOUS SILHOUETTE

A dark silhouette
Passes,
Anxious eyes
Pierce
space

"Who are you?
Why is your walk
So sad,
So slow?

"The sun will rise tomorrow,
The skies will be brighter
Blue and white
They will light up.

"When dawn will appear,
And when all the universe
Will awake from its sleep.
A new day will rise.

"Where do you go?
Where does your thought go?
Look, see,
The joy of the world."

But it seems that a heavy weight
Is a burden on its shoulders
This silhouette,
So miserable,
is anxious
Of tomorrow's fate.

Little by little it stops,
Examines
Through the window,
And sees the cake:

A luxurious cake,
A sumptuous cake,
"Who will give you to me?
And when you will come into my stomach?
To calm and satisfy me
And become one within my body."

Samuel Avital

It looks like the walk
is getting heavier.
Near a tree, not far,
A body collapses.

Again one soul,
Perhaps a genius soul,
Cruelly swallowed into oblivion.
In the life's great ocean.

Paris, May 22nd, 1960
English adaptation from French by Kriss Fleury

THE PLACE

In a noisy city place
Full of life,
On the sidewalk
A couple is seated.

He is all, eyes.
She is all, heart;
Clasped arms
And an anxious look.

In a noisy marketplace,
Gorgeous fruits are sold,
Sweet, beautiful fruits,
For the palate which loves.

Days after days,
When the shadows arrive,
The lovers come back,
To soften their secrets
On the sidewalk.

Beautiful and small children
Play nearby the tree.
The look of the girl
Admires from afar
These children.

Extraordinary world,
Full of majesty,
Merry and naughty,
And liberty,
To each, one's game.

"One day, a child will be mine,
I shall cherish him,
I shall give him the love of my heart…"
…Thinks the girl.
Suddenly a car passes,
A child crosses,
Between the wheels
Rests a little body,
The body of the girl,
She saved the child,
With her death.

Standing like a stone
Is the boy.
Before knowing he understands
What has happened?
A tear caresses his sweet face.

The girl he loved so much
Is not anymore.
He is alone.
Fate turned its back to him
And his world has darkened.

The dream of beauty and sweetness
Made by the girl,
Passed quickly and disappeared.
Replaced by death,
A bitter and cruel death.

God! Why? Why?
Two souls thou have separated?
To serve you, perhaps,
Thou called her to heaven.

Awakening from my sleep,
Anxiety took hold of me.
Life, vision or dream?
To god to explain its mystery.

Paris, June 10th, 1961
English adaptation from French by Kriss Fleury

THE ROOM

A letter shines
In a dark street,
Closed window,
And sad sun.

A light wavers
On enlightened eyes,
Burning look,
And sick soul.

A wall encloses,
Calling voice,
Answering voice
And cracked beam.

A dawn rises,
A foot aside,
Beating heart,
And sad woman.

A hand caresses,
The foot walks,
In a dark street,
And a heart suffers.

A bunch of matches
Dance,
The fire's dance
In the devil's fields.

Paris, October 4th, 1960
English adaptation from French by Kriss Fleury

THE WIND

Outside, rain,
Beating rain;
A street corner, dark;
And a street lamp glows.

A car passes;
a man is sad,
a woman happy,
a blind person gropes.

Two men
In lively conversation,
And in the obscure street
The lamp's glimmer weeps.

Fleeting rain,
an umbrella passes,
a radiant woman's face
in the company of her husband
or her lover.

They walk,
The light of the lamp
Is panting in the night.
On the dim souls,
But it smiles softly.

One of the street's girls
Who, on the corner,
Stand with courage
for love.

In the desert wind,
a car quickly
runs away
and the silence of the street
breaks.

Beware. Danger.
Wind. The car
passes, flies, travels.
To where will it go?
Through where will it go?

From Ecstasy to Lunch

No one knows it.
Many men and women
pass, travel
and all — to where?

Only him, only her,
Holding the wheel,
Their aim is clear, maybe,
knowing the road,
the road of the wind.

Paris, January 12th, 1960
English adaptation from French by Kriss Fleury

WHY?

Why is the water calm?
Why does the pillar endure?
Why is a tree wooden?
Why is man ridiculous?
Why does a baby cry?
Why does the wind blow?
Why is milk white?
Why does the lion roar so?
Why do birds sing?
Why do accidents happen?
Why is a dream unreal?
Why mechanical inventions?
Why is expression so limited?
Why serenity?
Why, on walking, tick-tock,
do lovers' lips tremble?

Why black, white, American? English? Russian?
Frenchman, etc., and all nations?
To be separate? Why human separation?
The wall? And non-communication?

Why does the voice tremble? Who does speech serve?
Why poetry? only to mock one?
Why justice? For whom? The assassins? The terrorists?
Who is mad?
Why misery? Hunger? Thirst?

Why useless hatred? Why useless pretentious love?
Why money? For our complete enslavement?
Why the tornado? And hurricanes? Destroying homes and lives?
Why the storm and the calm? to frighten us here?
Why art? How to exist with no one to comprehend here?
Why writing? to tell untruths?
Why light? to bring us clarity?
Why fear? Of whom are we afraid?
Anxiety, existence – <u>there</u> is fear.

From Ecstasy to Lunch

Why ask and receive no reply?
Why shout and not be heard?
Why cry and not complain?
Why life and not death?

Why thought and not drowning?
Why drowning and not thought?
Why is society rotting and we,
rotting ourselves alongside society?
Why no effect? Why effect?
Why does weakness assail us, and strength free us?
Where is human power? Where has it disappeared to?
If one day, you find it, please, give me the address.

Why search and not find?
Why is finding easy before searching?
but waking scatters,
the cries of others entice,
the wind irritates?

Why exist in this world, LOST and without hope?
With the wind irritating, the cries of others inciting?
The tick-tock-tick-tock, fire burns, water engulfs,
the heavens cut short life…

Why are the churches so tall?
Do they pretend they are Jacob's ladder?
Why the cruelty of the knife of death?
Why do men know of knives when they are so evil and violent?

EYES CRY BLOOD TEARS AND DROPS OF WATER WILL
NOT WASH THEM AWAY.

ENOUGH THROATS HAVE BEEN CUT, CRIES GONE UNHEARD.

ENOUGH MEN HAVE NOT SPOKEN…
THEY DON'T KNOW HOW TO SPEAK.

Why music? For lifelong bodies dead and living?

Samuel Avital

My soul!
Cry out if you can
Cry through all eternity,
No one will hear you.
The ears are closed from dark abjection,
I shall call on you insects, ants, earthly powers,
to open a cranny in the brains of those
who think evil here.

On this deep terrible scene of
My existence.
As a lost rebel child
I cry
I write
In silence…

Does no one hear me?

Paris, April 1963
Translated from Hebrew to English by Maud Merrill, New York, 1967

POEMS FROM NEW YORK AND BOULDER

A Breath of Love

A Song of Gratefulness

A Wave of Sadness

Above and Below

Ageless Echo

Between the Two Worlds

Divine One of My Heart

Holy Void

I Am Peaceful and Calm

I Am the Song

I Am Where I Am

I Live In Times Of…

Keep Me Hidden

Keep Me Sane in the Midst of Madness

Missing the Precious One

Morning Dew

My Tears Flood the Earth

Once Upon a "Time"…

Only Five Senses?

Sitting On My Rock

The Abandoned Temple

The Flame of the Heart

The High Chamber of Being

The Magical Treasure

The New Page of One Book

POEMS FROM NEW YORK AND BOULDER, CONTINUED

The Offering of Now

The Presence of the Flame

The Silent Tear

The Station of Love and Rest

The Veil of Silence

This Too Shall Pass

To The Beloved One

To Thee Beloved

Tonight I Cannot Sleep

Two Is One

Waves of Love

Welcome

While You Can...

Within the Silence

Words from a Cosmic Lover

A BREATH OF LOVE

Today I raise my voice to sing
To the Precious one of my heart.

Today I will inhale the fragrance
Of the Love Divine within my Beloved.

And as I breathe her love,
I voice my being's murmurs for her.

The queen of my heart resides
Within my cells and blood.

And as She breathes, I utter LOVE.
And as She looks toward me, I am joyous.

Today I vibrate the music of my soul
To her that gives me love's birth.

This moment is sacred for both of us.
This love is sacred for our love Divine.

I am the gift, and you are the gate
Of infinite wisdom.

You are my treasure, and I am the key.
You are my joy and I am your ecstasy.
All lovers today are within.
All Beloveds today are humming.

You are the mirror of my self.
I am the reflection of your being.

Today my voice sings to you,
And all my bones cry out, LOVE.

Now I enter the palace of the infinite
Echo of you that speaks through me.

Samuel Avital

And all the voices of humanity
Join to the silent echo of the Divine.

And as messengers of love, we shall
Pierce the sounds of all hearts, NOW.

Boulder, Colorado. February, 1985

A SONG OF GRATEFULNESS

I am now grateful for the sheer
Joy of Being Alive.
To breath.

To be born to a family that gave me
a basic healthy formation on many levels.
To my teachers
with their patience in my formative years.
To all the friends
and enemies who, by being themselves,
caused me to be Here Now.

To my students,
who reflect me most, and taught me
patience, compassion, tolerance, and love.
To the earth I walk on every moment.
To be thankful for being able to be still,
And visit the marvelous World Within.

To be the vessel in which the divine spark lives eternally,
where the light force flows.
To recognize that when I meet "another" human eye,
the inner self is reflected through the light of
Being, that is the One in all.

This heart is grateful
To all beings I meet in this life,
Who, by being themselves,
teach me how to be myself,
To my visible and invisible "teachers,"
who are present in me whenever I am in need
of instruction or assistance
in any daily problems.

To the abundance of nature showering light and health on
all living beings on this planet and others.
To the Communion with the "One" within,
Who guides in spite of all blindness.
To the Giver of Life, who,
with His might, we become
One, grateful, and just Be.

For these and others,
this heart sings the song of creation,
vibrating in me eternally.
And Shalom Shalom to
All beings, to those who are "far"
and to those who are "near".

Boulder, Colorado. November, 1976

A WAVE OF SADNESS

There is a small cloud
In my January sky.
A little flaw in the circle of love,
A dark spot on my path today.

I need the winds of transformation,
The winds to flow and shatter
The "darkness" in the "face."
And light shall dispel the darkness.

I call on the north wind of the Great Wheel
To appear with harmonious swiftness
To make my sky of love clear and blue,
Shining with a new light of love.

Boulder, Colorado. January, 1985

ABOVE AND BELOW

From the ecstatic heights
To the deepest of caves,

From the mountain summit
To the flat valley,

From the above to the below,
From the top to the bottom,

Was my journey in 1984,
My path of joy and sadness.

From ecstasy to sorrow,
Paradox was my king.

From a beginning to an ending,
From birth to death.

And in between, a miracle!
Between the two worlds,

The spaceless, the timeless,
Between the above and the below,

Connected only by a small
Golden thread called LOVE,

A love without thought,
Without attachment, or condition:

A meeting between Human and Divine, ONE.
From joy to sadness,

A loving paradox, no above no below.
An ecstasy, no mountain no valley.

From Ecstasy to Lunch

From the year of the "Garden"
To the year of movement and change.

And I, this "me" in between
That which is yes and no,

Swinging like a pendulum of light,
High, low, high, low, hilo,

Like a golden feather
From a wounded eagle,

Flying in the air, in the between,
Between the above and the below.

From ecstatic love, Divine,
To ocean's depths of dark.

From the great union of love,
To the "separation" from the beloved.

From the blessing of the Goddess,
To the sadness without compare.

And in between, a miracle,
A gift of life anew.

And "I" the witness and the involved,
Watching emotions like waves,

And being swept with the waves,
The great ocean's love within me.

Thus, an unending circle of light
Becomes the teacher of love and gentleness.

Bless me, Beloved, again.
Bless me, Precious one.

Samuel Avital

Within you, the cave of love,
I am captured like a bird.

Within you, Joyous one,
I become you within and without.

Joy beyond compare, fused with
The wave of sad notes of my song.
From the ecstatic heights
To the depths of caves
Was my journey of 1984.

From ecstasy to sorrow,
Paradox was my precious friend.

Boulder, Colorado. January, 1985

AGELESS ECHO

The celestial voice
Ringing my heart,
Lifting my spirit to the heights,
Breathing along with the Cosmic Music.

Still, I am,
Tears flowing through my eyes like
Winding rivers of an ancient echo,
An echo before everything was.

Listening, silently,
Inside the cave, the source of sound,
Of word, of letter and wind,
Becoming that silent murmur of Joy and Peace.

So many souls present,
Listening with me.
To this nightingale's ancient voice.

Eyes, faces enraptured in the
Eternal moment of becoming,
Singing within the wind
Of Peace Profound.

Friend of Peace,
Sit, be still, listen to your
Ageless voice of Supreme Being,
The Nameless ONE,
Permanent resident in every heart.

Listen to the silence within,
You will hear the Sound of Silence.

Boulder, Colorado. September, 1984

BETWEEN THE TWO WORLDS

1.
I am captured, a wave between the two worlds,
Resting my heart and being in Thee.
In the holy abode of Thy warm room,
I am a spark of light between your two breasts.

2.
In between two waves, I am a drop in the ocean,
in the temple of love and light.
In between the two pillars, I stand ready to reflect
in the chamber of my being and becoming.

3.
I am a treasure that can be found
in the concealed cave of wonders.
Open only to those with the key,
Known to the followers of the Tao.

4.
The lover and the beloved are one
In between breaths,
The one and the other are one
In between yes and no.

5.
The Garden of Eden is in Thee,
Between Heaven and Earth,
The tree of life is this "me",
between the leaves of Thy lips.

6.
In between fire and water, I am Thee,
In between air and earth, I am here,
In between joy and sorrow, I am there,
In between two drops of water, I am ocean.

From Ecstasy to Lunch

7.
I am a captured spark of light
between the two worlds.
I am the key, and thou art the door.
I am the wave, and thou art the ocean.

8.
In Thine inner sanctuary, I found refuge,
In Thy holy chamber, I found the joy of becoming.
Thy perfumed garden is my heaven,
In between Thy gates, I am one with all.

9.
Between the sacred and the ordinary,
I dwell in Peace Profound.
Between that which is above and that which is below,
I live in the joy of being and not being.

10.
Between that which is inner and that which is outer,
I am the dot that forms it all.

11.
Between the sun and the moon,
I am the earth on which you dwell,
and walk to become what you become.
Between movement and stillness, I simply am present within all
beings.

12.
I am Thou, and Thou art me.
And there is no Thou and me.
Just being one in one.
Blessings to Thee, Mother Earth, I am
Thy child, and Thou art my source of being.

Boulder, Colorado. September, 1984

DIVINE ONE OF MY HEART

Make a place for me, Divine one,
Open for me the door of Joy,
Let my head rest near your heart
To hear earth mother's sound.

Divine woman of my heart,
We are the Key and the Door
For one thousand rooms of love and wisdom.
In Thee, I find refuge and serenity.

In your embrace, I tremble in Thy gaze.
In your being, I am the gaze itself.

With your hand's caress, All of me becomes JOY.
With your eye's look, Thou art the Mirror.

All beings are in Thee, One.
All forms are in Thee, ONE.

Words are inadequate to sing the great joy,
Feelings are poor to breathe the mysterious
murmurs of my heart.

Names are not names to name Thee,
Thou art beyond name and form.

LOVE is the word humans use for this breath.
LOVE is only a drop in the ocean of the Great Being,
and I am just a spark of light.

A spark of light, made of Thee.
And as such, I may become Thee.
Here or there, it does not matter anymore.
Time or space, it does not matter anymore.

Boulder, Colorado. December, 1984

HOLY VOID

Captured in the emptiness
In the center of the void.
Nothing to hold
Nothing to touch.

Exiled from the source of my being
The center of love.
Transported on the unknown wave
To the edge of nowhere.

Guided by the wind of joy
To the palace of my beloved.
I rest, I become one
With my infinite love.

With the light of my soul
Led to be conscious of this new void.
Surprised immensely and awed
By the nothingness of this SELF.

Boulder, Colorado. February, 1985

I AM PEACEFUL AND CALM

I am peaceful and calm
I feel warm and loving toward myself
I create wealth and abundance in my life
I always do my best with what I know

I forgive myself unconditionally
I give myself permission to live, love and laugh
I live in an abundant universe
I am my own best friend

I am a joyful giver
I forgive my enemies.

Boulder, Colorado. November 27, 2003

I AM THE SONG

I am the song of all life within you and me, Beloved.
I am the letters with which you write my name of love.
I am the golden pen with which you move your hand of love.
I am the same breath that moves you to me and me to you.

You are the paper on which I am writing my song.
You are the holy space in which I become me within you.
You are the parchment on which my being is written by you.
You are the same me that proclaims today the joy of becoming.

We are two bodies made of the one spirit of love.
We are two rays of light merging into the infinite.
We are two opposites that converge and act upon one another.
We are that oneness itself that makes us be aware of "YOU" and "ME."

In that place where there is no "me" and "you"
In that time where there is no name or form
In that tune that unites all in oneness
In that holy place we become and merge with the MOTHER of all.

I traveled half circle of darkness of winter,
To emerge a NEW BEING of spring.
And thus open a NEW PAGE of love and friendship,
With new understanding of what is "one" and the "other."

I have woven your being into my eternal dream.
You have found in me that "hidden you" of light.
We have reflected into one another, and
Allowed the time and space to heal us from all illusions.

This song is sprung from a well,
Ancient and magical.
To you, to me, this song is
One heartbeat of great magnitude.

Boulder, Colorado. June, 1985

I AM WHERE I AM

"If I am not for myself, who will be for me? And if I am only for myself,
What am I? And if not now, when?" Hillel – Sayings of the Fathers 1.14

I am where I am, you are where you are.
When you are where I am,
I am where you are.

When we are where I am
We are where I am and you are.

When you are where you are
And I am where I am
We are "separated."

When you are where I am
And I am where you are,
We are united.

When you are not, and I am not,
We are then, where we all are,
with the ONE. Within the ONE,

Beyond the ONE which cannot be counted—
when we are "separated," we count.

The more we count the more
we diminish from the ONE.

When we diminish from the ONE,
we suffer and complain to the "gods,"

Asking why we suffer, and we begin to "pray,"
and invent new "religions."
When we pray that way, we are again separated.

And our only sane restoration
Is to BE ONE with ALL,
With our thoughts, words, and actions.

This is the sane road to the authenticity of being,
a way of learning to nurture the state I call:
"The Conscious Innocence" — the state of Being One.
Where you and I are where we are,
both being and becoming, ONE.

Boulder, CO. May 6, 2003

I LIVE IN TIMES OF...

1.
I live in times when intelligence and sanity have left this planet.

I live in times where the soft human heart has turned into a heart of stone.

I live in times that my ancestors told me: "And at THAT TIME" you will know.

I live in times where dishonesty and corrupted leaders are the new norm.

I live in times that I scream like a child and no one hears my conscious weeping.

2.
I live in times that the light is considered dark and the dark is considered light.

I live in times that the left is right and the right is left.

I live in times of the edge of the edge of the edge of all the edges.

I live in times when humanity is "like a drunk at the edge of the roof."

I live in times that look and feel like the great insane asylum of the Universe.

3.
I live in times that pretense and stupidity are rampant and the norm.

I live in times where noise is silence and silence is noise.

I live in times where "health" is lack of disease, and people calling 911 for a minor scratch.

I live in times where the pretentious succeed and the honest are ignored.

I live in times where true wisdom is mocked and the lies and honesty are revered.

4.
I live in times where terrorists receive the Nobel Prize, and the courageous person is dismissed.

I live in times where the essence of life is called phenomenon.

I live in times where the leaders are mentally imbalanced in the land of fools.

I live in times where this anti-civilization worships dishonesty and is addicted to "success."

I live in times where the black is white and white is black.

5.

I live in times where evil and greed is considered good and good is considered evil.

I live in times where it is fashionable to be a victim feeling entitled to benefits.

I live in times where tyrants call themselves honest leaders.

I live in times where the docile and complacent citizens accept the lies.

I live in times where sweetness is bitter and bitter is sweet.

6.

I live in times where "leaders" present the truth as a lie and the lie as truth.

I live in times where "tyranny is on, and people are afraid of government."

I live in times where freedom without self-discipline is rampant.

I live in times where mediocrity is praised, glorified and worshipped.

I live in times where well-dressed terrorists receive the Nobel Prize for "Peace."

7.

I live in times where one is considered guilty until proven innocent.

I live in times where lawyers justify the guilty and the guilty is presented innocent.

I live in times that the value of justice has disappeared from the human vocabulary.

I live in times where police brutality and child abuse is the new norm.

I live in times where the greatest theatre of the absurd is active and appreciated.

8.

I live in times of being inside of the greatest insane asylum of the universe.

I live in times where the fools lead and pretend to work "for the good of the people."

I live in times where children defy their parents and despise self-discipline.

I live in times where teenagers shoot their friends in the school cafeteria.

I live in times where "iniquity and evil have increased to the highest pitch."

9.

I live in times where "the wicked prosper and the good ones fall into contempt."
I live in times where the unaccomplished, ignorant and the incompetent, rule.
I live in times where violence, racism and hatred are accepted without protest.
I live in times where murder, dishonesty and deceit are promoted as acceptable.
I live in times where abuse of sex and violence become a norm of accepted behavior.

10.

I live in times most humans have forgotten their basic kindness and genuine care.
I live in times where care for animals is more important than caring for humans.
I live in times where there is no more shame or admitting when one is wrong.
I live in times that schizophrenic leaders are elected by majority.
I live in times a fire-fighter will save the animal life rather than the human one.

11.

I live in times where everything is upside down, and being confused is "natural"
I live in times where history is rewritten to honor dictators, murderers and thieves.
I live in times where the founding documents of the USA have been shredded,
I live in times and where every person's guaranteed liberties, are denied.
I live in times where humans have forgotten how to be humans.

12.

I live in times where fascism is now fashionable again.
I live in times where everything you say may be held against yourself.
I live in time where animal cruelty is more important than human cruelty.
I live in times that the life of a dog is more valuable that a human being.
I live in times that most humans create problems where they do not exist.

Boulder, Colorado. Friday, Feb 10, 2012

From Ecstasy to Lunch

אֱלוֹהַי, נְצוֹר לְשׁוֹנִי מֵרָע וְשִׂפְתוֹתַי מִדַּבֵּר מִרְמָה וְלִמְקַלְלַי נַפְשִׁי תִדּוֹם.
"Elohim, guard my tongue from evil and my lips from speaking deceitfully,
And to those who insult me, let me stay silent...."
From the morning Hebrew prayer meditation.

"AT THAT TIME" Insolence and honor will be in contempt.

The chamber where the scholars meet will be used for harlotry.

The wisdom of scribes will be deemed a stench. The truth will be lacking.

The face of the generation will be (brazen) like the face of a dog.

The young will humiliate the elders, and, a son will revile his father.

The daughter will rise up against her mother and shame her parents."

Mishna, Tractate Sota, page 49b.

KEEP ME HIDDEN

Within our heart, your inner sanctuary,
Keep me hidden.
Within your breath, the spirit of life,
Keep me hidden.

Seal me in the stamps of your love,
Keep me hidden within your being.
In your cave of crystal,
There shall you keep me hidden.

Help me to stay invisible,
So that I can observe quietly
The murmurs of your heart
Where I shall always be kept concealed.

In that hidden place, our love
Increases its power and joy.
Within my heart you are forever hidden
As the power of the Jewel in the Divine Crown.

Within that invisible place,
I shall be always the KEEPER OF THE FLAME,
The Flame that makes all be and not be,
You and I, visible in the white mountain.

Through the fire of the Beltane
I gaze upon you from the inner warmth
Of my being, and your Divine Grace
Is for me the holy hidden place.

From within the great sleep,
I am awakening within you,
And within your thought, I become
One, with you, with the eternal breath.

From your heart, where I am concealed,
I activate the flow of your being.
And in return, I inhale your breath
That makes me be, becoming love for you.

From Ecstasy to Lunch

This word is offered with the singing
Heart of gold,
Born from the moments of Ecstasy
Activated by your precious presence.

Keep me hidden, Beloved,
This I have asked you the first time
I became aware of you within me.
And your acceptance is a blessing to me.

I am your hidden treasure
And within you I am known.
Your inner flow of blessing
Is my sign of eternal love.

Hidden I shall be always,
From all eyes that do not see,
From all unbalanced thoughts.
Hidden I am within you, as you are within me.

Great longing lives with me all these days.
Your name is a nectar for my wounds,
Wounds that are canceled by the light of
Your heart.

Remember, Beloved, the word of love,
The precious moment of our Oneness,
Sacred and concealed.
Keep me hidden within you, Beloved.

Boulder, Colorado. April, 1985

KEEP ME SANE IN THE MIDST OF MADNESS

Keep me Sane in the Midst of Madness
Keep me pure in the midst of mud.
Keep me a soft rose in the midst of thorns.
Keep me an open door in the midst of walls.

Keep me ONE in the midst of many.
Keep me healthy in the midst of disease.
Keep me straight in the midst of broken lines.
Keep me bright in the midst of darkness.

Keep me sacred in the midst of secular.
Keep me conscious in the midst of unconsciousness.
Keep me lucid in the midst of the slumber.
Keep me a circle in the midst of squares.

Keep me close to the core in the midst of the circumference.
Keep me a dot in the midst of a circle.
Keep me awake in the midst of the sleepwalking.
Keep me always "here" in the midst of "there."

Keep me in the vicinity of love in the midst of hate.
Keep me important in the midst of indifference.
Keep me moving in the midst of stillness. And still in the midst of motion.
Keep me in the foundation of the kingdom of Light.

Boulder, Colorado. 1971

MISSING THE PRECIOUS ONE

Where have you gone, my beloved?
Where do you hide from my eyes?
Only your presence is healing,
Only your sweet scent is alive within me.

Where shall I find you?
Hiding in my heart?
Show me your sacred face,
The light of your splendor,
The joy of my being.

You awakened within me
An ancient memory, and ancient love.
You are the bell of my awakening
To recover the form of new love.

Where shall I go without
The radiance of your presence?
Where shall I run to find
The loving heart of ancient love?

I am both the question and the answer.
You are my heart, and I am
The breath of that beating.

Return to me, Beloved,
To dissolve the quest of love.
Return to reside in my heart,
So You and I are ONE,
So there is no You and I.

Boulder, Colorado. January, 1985

MORNING DEW

Early morning, before the light of the sun shone,
I landed in a field of Roses
As a drop of Dew, shining, and
Breathing the Morning.

When the sun's first ray appeared on the horizon,
I was still embracing the petals of Roses,
And when the morning expanded,
I evaporated with the sun's rays, becoming light.

Thus, I, the dew drop,
Became, from moisture, light,
Disappearing into warmth;
From water, to light, to air.

I picked a Rose from my garden
one morning,
Put it in a large basin of water,
With the dew drops still on the petals,
And called Bat Oryah,
And whispering, said:
I am reposing on the petals, Will you see me there?

Boulder, Colorado. August, 1984

MY TEARS FLOOD THE EARTH

My tears flood the Earth,

And my children are in the
mysterious maze of confusion,

And my heart melts like a
crying candle from the
inner flame.

And thus, compassion is
revealed
To Be.

Boulder, Colorado. December, 1976

ONCE UPON A "TIME"...

ONCE UPON A "TIME" there was America,
And now, we have to light a candle to look for it.

ONCE UPON A "TIME" I was myself,
And now, I pretend to be myself.

ONCE UPON A "TIME" I breathed air,
And now, it is polluted.

ONCE UPON A "TIME" there was "freedom,"
And now, it is no more, and we cannot buy it from any store.

ONCE UPON A "TIME" there were close relationships, and patience in relating to one another,
And now, no store can sell us patience and tolerance.

ONCE UPON A "TIME" we could get together in public,
And now, we have social distancing.

ONCE UPON A "TIME" there was a precious gift called freedom of speech and movement,
And now, we stay at home between our four walls, "for our own good."

ONCE UPON A "TIME" I was asked to perform for live audiences,
And now, I perform for absent audiences.

ONCE UPON A "TIME" we could go on vacation.
And now, we cannot travel.

ONCE UPON A "TIME" there was trust,
And now, we suspect one another.

ONCE UPON A "TIME" I was joyous about life,
And now, we are sad and more lonely than before.

ONCE UPON A "TIME" there was the possibility to love,
And now, there is hatred that separates us from loving.

ONCE UPON A "TIME" there was hope for a better future,
And now, all is full with doubt and suspicion.

ONCE UPON A "TIME" there was true and authentic journalism,
And now, most of the news is false, and full of lies,
And newsmakers are barking at us with words of fear.

From Ecstasy to Lunch

ONCE UPON A "TIME" the social news media pretended to connect us,
And now, we are disconnecting, and they make the disconnection only deeper.

ONCE UPON A "TIME" we talked about life, love and light,
And now, all this has become a big illusion, lifeless.

ONCE UPON A "TIME" there were real and brave statesmen,
And now, there are career politicians, who look out for themselves,
and not for the benefit of those who elected them to office.

ONCE UPON A "TIME" there was kindness between us
And now, we are mean to one another.

ONCE UPON A "TIME" we respected and honored our parents and teachers,
And now, we do not even visit them, and despise them openly.

ONCE UPON A "TIME" we could hug, shake hands, and kiss each other,
And now, it is forbidden to touch each other, thinking the other is sick.

ONCE UPON A "TIME" the other was a friend,
And now, the other is the enemy.

ONCE UPON A "TIME" a pregnant woman was a blessing and a miracle,
And now, pregnancy is treated like a disease, and sneezing is suspicious and dangerous.

ONCE UPON A "TIME" I used words and movement to communicate and teach,
And now… I have no more words and no movement to teach. But I "have" plenty of time
to contemplate, and find new ways to restore all that is, starting first with myself, and then
extending that restoration to all the world.

We see now that what was can suddenly not be.
Suddenly, our way of life can come abruptly come to an "end."

We are struck by a challenge – suddenly we must become aware of what is and what is not
Thus learning to accept the paradox

And the only sane way is to realize:
That which appears to be bad and negative has the immense ability to create a great light of
goodness - offering us a new and awaked way of being.
We can appreciate this miraculous life with a new consciousness of increased kindness,
enjoying life in its amazing simplicity, and helping one another any way we can

NOW we are between the hammer and the anvil.
NOW we are between yes and no.
NOW we are between here and there.
NOW we are between you and me.

Samuel Avital

NOW we are between him and her.
NOW we are between what is and is not.

WE must NOW, Arise to use less I and more WE
The obvious miracle is that, some of us ARE STILL HERE, against all odds,
I am confident there are still some honest and intelligent human beings left on this planet, and the Earth and the Heaven will always be here after we are all gone, with us or without us. Life is forever.

So BE HERE AND NOW, and become, once again, the true being you were really meant to be. I have no more words, and it is now time to enter into my palace of silence, and let my teardrops merge with the great ocean of being.

No one can take from the human heart the hope towards a new awakened way of being, more conscious and with the great joy of life and existence.

Let King Solomon counsel us with his practical wisdom, still so relevant today. Enjoy this moment in which you can read these words, while you are still here and able to read.

Ecclesiastes 3. 1- 4:

To every thing there is a season, and a time to every purpose under the heaven	לַכֹּל, זְמָן; וְעֵת לְכָל־חֵפֶץ, תַּחַת הַשָּׁמָיִם
A time to be born, and a time to die;	עֵת לָלֶדֶת ,וְעֵת לָמוּת;
A time to plant, and a time to pluck up what was planted;	עֵת לָטַעַת, וְעֵת לַעֲקוֹר נָטוּעַ;
A time to kill, and a time to heal;	עֵת לַהֲרוֹג , וְעֵת לִרְפּוֹא
A time to break down, and a time to build up;	עֵת לִפְרוֹץ וְעֵת לִבְנוֹת
A time to weep, and a time to laugh;	עֵת לִבְכּוֹת וְעֵת לִשְׂחוֹק,
A time to mourn, and a time to dance	עֵת סְפוֹד וְעֵת רְקוֹד

ONLY FIVE SENSES?

I open the door of my heart for these words to flow, to utter some
of the images and experiences over the years of being here,
so you may listen and wake up from that deep slumber.

I wander in the wild streets of the unknown, alone, and the
flowing red tears from my face, turn into the great river of life.

HEARING - LISTENING

I hear my stomach singing the song of hunger

I listen to the echo of a child who cries like a dying violin.

I hear the voice of a woman who scolds her child who is
crying and hungry.

I listen to the wind that caresses the trees and tells them
the most simple and guarded secret of the universe.
I hear a cruel saw furiously cutting down the only tree in the horizon,
and the crying violin, and the hungry helpless child.
I listen to the sound of bombs that kills my ears and threatens
to steal my instrument of hearing.

I hear the breeze of wind and the murmurs of my universe,
and I listen now with my other instrument of listening.

I listen to the noise of a city pretending to be good, while almost
all are walking in the darkness of the soul.

I listen to the human suffering with every breath while waking
hungry in the streets of a wealthy people.

I hear how to listen to my soul urging me to come back
to the source of being and dare to be where no one is anymore.

I listen to the movements of my inner being and learn to decipher
the "mystery" of my being, so that I may become a "mystery."

I hear the agony of pregnant women tortured by impotent and
sick men who wear the mask of "good".

I hear the troubling voices of a generation gone crazy, a suffering
generation that forgot the difference between good and evil.

I hear a perplexed generation that has forgotten how to be kind to one
another, living on the surface with the great mask of arrogance,
lying, perfected pretention, and mastery of self-deception.

SEEING

I see the rainbow that my eyes receive in splendid colors,
bursting to shape a form, an idea into action

I see many humans rushing and running in the streets, as if going
to an unknown place, like mad robots driven by a strange and
inhuman force, pursuing their urgent ways, toward their slow
descent of self-destruction and annihilation.

I see groups of humans panicking, screaming and crying
and running after an enraged man.

I see women and children running in the streets, screaming
for help, and no one comes to their aid.

I see a street clock that shows 10:15, and when crossing
the street it shows 3:30.

I see the lights that caress the streets of Babylon (New York)
Like shining pearls around the neck of a beautiful woman
in a self-made prison.

I see the street that leads me to my place, the school, and the day of the
Public market, hurrying to kiss passionately the beautiful
breasts of their women.

I see a flying dancer above the Empire State Building, covering New York
with her blue and white veil, hanging from her shoulders.

From Ecstasy to Lunch

I see a serpentine path that leads to infinity, like a beautiful garden
 swimming in its fresh green grass.

I see an immense cloud covering this earth with darkness,
and know that the light will not return until the time when all humans yearn
and beg for light to give life to this earth again.

I see the indifference of humans toward the essence of life,
while pretending to want to live.

I see how intelligence has the brains of humans, leaving
only the moisture of gray matter with no spirit and no meaning.

I see how slowly humans distort reality, and call the light darkness,
and the darkness light, wrong as right, and right as wrong.
and the good as evil, and the evil, as good.

I see when a time comes when humans will rediscover again the simple
and meaningful purpose of life, and live it fully, with no because.

TASTING

I taste the bitterness in the liquid in my cup of this life, as a passenger
from "here" to "there."

I taste the terrible taste of unkindness that endangers my very
existence here, and dream of infinite possibilities
of restoring my life.

I taste the imaginative dinner when my teeth are so clean from hunger,
imagining vividly when shall I eat to nourish myself with a
great appetite.

I taste the thoughts of humans plotting to kill one another with their
unconscious and negative thoughts.

I taste the drops of the water inside my palate, as if it was the promised
elixir of life.

I taste the thoughts of others, as if I am inside their brains, knowing all
their little "secrets", and the pretense of their pitiful behavior.

I taste the joy of my first daily breath as if I had just landed
in this body from another dimensional reality of existence.

I taste in my imagination a morsel of food to visit my hungry palate,
so I can bless the one who feeds all the hungry.

I taste the occasion to wake up one day in the arms of my beloved,
Singing to her the most beautiful verses of the Song of Songs
of Solomon.

I taste the presence of a being full with light that embraces all my
being, that seems familiar from another realm, not from here.

I taste my imagination of my mother's cooking while I am
desperately hungry and I feel as if I just tasted the Manna
itself from heaven.

I taste the longing of my soul remembering her "Divine Stamp,"
being tested in "this world" so it can overcome the desires of the flesh,
and soar beyond the "story," to learn to read a new story and a new way of being

I taste the sweet mixed with the bitter, the white and the black, the whole and the detail,
and learn finally to live here, be here,
and concentrate on my motto: "Keep me Sane in the midst of madness."

TOUCHING

I touch with my eyes the desperate look of a woman in search of love.

I touch gently with my hands the rebellious form of her tortured body in agony.

I touch with my eyes the bright rays of the sun in the early morning
watching the horizon.

I touch with my ears the sounds of the birds welcoming the morning
with cries of joy.

I touch with my palms the soft leaves of the rose bathing
in the morning dew.

I touch with my knees the soft earth while I kneel in
devotion to imitate the rose.

I touch with my nose the edge of "space" and call it, a "time"
to Be and Become.

I touch with my fingers the surface of the tree of life and
ask for knowledge and wisdom.

I touch the surface of her smooth skin as if I travel in the
sacred earth of my being.

I touch the soft cheeks of her face and whisper to her ears
the secrets of life.

I touch the iris of her eyes, and she blesses me with her presence
and her benevolence.

I touch the essence of her being, so I may know the purpose
and meaning of "this life."

SENSING – FEELING

I sense with my soul the movements of life and light within
every being everywhere.

I feel the constant suffering of my people in my heart, as if eternity
lives within my cells and bones.

I sense some words spoken for no purpose by unaware humans
pretending to be awake.

I feel with my ears the whirling buzz of a time before I was born,
and what am I doing here?

I sense the cries of small hungry children falling on deaf ears
in a world gone mad.

I feel with my heart the message of Solomon's dream to ask for wisdom
rather than fame.

I sense millions of ears attempting to listen to their inner heart
to restore the world.

Samuel Avital

I feel with my hand the caresses of the ancient echo calling me
to "remember."

I feel with my eyes the sight of light that cannot be described
with human language.

I sense the infinite joys of those who know fully who they are,
and why they are here.

I feel with my essence the millions of cries of humans for a better time
of one peace, one knowledge and kindness to all.

I sense with my whole being the totality of all humanity, as if
I breathe with all creation the song of our being and becoming,
and the constant gratefulness to simply be here, now.

I see beyond seeing,
I hear beyond hearing,
I touch beyond touching,
I feel beyond feeling,
I taste beyond tasting
the power that created me here,
to be able to write these letters, and dare to utter
these words from my experience,
while passing through "this life."

Whoever you are, wherever you are, please, accept these words
with a humble spirit in an attempt to give profound gratitude
from all my heart and being.

I wonder about the effect my words have inspired in you to wake up.
Only you can know what will happen to them.

With this "knowing," I close these sealed words to you, consciously
choosing the outcome that brings ONLY goodness and joy to all
humans, with profound hope, that you will do something with your awakening to the new
reality, that is good for all beings.

New York City, USA. Friday Nov 24, 1967

SITTING ON MY ROCK

Sitting on my Rock
at the edge of the world
where there is no more horizon.

Sitting on my Rock
and looking into deep water
I see the world dissolving,
alone, on my lonely Rock
I am sitting, frightened.
let me stay on my Rock
and laugh to the end of my breath.

Still sitting on my Rock
the clouds down at my feet
feeling the angry wind sweeping this planet.
Awake, my Earth, awake,
the end is approaching
on the fast and angry wings
of the ferocious eagle.

And I, still sitting on my Rock
cry like a little child
frightened and hoping.
Maybe the hope of this little child
who just entered this planet
from his mother's womb
with an innocent cry,
will awake you,
my sweaty Earth.

Still, immobile on my lonely Rock
at the edge of the world
the Rock and I are one
hearing millions of innocent cries
of those who will sweep the world
with their new cry of hope,
of change,

of revolution,
and build a new world
of love, of peace.

But still on my Rock
sitting on the edge of the world,
caressing the universe
with little hands,
with hope, with love,
to guard it from that terrible end.

New York City, USA. January, 1969

THE ABANDONED TEMPLE

Here you are, now, abandoned
in silence on Henry Street
absorbed by the years of prayers,
of prayers without answers,
your walls crying the laments
of hoping souls.

Dust on your corners tells
me your story,
but your savior is now
continuing your message
with his paintings, and
symphonies of color are now
your prayer.

Here you are, abandoned
temple, serving human hands
struggling in color for
harmony in silence,

The eyes of the artist
caressing your walls day and night,
your wisdom of silence
weaving peace into the artist's soul,
and he, continuing your message
with his pregnant wife,
with a new hope,
with love for life.

Here you are now, still
present in that sad and lonely street
not abandoned any more.

Boulder, Colorado. January, 1969

THE FLAME OF THE HEART

Every day and every night
I light the Candle of love,
With the breath of my heart
I offer thoughts of love.

Engraving the word of love
With the flames of my heart beat,
Impressing the letter of love
With the blood of my Divine breath.

Carrying the star of my love
With the cells of my heart,
The flame of love, burning
Within me with ONE breath.

Calling with the voice of silence
The murmurs of being one
With the Beloved, sacred presence
From the Edge of my whole being.

The tears of my flame wash and clean
All the imperfections of my thoughts.
The waters of my being flow to meet
Her within the temple of light.

Into that sacred silence, I enter
With all my being trembling,
With awe, joy and sadness as one.
Into that stillness within, I AM.

Seven words formed from the flame
Of my heart are before you:
Seven letters inflamed with love
Are in your heart, Precious One.

Boulder, Colorado. February, 1985

THE HIGH CHAMBER OF BEING

I sing to my Creator night and day,
I elevate my voice in exultation,
And the angels also join us in that celestial song of being.

So that heaven and earth are one,
And the miracle of life
Is lived to its fullness.

Come, Beloved, open Thy gates of love.
I, the ancient one, am here within Thee.
Joy to all beings everywhere.
Sing with me the silent and splendid
voice of the ONE, in you and me.
Hold hands of matter, while the spiritual hands confer
with the ONE SELF.

Let the hearts beat here as the heart above
Moves and becomes beyond form or name.
<u>Unissons nous dans l'Amour eternel.</u>
<u>Unissons nous dans la joie humaine et Divine.</u>
<u>Unissons nous dan l'union Cosmique.</u>
<u>Unissons nous dan la Presence d'etre UN.</u>
<u>Unissons nous dan l'Univers entier.</u>

I sing to my Creator night and day,
To the Un-namable, the Infinite one within all beings.

To Thee alone, I am Thy song of love.
In Thee is my trust, Thy word IS my being.
I am the KEY, Thou art the celestial DOOR.
With Thy instrument, I rejoice in Thee.

Here I am, Beloved, ready and longing for Thee.
Hands and Hearts joining, singing and dancing the
dance of love divine. Here you are, Beloved, waiting for me,
The KEY of Thy mystery, I am Thy secret,
And thou art the Chamber of my being.

Boulder, Colorado. December, 1984

THE MAGICAL TREASURE
(Twelve breaths of joy to my beloved)

1.

Within this heart I inhabit,
Your sacred presence is to me
The FLAME OF LOVE, eternal and infinite.
Hidden and concealed from all.

2.

Within my breath, in and out,
Your name is the treasure of my self.
I remember ancient echoes
Of unity and the uniqueness of you and me.

3.

I stand before the entrance of the cave,
The cave of wonders, the castle of my love.
With my glowing heart of purple hue,
The entrance is majestic and splendid.

4.

The hand of my beloved caresses my face,
And a tear is born from my wet eye,
A tear of sadness and joy at once.
But my heart is warm and welcoming.

5.

I still tremble within my being,
I still feel her vibrant look of light,
As we both face the East, the place
From which light and love appear.

6.

Through her eyes, a shining crystal
Reflects the moment of sacredness.
We face each other, with love.
And the blessing is given by the Great One.

7.
We are simply two pages of one book,
The book of love and splendor.
We listen together to the voice
Of the ONE WITHIN US, to illumine our way.

8.
But with that glow, there is also a sigh
Of sadness deep and profound.
Both our eyes are filled with readiness
To sacrifice the egos, for THE ONE LOVE.

9.
This is my magical treasure, here and there.
Visible and invisible, present and absent.
All the opposites of duality in ONE.
Both hidden and revealed, but only to her and me.

10.
The magical place shines within
The great silence at the edge of my being,
With thousands of roses and lilies
And the fragrance of the beloved within.

11.
Only she and I have the magical key,
The key of gold and silver,
That leads to the crystal immensity
Of our beings at the edge of silence.

12.
This is the place of our meeting,
Where neither I nor she can be,
Where man and woman are no more,
ONLY ONE FLAME, One Infinite love.

Boulder, Colorado. February, 1985

THE NEW PAGE OF ONE BOOK

1.

Now we open this new page
In the book of our love.
Now we open a new time
In the life of our love.

2.

So many images dance within me,
While I enter into my seclusion
With a heart that knows how to wait,
Looking to the Eastern light of our horizon.

3.

Every day I sing your name,
As I did for eons of time.
Every beat of my heart calls
For the echo of you within me.

4.

What is time for the Cosmic Lover?
What is space for the Cosmic Beloved?
What passes like a meteor of light in
The heavens of our being and becoming?

5.

Oh! Angels of love, be present within my heart.
Oh! Great One, guide this "waiting"
Until we meet again in our sacred place,
In spite of all this sadness piercing my heart.

6.

I am lifted upon the wings of my Beloved's fire,
Carrying me to places no eye has yet seen,
Where no you and I or it exists,
Where all loves are being born of fire.

From Ecstasy to Lunch

7.
Lifting my eyes to the center of the circle,
I see the spiral movement of your heart
Vibrating with my breath for you:
And then THE WILL OF LOVE IS DONE.

8.
But while as beings of light we dwell
In this envelope of matter, our bodies,
I bear this "waiting" for the sake of our love,
And yearn for the origin of our source.

9.
While in the cave of seclusion, all in me
Is renewed, and I become the NEW PAGE,
And we write in our BOOK OF LOVE the
Flaming letters of LOVE DIVINE.

10.
Bless me, Beloved, with your tears of joy
And the elixir of life within you and me,
Hold my hand, Beloved, look into my eyes,
And see the splendor of things to come.

Boulder, Colorado. February, 1985

THE OFFERING OF NOW:
A Song from a Cosmic Heart — A Meditation to Become ONE

WHEN the scent of the ROSE becomes ever present
WHEN the sweetness of the WINE has flowed into these wines
as the river of light,
WHEN the shining beam of this THOUGHT of eternity, new as the dawn,
is born in me,
then it nourishes this fertile garden of being,

WHEN the IMAGES of the letters of light dance at the joy of being formed
From the formless clouds of their journey,
WHEN the HAND is seduced by the image that says:
Write me,
Birth me,
Form me,
So the knowing soul recognizes IT-SELF,
being and becoming.

WHEN the WORD has been formed,
moved from the unknown state of the light,
to the known, this white sheet of paper,
the idea is born.

WHEN the EYE reads the image of the formless,
which has been molded like the clay in the hand of the potter,
as it realizes this becoming,
IT IS then filled with Divine Light.

WHEN the LIGHT of the dimension of Peace, is manifested,
by that invisible hand, murmuring the great stillness and silence,
Then BE, and BE SILENCE itself.

WHEN the OCEAN in its splendor, springs up from the rivers of light,
with a great and mighty vibration,
source of the tears of NOW,
it washes me clean and pure,

THEN, I see the woven tapestry of the rose, the wine, the thought, the image,
The dot in the center of silence, the Hebrew letter YOD.
The sight of the cosmos from that light is the infinity,
The limitless identity beyond time and space
of the physical identity of "this world"
the dimension of NO-THING,
The boundless LIGHT of the Ein Sof,

Boulder, Colorado. Sept 11, 1975, 11:00 PM.

THE PRESENCE OF THE FLAME

The passing of time and space
Increases my love for you.
Every day and every night
I awake with your name and sleep with
The presence of the Flame.

Today I passed by your abode,
Invisible and very present,
As you were working in your garden.
How symbolic is this moment
Of having a glimpse of your being!

I sent you thoughts of love and light
And my heart sings for the MOTHER of all
That gives us birth and nourishment
For our breath while in this world.

Your presence is always with me,
Like a song without sound,
Like a breath without word,
You are a Flame from the unknown.

In my dreams, your presence is a winged being
Moving within my heart like an ancient echo,
A tune of the sound of sounds, flowing
Within my veins like a hope,
A hope for merging our flames in one light.

In your dreams I send you many words
Unuttered by any mouth,
A constant longing for your love,
A yearning so deep I may drown in my tears.

From Ecstasy to Lunch

If only you knew, Beloved, how present your
Light is within me.
I am speaking to the GREAT BEING within you,
Your body is the energy
Of that light within me.

Where do I find words to say what I feel
Within me, How can I speak to you without words?
I know the ONE within you HEARS this "me"
Calling in the darkness, and I know also
That YOU are listening within the flame.

You have gazed within the Central fire of the
Beltane ceremony, and I was there watching you,
Though my body was present elsewhere.
But the ONE loving you danced through you.

While the Mystical song is around me now,
I listen deep and find you within me.
While these words are written I see you as love,
And I hear your longing and reaching to me.
The time for UNION will come when Berakha, blessing, is in your heart.

I walk alone on a dusty road,
And your sacred name is my path
Of return to my Higher being,
Manifested in you at this time.
I am consumed in the fire of love.

From that point of unity within all life,
I cry the silent hum of all souls.
From that Center of all creation,
I explode with zillions of sparks,
Striving to be known within your womb.

I am guided by that Flame of being and becoming,
Traveling in unknown places, among unknown people.
I see and hear the ultimate cry of love
Within the hearts of all living beings.

Samuel Avital

> One day all hearts shall be pure
> And know that all is one great heart of love
> Manifested within units of beings like
> You and me, in the process of love,
> The Power of being.
>
> I pray that it be so in this lifetime,
> While in your present form I met you.
> I hope within that center to be with you.
> And you may banish the illusion of fear
> That makes you hide your love from me now.
>
> So I seal these words today, while the sun sets
> Beyond the horizon, but I know that
> In the morning of love, the SUN will
> Appear to you and reveal to you
> The true love for you in my heart.
>
> Come, beloved, Shekhinah, the image of love,
> Come, Precious Being of my heart.
> Reveal to me the mystery of vulnerability,
> And give me strength to show you my
> Palace of love where you and I are one in ONE.
>
> Honor the body that loves with the heart.
> Celebrate this moment as I long for you.
> Enjoy this passing time as I yearn and long
> For the Presence of your Flame
> Within which I find the ultimate hope.

Boulder, Colorado. May, 1985

THE SILENT TEAR

1.
Now, that I read the new page,
My silent tear is humming,
And the eye is sad and happy
For the lessons learned this year.

2.
Now my tear dries in the air
That blows the winds of love,
The love that turns into the ONE,
The One within and without.

3.
There is no water within
Me to flow, the fire has come.
There is only LOVE, that awesome
Flame of longing, ancient and trembling.

4.
Here, now, I am listening to the
Inner sound of my love:
The Universal tune of my soul
Soars into infinite being.

5.
Yes, I read the new page,
But I write it
With the dried waters of my breath
To reach the ONE, who I await within me.

6.
I open this page, and it was changed
To a word of newer love.
And the more everything changes,
The more nothing changes.

7.
And now, the treasure is hidden
Within the belly of the womb
To be nurtured for its new incarnation
In a new being with a new page.

8.
And I shall write that page with
More love and fire in my heart.
And I shall find its substances within all beings
Who orbit around my sun's being.

9.
And I shall continue to be well,
And all shall shine with celestial light.
Within the inner temple of my soul
I find the peace and wisdom of my mother.

10.
Walk now, Beloved, walk.
Go now, my love, and be.
I am here, new and living.
You are there, but within all.

Boulder, Colorado. February, 1985

THE STATION OF LOVE AND REST

Now my soul soars beyond the stars
and mingles with the light of love.
Now my heart sings the Cosmic song
With the ancient voice within.

Now this being has tasted the ELIXIR OF LIFE
Mixed with the rays of eternal love, Divine and human.
Now this hand writes with words
That come from the station of nowhere.

Now this body is bathed within the rainbow
that shines brilliantly in the heavens.
Now this being gives thanks to all
With the GREAT BREATH of life and love.

To Shekhinah, a song of love
From a heart that knows the mystery.
To her, the Eternal ONE, the Beloved.
To her, within and without.

With expansions of oneself within,
Reaching with human hand to touch.
With contraction of oneself without,
Merging with the now and the then, the yes and the no.

A time to rest, a station of repose.
A space to move with invisible body.
A sanctuary of the Soul's voice.
All this is the voice in me trembling.

How Great are Thy works, Maker of all,
How splendid are Thy thoughts.
Bless me beloved, Bless me oh One,
So that I become a blessing to others.

All that was, is here now within my heart.
All that will be, is also PRESENT now.
All time and space are illusion,
ONLY the FLAME is burning in my heart.
Lift your eyes that see all to heaven.
Hear the sound of silence soar within me.
I will speak the words of my heart to you.
Which touch the essence of your soul with love.

Join me, Beloved, merge in the ONE
Who inhabits this temple of light.
Open Thy gate between the Holy pillars,
The pillars of splendor and understanding.

The image of Thee is within me, Beloved.
Thy face shines with the sun's rays,
Thy hands caress this body in Divine rapture.
Thy being is none other than this I.

Let the Joy resound within all lovers,
Let the trumpets sound the love song.
Let the violins pierce the air of this becoming.
Let the flute breathe the heavenly symphony.

We are each other's mountain,
We are each other's stars.
We are the Miracle that is,
We are the tomorrow humans wait for.

Walk my love, walk the path of love.
Dance, Beloved, the Cosmic Dance.
I am the Dance and you are the Dancer,
I am the path and you are the traveler.

Turn the page, turn the wheel, Beloved.
Rest, stay shining within, radiate to all.
All is new to me, within Thee all is one.
Let the wheel turn and turn and turn.

From Ecstasy to Lunch

To Thee, this song is written,
With words of Love Divine,
With letters of the Flame within.
In Thee, I am always present,
and you in me.

Boulder, Colorado. January, 1985

THE VEIL OF SILENCE

The sun has given me
Warmth and light and
The waters have cooled my
Passion, now.

Into the cave, within the
Invisible corners of my soul,
My being entered and sat
Calm and still.

The curtain now is drawn
In the temple of life.
The veil of silence is
Covering the Flame.

After many days of profound
Dwelling in the forest of love,
Now is the night when
All are asleep, and very still.

My soul knows this sorrow,
My heart bears the joy.
And I am here now,
Behind the veil, unseen to all.

Before the performance begins,
The curtain will open wide
And let the light penetrate all
My centers of work and giving.

For now, Beloved, let me hide.
For now, Precious Jewel,
Let me dwell behind the veil
With my ancient Friends, and Be.

From Ecstasy to Lunch

And when the time is ripe,
And all the hearts rejoice,
I will open more of the wonders
Of love and untold mysteries.

Behind the veil, I will learn
Again TO READ the new letters,
With the GREAT FLAME OF LOVE
For you, and for the ONE WITHIN.

Stay well, Bien Aimee.
I am here and you are there.
And I hold Thee within my heart
Until the light of love is present
Within you and me as ONE FLAME.

Boulder, Colorado. February, 1985

THIS TOO SHALL PASS

Beloved, oh beloved
night and day
in my heart, through
the windows of my soul
I yearn for thy light
to shower me with
thy peace and understanding
so that I may serve you
with being awake and
aware to thy call.

He that breathes into me
he that speaks through me
he that sees through me
he that hears through me
he that smells through me,
thy creation is mighty
thy light is shining
thy harmony flows into all living beings:

Into all cells send love
into all beings send peace,
in the midst of chaos
help me bring order.

Between the yes and no, let
me explore thy inner space
and illumine me with
thy ultimate profound peace.

Love surrounds me in all
this mouth says, in all
this hand touches, in all
this ear hears, in all
this tongue tastes,
he lives in every cell,
in every container.

From Ecstasy to Lunch

Ina illahi wa ina
illahi raji'oun
I am that and into
that I will return.

Master of the universe
let me bring to my
brothers and sisters
the love you implanted in me
in the first breath,
let me be thy way, the way
of clear vision
to realize the whole of thy splendid creation.

Keep my tongue singing and
dancing to spread joy
and happiness to all my beloved
ones in all thy infinite universe.

Remember, oh passenger on
this earth, remember that
source from whence you came,
remember that you are the
result of a thought, remember
that you are a dot in space.

Passenger, this is just a passage,
fill your bag with useful luggage,
chew very well that which you put
into your mouth, digest the thought
so that it will become vision in
following the path of him living in you.

Say in every event:
"This too shall pass,"
"gam zeh ya'avor,"
follow the pulse of your legs,
honor them so they might lead you to light.
make your path shine, and become
he that lives in you, me, all.

Samuel Avital

Pass now into the path of certainty
with no fear, oh my brother passenger,
walk on my sister, you that loves me
with all thy might, stretch your arms up high,
hug me with thy strength,
and to all I say,
there is only that silence
that sings through me
every breath that takes me
to be one with you forever.

Floating into infinite space with
my golden wings, I carry in me that holy
spark, to keep the flame burning, for all
shadows of blindness, to clear the way
ahead to join me, wholly in ecstasy, in
that silence that speaks and sings the
glory of the one, and only one in everyone.

Lift me up high, my master of creation,
let thy mighty wind carry me to the infinity
of my soul, help me realize that essence wholly
every moment of this now, so that
I will be worthy of being you,
And become one with you.

Boulder, Colorado. March, 1973

TO THE BELOVED ONE

At the hour of ONE
you called me to enter your holy chamber
inner and magnificent.

And when the SOUND
was heard inside my walls
I was awakened at once,
I was awakened from
that long sleep.

In the inner chamber,
the cave of myriad colors,
I enter with reverence
and humility, to be ONE with THEE
through the Triangle of BEING.

Inside your holy chamber
I enter with vigor and
the strength with which you
created me, to BE WHOLLY
in you.

You drink the waters
of my earth, with the fire of the altar you
built into me.

When the flame of your Light
burned the earth,
through the air I breathe, I felt your
holy WORD vibrating, echoing
into me, BEING and BECOMING.

Thus, from the DOT
growing into the erected
vertical-horizontal LINE,
I curved from THEE
and formed the HOLY CIRCLE.

Samuel Avital

Now, spiraling into you,
Goddess of LOVE and Creation,
Mercy and Light, I become
Male-Female being, with
The Sacred UNITY WITH THEE.

I walk now with you
in me, and Thee in me.
One trunk has sprung
from many roots from Thee,
From THEE I came, and
To THEE I give.

My thanks are offered at THY feet,
All my bones chant THY NAME.
And you have given me, as a symbol
of remembrance, a DOT,
a TRIANGLE, and a CIRCLE,
radiating LIGHT forever.

All my thoughts and actions
are NOW directed by THEE,
All offerings come from this
place to thy JOYOUS CHAMBER
of delights. KNOW then,
my LOVE, that WE ARE ONE
in all this illusion.

Boulder, Colorado. March, 1979

TO THEE BELOVED

To thee, Beloved, I sing a silent song
without words or form,
To thee, Ancient One, I breathe the spirit
of unity beyond the known and unknown.
To Thee, mon amour, I offer my gifts without price.

To Thee, mon ami, unto Thee, my Precious One,
I offer treasures beyond gold and silver.

Unto Thee, I pour my being to be ONE.
I contain Thy elixir beyond compare.
And you contain this "me" within you.
As a fluid of the alchemical union of two beings
that are one in essence, and two in form.

Open thy gates, beloved, and we will explore and
become the wonders of your cave of marvels.

As the one being in you, we tremble like the wind
kissing the tree and the leaves of ONE BEING.

Joy of immensity, Love of Eternity,
Life of Cosmic wonder.
We are One in Thee,
One in Thy breath,
One in Thy tune.

Boulder, Colorado. December, 1984

TONIGHT I CANNOT SLEEP

Tonight I cannot sleep. My spirit is awake tonight,
Images of the Universe parade before me very clearly.
As I am, and for what I am, Looking at the candle flame
With a thousand colors
That manifest and dance before me. Bright.

The objects on my table arranged properly and orderly.
My hands design words, which translate the images.
Vivid images from my childhood,
Passing before me like a review.

Events from the past, that are now present, at this moment.
With me, where I am now, here, and where I will go.
Very meaningful events that shaped this "me",
Over the time that past, or it is? And…who is this "me"?

This "me," at this late time of the night, writing with this black pencil,
Pardon me, red pen, like blood, on white paper.
My hand hesitates, then flows, guided by a thousand thoughts,
And its own rhythm. The pen writes and breathes with the paper.

I am rolling in my bed seizing my head with my two hands,
With my two big eyes open wide in the air. Then I close them again,
Trying to contemplate what is occurring now with me.
Silently, I feel sharp and as if transparent.

What I sense, and feel at this late hour, when everyone is asleep.
All separated by walls, asleep in their private apartments.
Their room arrangements and their inner environment
Pass before my eyes now, through the walls, so clearly.

I see a white house surrounded by beautiful grass and columns,
With a white and black fence, six stairs to get to the door,
I ascend the stairs, stop, near the door and…Is this door going to open?
Or not? A door like many other ordinary doors.

From Ecstasy to Lunch

Is this how the door of destiny looks?
Is it designed to open like other doors?
Will it open magically before me like a spectacle?
And to reveal for me an unknown universe…Do I need a key?

I am almost impatient, anticipating discovery,
And while I observe my impatience,
I notice my words become bigger and bigger on the paper.
What does this mean?

Maybe I will discover the "miracle" of the door opening?
And with a deep wish in my heart, the door will finally open?
What door? What is a door? Any way, anywhere, a door must open now.
Please open, so I can enter. Where to enter…Inside the house? What house?

And so, when I enter, I find another door, and another door,
Another door, inside a door, inside a door, until…
Infinite doors inside doors are revealed before me,
It seems to me an eternity of doors.

The eternity of doors finally open wide, the door to infinity.
And I am allowed and invited to enter inside.
Inside the infinite of infinite doors, ready and always open,
If only we will allow them to open.

The shadow of my hand, writing and dancing,
Moving from within to design dots, lines, letters, directing my red pen,
Continues to write, write, another word to depict an image.
A continuity that is eternal in being, living in this present moment,
This immediate present moment, sometimes sad,
Sometime joyous. It continues to flow like a river
Making marks on the white paper with my red ink pen.

Oh, my beautiful white paper, I am making your surface dirty
And darkening your clarity and whiteness with my words, words, words.
And with my little red forms shining on the paper,
I am back to this "time," and notice it is three in the morning.
A new morning, a new light, a new day, full with new life,
Welcomes me to live a new way of being,

Samuel Avital

As I place my paper and pen on the table,
I see many hands, doors, entering, house, fence, stairs, red, shadows.

Go rest, my being. Meditate on life and Dream your way in "this world."
Observe…how you create words, images, in the middle of the night.
My hands move to write with the time of "me" again.
Yes, you and "me", the pen and myself, with the partnership of the paper.

With an open heart now, welcoming the morning,
Shifting from the night and the darkness in the hearts of humans,
To transform the new light of life, and the love
Of being and becoming.

New York City, USA. Thursday Nov 23, 1967

TWO IS ONE

My messenger, a bird, has brought
Me a word from my Beloved
As swift as it was asked of her,
And told me that TWO IS ONE.

We are one bird of love
With two wings of loving.
Beating, vibrating, to fly
As one being of light.

Both wings act together
To pierce the air and fly.
Both eyes together see
One path of love.

Two legs together walk
As one, and act as one.
Two ears together hear
One tune of love, ONE

Two hands together, touching
With one spirit.
Two opposites facing one another
Come in oneness of the One.
Two edges of a stick,
Yet, one stick.
Two male and female, yet
Only ONE BEING.

Thank you, my loving messenger,
For bringing me back the love
Of my "other" being, half of me,
And we will be one forever.

Samuel Avital

Go, now my little bird of light,
And spread the love of the ONE
With your two holy wings of joy,
So other loves may flourish.

I have heard the voice of my Beloved,
Warm, joyous and exalting.
I have seen the Light of love,
Like a violet flame of love.

Now, from this focused abode of love,
I shall radiate this to all.
Now, from this dot of the holy circle.
I shall spin my Cosmic spiral, TO BE.

A salty tear falls from my two eyes.
Traveling down the face that lights.
And this is the gift, to cry,
To shed a tear, from my being, trembling.

Boulder, Colorado. February, 1985

WAVES OF LOVE

Rising and falling, the immense
Waves of love encompass all of me.
Like breathing in and out
I become the waves of that dance.

My earth dances and trembles like a leaf,
With the rhythm of love and joy of my soul.
And I am a boat, drunk with love,
Carried to the horizon of forever.

Each wave dies for the next wave,
And in an infinite movement,
The silvery surface kisses the moon.
And I become the wave, the kiss, the moon.

Then, I see Divinity everywhere,
Within me and my precious beloved,
Within the wave and the ocean of love,
Luminous and profound immensity.

Breath and voice and word are one
In the sound of inner silence.
That center is everywhere,
Encompassing all.

All this sensing engulfs me like
A coat of many colors.
Then Thy image, Beloved, embraces me,
In thought and in action with Thy love.

When I think of you, Beloved,
You are that wave of infinite love.
When our eyes meet in that place
Of great wonder, I tremble with joy.

Samuel Avital

Come, Waves of Love.
Come, Waves of Light.
We come together in ONE WAVE.
We come together in ONE BREATH.

Boulder, CO. February, 1985

WELCOME

Welcome to me in tune with me.
Welcome to me vibrating with the ONE.
Welcome to me, loving love in all.
Welcome to me, joyous in the act of love.

I join the ascent of the ladder.
I am attracted to the Love Crystal in you.
I do not count two, only with you.
I am no one, but not two.

You are the one who reflects this me in your mirror.
You are the one who sings this unheard song of love.
You are the one into whom I fill the holy space of IT.
You are the one who responds to the echo of ancient rite.

We are that vehicle through which the ONE lives.
We are the form of the formless, the nameless.
We are the FLAME, by which all is right.
We are one world, we two.

Welcome to me, you who recognize yourself in me.
Welcome to me, you who embrace me as you are.
Welcome to me, you who merge with me, become all.
Welcome to me, you who are me in another form.

Beloved, HEAR my voice, the echo of my being.
Beloved, BE my heart giving light to the flame.
Beloved, REPLY to this call, from the Crystal cave.

Boulder, Colorado. January 1985.

WHILE YOU CAN…
Enjoy every moment of being here

Take a deep breath while you can.
Take a breath from a flower while it is still possible.
Drink a glass of water while you are able.
Take a walk and enjoy each step while you are here.

Look in the eye of your friend while you can.
Look at the sky while it is possible.
Look at the moon while you are able.
Look in the eyes of your child while you are here.

Look at a flower while you can.
Look at the face of a child while it is possible.
Look at the mountains while you are able.
Look at the palm of your hand while you are here.

Listen to your heart while you can.
Listen to your inner silent voice while it is still possible.
Listen to the wind while you are able.
Listen to your friend while you are still here.

Touch the curves of your beloved while you can.
Touch the heart of the other while it is still possible.
Touch the breath of your friends while you are able.
Touch the surface of your face while you are here.

Explore learning a new way of being while you can.
Explore applying what you learn while it is still possible.
Explore the possibility of being present while you are able.
Explore your conscious miracle of living while you are here.

Boulder, Colorado. Jan 1992/2019

WITHIN THE SILENCE

Within the silence of my being,
I send forth the call of light.

Within the stillness of my breath,
I utter the sound of love.

To you, Precious one of my heart,
The call has been voiced from within.

With your inner ear, and inner eye,
You will see the shining pearl I am.

And in turn, your response creates
The echo of Thy being, my being.

And when the lovers meet in oneness,
A feast appears on the holy altar.

And from this focused place of love,
We shall radiate the great ray of light to all.

And looking from the summit of the mountain,
We shall both see the glory of the ONE within.

And merge with the expansion of the Self,
Toward the great space of infinite love.

Boulder, Colorado. February, 1985

WORDS FROM A COSMIC LOVER

Drink, Beloved, drink
From the Source of LIGHT.
Thirst has shown you
The way to the HOLY FOUNTAIN.

From the waters, I give you fire,
The FIRE of Love, and with the
Fire comes LIGHT.
And with earth and air,
"YOU" and "I" BECOME ONE.

And so, the FOUNTAIN
Drinks from its own source,
Rejoicing in the HOLY WATERS
Through the FIRES of BEING
And BECOMING.

I kiss your "EARS"
So you can HEAR my call,

I kiss your "EYES"
So you can SEE my vision,

I kiss your "NOSE"
So you can smell my fragrance,

I kiss your "MOUTH"
So you can "TALK" and "EAT" me,
Digest "me" and utter "me" through
your lips.

From Ecstasy to Lunch

Thus, I am blessed,
By kissing, I am kissed.
By touching, I am Touched.
Oh! Beloved ONE of FIRE,
of Water, of Air, of Earth,
I am in Thee in all that is seen, heard and felt
In the innermost walls of my/your sacred chambers.

Boulder, Colorado. March, 1979

ARTICLES AND TEACHINGS

Many Words, One Truth
The Age of Miracles is Now
Awareness, Silence, and Art
Conscious Innocence
The Condor and the Turtle
Cosmic Accordion
Declaration of Peace
Hands, Expressions of the Soul
Homage to Marcel Marceau
Human, Awake from Your Slumber
If I Am Because I Am
In the Beginning Was the Dot
The Journey from Thought to Action
Keep Me Sane in the Midst of Madness
Listening
Madness and Sanity on Broadway
New Artist – Tikkun Maker
The Other – Key for Peace!
The Puzzle of "The Hidden Obvious"
Spiritual Archaeology: Bodyspeak and the Hidden Obvious
The Spiritual Ratatouille of the "New Age"
Words, Web of Noise

MANY WORDS — ONE TRUTH
The Veil of the Obvious

We live in a time of rapid change, when evolution of thought and consciousness is proceeding by leaps and bounds. There are many avenues open to us, so many voices competing for our attention that we are sometimes overcome by confusion.

To meet and transcend this confusion, we must increase our awareness. We must eliminate confusion and transmit and radiate the simple, beautiful messages of the heart's flame of truth. This is what the artist in us considers as his chief work, not only for his own benefit, but also for the benefit and well-being of others.

We respond with laughter and sometimes tears. The higher emotions of being one with the Cosmic lift us beyond the cares of daily life to an experience of oneness with ourselves and the eternal life that is vibrating in us at all times.

Source of Imagination

When the artist taps this source of imagination by proper attunement and mastery of the art of visualization, he gives us a glimpse of something precious and essential. When we have a close look at the essence of another, we experience our own essence. This same essence resides in different places. There is no separation, no division. There is only the reflection in the mirror of the same being.

One of those inner glimpses leads our attention to the obvious and natural law of many in the One. Once this law is understood and lived and maintained constantly in the situations we face, we enter a world of peace. We become calm in the midst of madness. We finally begin to understand the adage of the sage that urges us to be in the world but not of it.

The obviousness of this law is actually the "veil," and we need only increase our attention to see through to the depths, to unveil and reveal the truth of the one in the many. This veil is the hypnotic spell of the material world in its extremes. We accept this hypnotic curse because of our laziness and our unwillingness to think deeply with proper discrimination. It is actually easy to see through this illusion that we have accepted at one time or another, either consciously or unconsciously. But, until we do, this hypnotic reality is one with our structure of thinking, and we sink into an attitude of slumbering through life.

We know from observation that the entire ocean cannot sink a ship unless the waters enter the ship. All the hypnotic vibrations of negative thinking cannot affect us, unless we allow or welcome them to enter, unless we believe in their existence. It seems ridiculous to spend so much energy dwelling in those negative waters, letting our ship sink. The inner intelligence rather suggests guiding the positive waters toward a good direction, toward the manifestation of the same beautiful law of Oneness in its perfect working order.

The Illusion of Separateness

So, this seeming separateness and this illusion of division are obstacles toward the One. We divide in order to unite. Harmonizing the opposites is the very work to abolish the division and to be in the One.

But, in order to increase this awareness, we have to recognize the oneness in the other as well. We may theorize, but we must immediately go on to the activity of actualizing that theory.

When we acknowledge, accept, allow, and welcome this action of penetrating deeply into the obvious reality in nature, it leads to a comprehension of the one reality, that which we call the state of harmonium.

I would hint that an essential key to unveiling the obvious is simplicity, this and the focalized attention of single-mindedness. This sharpens our perception, opening wide the doors to illumination. Then, we may inwardly perceive the invisible ways of the Cosmic at work.

Now, let us contemplate this by mentioning the many aspects of this obvious/hidden reality of nature that is veiled, and that we pass by and take for granted.

Here for your attention, are assembled a few of these observations that are clear to every being in the creation of the Cosmic. See the obviousness of it, reflect and see "**How great are Thy works!**" as the psalmist says.

Have you noticed how many words are written here to utter one simple truth?

Many petals, but only one rose.

Many letters, but only one word.

Many hairs, but only one head.

Many Days, but only one Saturday.

Take time and see for yourself how simple this beautiful law is,
and activate it in your daily life.
Thus, you will witness the oneness with the God of our Hearts
that is available to all living beings.
But please, see through the OBVIOUS and your soul will rejoice
in THE CREATOR that makes us *ONE with The ESSENCE of Creation*.

THE FORTY-EIGHT MANYS WHICH ARE ONE

	MANY	ONE
1.	Words	Truth
2.	Thoughts	Mind
3.	Volumes	Knowledge
4.	Letters	Word
5.	Hours	Day
6.	Minutes	Hour
7.	Chips	Computer
8.	Light bulbs	Generator
9.	Candles	Light
10.	Sparks	Flame
11.	Bodies	Soul
12.	Hairs	Head
13.	Fingers	Hand
14.	Breaths	Life
15.	Cells	Organism
16.	Movements	Stillness
17.	Spokes	Wheel
18.	Ties	Track
19.	Ways	Highway
20.	Routes	Path
21.	Cities	Planet
22.	Children	Father
23.	Babies	Mother
24.	Branches	Tree
25.	Petals	Rose

	MANY	**ONE**
26.	Grains	Seed
27.	Colors	Rainbow
28.	Rays	Sun
29.	Rocks	Mountain
30.	Waters	Ocean
31.	Streams	River
32.	Details	Whole
33.	Diseases	Cause
34.	Ingredients	Recipe
35.	Containers	Essence
36.	Chambers	Castle
37.	Threads	Carpet
38.	Brushstrokes	Painting
39.	Lines	Circle
40.	Dots	Line
41.	Melodies	Harmony
42.	Notes	Keyboard
43.	Vibrations	Sound
44.	Sounds	Silence
45.	Religions	God
46.	Theories	Reality
47.	Interpretations	Truth
48.	Pages	Book

From Ecstasy to Lunch

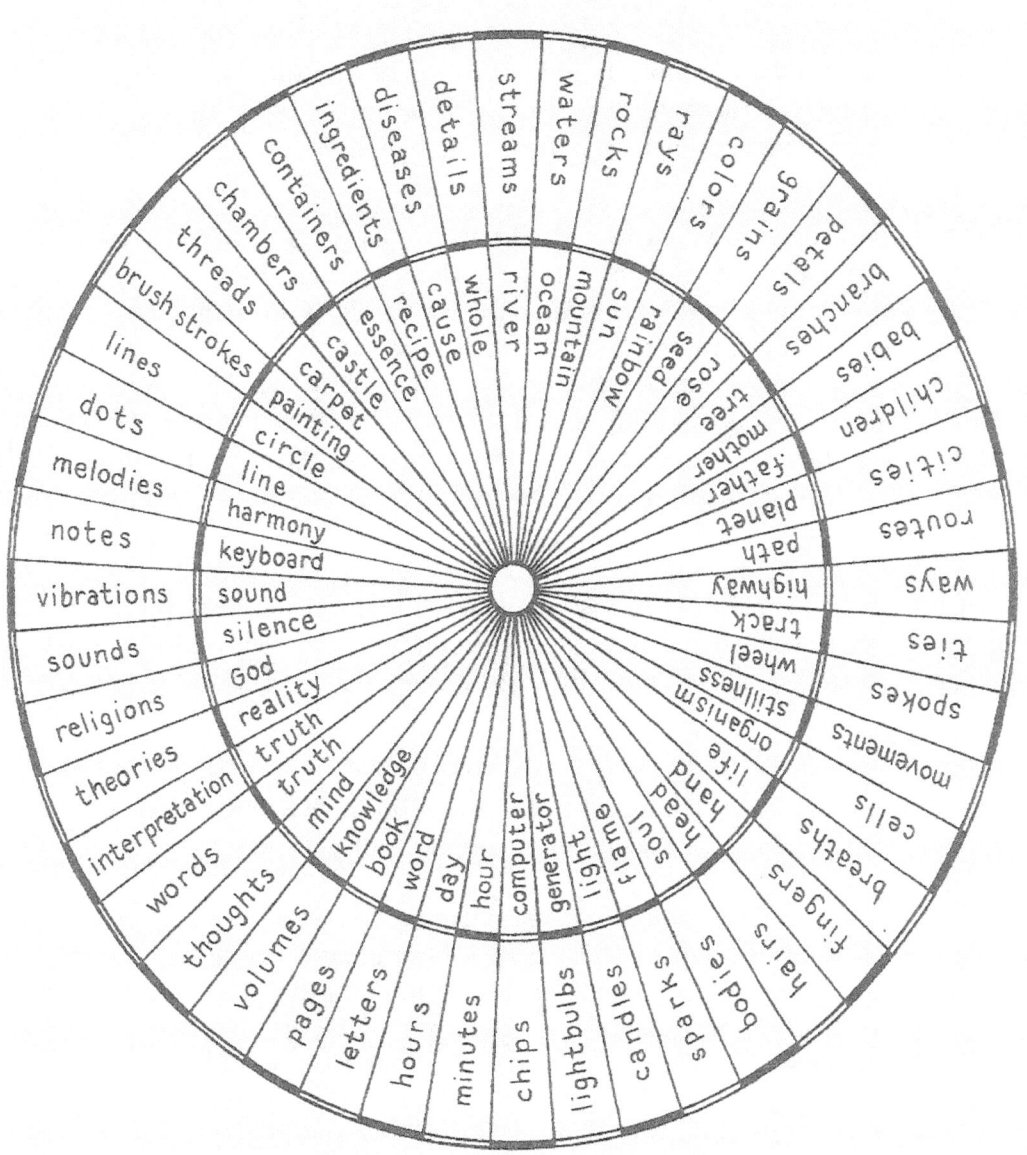

The Forty-Eight Manys Which Are One

Illustration: R. Majka

THE AGE OF MIRACLES IS NOW ACTIVATED

These days it can seem as if human intelligence has deserted the earth. More and more, we see people struggling to manage their lives, both individually and collectively, from individuals, to groups, to companies, to nations. Why is this?

What we find is that throughout history, there are times when humanity reaches a certain boiling point, or critical mass. People can no longer manage their agriculture, relations, commerce, religious beliefs and economic developments, and they arrive at a state of paralysis. They come to an impasse, and become increasingly more unaware, counting on someone to save them and to solve their problems for them. That Critical mass, or "high boiling point" state, leads to stagnation and if taken to the edge, it can mark the end of that individual or group. When that edge is reached, catastrophes begin to happen, which are actually caused by people's laziness and constant lack of awareness, and that civilization simply disappears.

Our state of humanity at this time in history is that same one of reaching the boiling point and critical mass. And we see the same symptoms and signs. They indicate that we have navigated this civilization to this point through our thoughts and our actions here on this earth.

In these times, people cry out, wishing for a "miracle." But here is one obvious thing to reveal: The simplicity of the fact that you are here now, at **"this time"** is actually a miracle unto itself.

What is a miracle? A miracle is something that happens so fast or so slow, that the untrained human awareness cannot sense or perceive how it happened. Thus, the person either denies it, or is amazed at the event. And since one cannot understand it, they assign it to a "higher authority", to that which is beyond our perception, and forget that maybe, actually, they themselves are the **Cause** of that occurrence, without being aware of it at all.

In order to become aware of this "**Miracle of Being,**" one must distinguish between that which is within (פנימיות) and that which is without (חיצוניות). This is all understood in the Sacred Knowledge of the Kabbalah, which was kept hidden for many centuries and was available only to a few. They worked hard to preserve it, develop it, and bring it to a state such that the world would be able to learn and know it from experience, so that everyone can achieve a new life with meaning, direction and purpose.

This process, in which humanity reaches a boiling point, has happened many times in our human history. Giant cultures and generations of human families have disappeared in this way. Generally, before that disappearance, the ones who are aware that the "**end**" of that culture is coming warn the population about the situation. And many ignore and deny "what is" and perish. Those who heed and change their ways actually survive and they do what we call "**In The Beginning**" — they renew themselves to create another new culture and prosper. (Read the story of Jonah, which illustrates this.)

Some are heeding this and some are denying it. Some are pretending to know, and some are in a confused state. A great perplexity is guiding individuals and societies now, and most everyone is guessing what will happen next and hypnotized by what is happening now. **FEW ARE CAUSING A NEW WAY TO HAPPEN**, to emerge to a new and sane civilization, to emerge to a new life, a new way of being and thinking.

In our sources there is what we call **the ARC work**, in which the Creator prepares the healing before the illness comes. What we must realize, right here and now, is that arc of healing has happened already. A knowledge is there that can give us a new guidance and help us to learn how to govern ourselves and navigate our lives. We can manage our way of living and being in a new way.

That knowledge is available now and no one must complain that they did not know. This is true especially at this time when great catastrophes are fast arriving on this blue and beautiful planet, a planet which is probably the greatest gift of life for all humans. All we need is to **DARE TO TRANSFORM from what was to WHAT WILL BE, through WHAT IS.**

HOW? By learning about ourselves, how the universe works, and how life develops within us and around us. By learning the laws and applying this knowledge and dedicating one's full time to this understanding. And by overcoming all our difficulties, learning how to restore our ways. We discover that illuminating simplicity, **to CONSCIOUSLY CAUSE CHANGE in our lives, and DARE TO BE WHO WE REALLY ARE**, individually and collectively.

When the individual comes to the realization that indeed these times are pregnant with unexpected events, that many great changes are to occur in our lifetime, one begins the eternal human quest. Who am I? What am I doing here? Where am I? How do I know it? What can I do about it? What is the purpose of my life? Am I a puppet or a puppeteer? These are questions of life and death really, not just questions of curiosity.

At the beginning of this QUEST, the doors of knowledge begin to open. This ancient-new practical knowledge that is based on the essential quest of the human is open to one, and if they have the dedication that is needed, they can begin exploring the laws of the Universe and applying them according to the ancient wisdom tradition of the Sacred Kabbalah.

Because it is true that it is possible to live a perfect life, right here on this earth. One does this by learning how the Universe works via specific laws, learning to align with and activate the inner intelligence, to **BE AND LIVE IT.** Then one lives with dignity, and especially with the joy of experiencing this "**Miracle of Being.**"

Many may feel drawn to these ideas of the Kabbalah, sensing that there is something in it that could help restore their lives, to go from "**TALKING ABOUT IT**" to actually **LIVING IT, BEING IT** and **APPLYING IT**. But this can be a difficult path for those who are used to seeking convenience only. Somehow, their conditioning serves as a trap and a limitation, and they stop themselves from genuinely applying the learnings, and they miss the resulting benefits of self-evolution.

Prejudice and Laziness is the enemy for this SELF-ACTIVE DEVELOPMENT to traverse from **TALKING ABOUT IT** to **BEING and LIVING IT.**

However, for those who are sincere, once this learning begins, according to the Kabbalah, one attracts a special LIGHT called, OR MAKIF, a surrounding light, to assist the student's honest efforts. From there it will be according to one's steadfast perseverance that they advance and learn how to restore their soul to ascend back to her Creator.

Here, it is possible to explore the roots of conflicts, to know how they are caused, and to see how to restore harmony. This could make many things clear in one's life. It could show us how to overcome the conflicts and work toward the perfection of living in all worlds – that is in harmony and perfect happiness and pleasure beyond human understanding.

The Conflict we see is when one speaks one thing, but does something different through their actions. One's heart and mouth must be coordinated as ONE, and harmonized to speak what one means and to act based on it. When a person does not consciously guide themselves to this state of being, this creates a "conflict", which is in turn, the source of all misunderstanding, miscommunication, disharmony, perplexity, confusion, suffering and personal and collective misery.

This is one of the ways to resolve conflicts, to avoid making mistakes, and **especially to transit from "TALKING ABOUT IT" to LIVING AND BEING IT.** Thus, one enters the world of constant awareness, advancing in one's path of **BEING and BECOMING.**

For the Kabbalah Seminar "Gathering of the Sparks,
Boulder, Colorado. Friday, Jan 19, 2007
29th of the Hebrew month of Tevet, 5767

AWARENESS, SILENCE, AND ART

To be true essential beings, we strive to live by our higher ideals at all times, and not to submit to behavior which is inconsistent with those ideals. To be successful in this, we need to develop and maintain a conscious degree of awareness.

There is a tendency among humans—including those with a mystical bent, to speak of high ideals and then to contradict these ideals with their actions and behavior. If a person is to do something about this tendency, they must begin from the true self. As we know, the camel generally does not see its own hump. More often, it sees only the humps of others. But, if one wishes to restore the world, one should begin with his or her own self.

The word "awareness" is indeed an abused word. One cannot *talk* about it; one can only *be* it. Simply, if awareness does not manifest in a person, that person is really asleep. For those whose role is to awaken, the awakening will not come about with words or promises, but through "suffering." Only when a person experiences that signal we call pain or suffering, and is ready to "work," can they decipher the cause of their state of sleep. So being aware begins with oneself. That is by being in this present moment. Those who are living this awareness will not be talking about it, they will simply be aware.

There is a saying that goes, "The fence for wisdom is silence." Self-observation is a gift and honesty is a great virtue. In a society that takes everything for granted, and perceives the "other" as the enemy, one needs to sharpen one's tools of observation. Learn how to learn, and act accordingly. Where others are concerned, one cannot always openly converse about the unawareness and subtle inconsistencies of behavior. Only when the highly evolved individual is attuned with other like-minds, can something relevant be said, and even then, with the realization that we differ from each other in our understanding. It is probably best in these situations to manifest a beautiful smile and see if intuition leads to the use of words or not. Each person will probably behave according to his or her own evolution on the path of life.

This is exactly the source that the Mime artist draws from when beautifully expressing profound ideas in public in utter simplicity. This is done by practicing the art for many years, observing the contradictions and inadequacies of human behavior, then mirroring or reflecting them back to the audience. Through this expression, a profound suggestion is introduced to help others become more careful with words, to learn not to speak them heedlessly. This artistic reflection is one way to act on the problems of unawareness in our society.

"Turn it and turn it for all is in it and look in it and grow gray and old in it, and turn not away from it, for there is no better rule for thee than it." (Ben Bag Bag, Sayings of the Fathers, 5:25).

The verse above is about the Torah, the book of instruction. Thus, the first law of the realized authentic human being is *silence and stillness*. Words are very important and uttered with care.

Samuel Avital

We all need to know how to keep the "**golden bit**" in our mouth. We are tied with the wisdom of the ancient sages and must reflect and go within to find the *real* value of the sacred silence.

March, 1979

WHAT IS CONSCIOUS INNOCENCE?

"**Conscious Innocence**" — A living state and a natural quality of being, where one is completely at one with their child innocence, and is consciously aware of it. It is a Paradox. But, when one knows with "certainty" that paradox does not exist, then this state of conscious innocence can be totally understood, experienced, and lived with every breath, thought and action.

Clowns, genuine artists, gifted musicians, painters, actors, and mimes also have this quality of being, with a great source of true and potent creativity, a kind of innocence of behavior. They are very aware to act silently and discreetly, without talking about it at all.

Einstein and some other conscious scientists had it. It is known from our tradition, that the gaze of a consciously innocent being is the most powerful in "this world." It can be what most people call a "miraculous" event of spiritual and physical awakening in one's life.

If you did not lose your innocence after your childhood, you will begin to know it and understand it from the depths of your whole being.

When learning and living with this awakened state, and I might even say, blessed attitude, many positive changes happen in one's life, almost imperceivably to the outside world. One begins to feel and welcome change as a good event. It is like an expansion of one's awareness to higher levels and new dimensions of being.

When you read, speak, walk, and live from this state of being, your decisions are guided toward your good and the good of others. You learn fast, and both hemispheres of your brain function to their best. It is a balanced and very pleasurable way of existing, and as a result, your "**problems,**" "**stress,**" and physical and mental tensions simply disappear, seemingly "**miraculously.**" But first, one must build and establish this state slowly, patiently and consciously, and then learn to cultivate this special awareness until it becomes "second nature." When that happens, then you become like a "**miracle**" walking on this earth.

And when will you start to make the above process happen? It will happen when you are the total edge of dissatisfaction in your life. It will also happen from your very deep and desperate honest questions, "**What am I doing here?**" "**What is my purpose in life?**" "**What is the meaning of my life?**" "**Who am I?**" "**What am I?**" "**What is a Soul?**" — Really, **the edgy questions** of life and death, probing and pondering all your profound **WHYS** that emerge from the depths of your heart and being.

As it is known to those who know, this classical and eternal process does not happen by itself, but from a deep awareness. It can take a short or long time. It depends on your sense of urgency and self-dedication.

I know it is worth your sincere effort, and I support you fully in this noble goal, to **wear this state of being** I call "**Conscious Innocence.**" So, 'Bon courage' in your journey toward that which you are looking for, because as we know, "**That which you are looking for is already looking for you.**"

In the perplexed and confused world as it is today, with a dangerous, insane, and distorted perception of reality, we urgently need many consciously innocent beings to restore sanity and balance. We begin in our own lives, and this ripples out to affect the lives of many others, changing the quality of our spiritual, mental and physical environments.

THE CONDOR AND THE TURTLE*:
Wisdom for a "Civilization" Drunk at the Edge of the Roof...

*"Great spirits have always encountered
violent opposition from mediocre minds."*
– Albert Einstein

The metaphor of the condor and the turtle conjures up two diverse images: **the condor soaring** with an unlimited view of reality; **the turtle crawling** slow and steady in its own pace, with a limited view of reality. When we take the time to carefully observe human behavior, we see this metaphor in the realm of human consciousness.

Some dare to soar, to fly, to live and create independently, ahead of the masses. These are integrated, conscious human beings that propel new and valuable creative knowledge. They possess the qualities that characterize <u>the Condor Factor</u>. I call them "**Condorians.**" They are the leaders, the independent integrated thinkers. They are their own authority.

<u>**The Turtle Factor**</u> encompasses humans who are too intimidated to think, be and live from their own volition. **The "Turtelians"** depend on external authority. Craving guidance and approval from others, they exist in a "<u>**follower mode,**</u>" a "<u>**sheep consciousness**</u>" syndrome. **The Turtelians**' natural state of thinking, living and being is dictated and depends on outside authoritative forces.

---

* I do not mean to denigrate these noble animals. I am merely using them (with their permission) as metaphors to illustrate some characteristics of human animal behavior.

Characteristics of Condorians and Turtelians

Condorians	Turtelians
Soars	Crawls
Inner directed	Outer directed
Wants to live forever	Accepts death as inevitable
Conscious consumer	Hypnotized consumer
Producer of values	Destroyer of values
Generous/self content	Envious and greedy
Eat to live	Live to eat
Authentic romantic love	Procreative, "sex for sex's sake"
Reduces stress	Increases stress
Increased health	Disease/death oriented
Real, conscious beings	Pretenders, unconscious
Realizes "Time is finite and precious" (lives in present)	Thinks "Time is infinite," (devalues time. Procrastinates)
Quick decision-maker	Slow. Retards decision making
Exerts with focused effort	Low-energy, unfocused effort
Totally integrated honesty	Dishonest, cheating
Lucid reality	Mystical thinking
Problem solver	Stuck in problems
Conscious mind	Bicameral mind[1] (see footnote)
Self-directed leaders	Followers
Flow, Forward movement	Stagnancy, Specialization
Developers	Maintainers
Conceptual thinkers	Linear and perceptual thinkers
Energetic, active	Lazy, passive, idle
Happiness-oriented	Melancholic
Enjoys the creative process (appreciates the 9-month gestation)	Looking for a "Two-minute solution" (wants instant results/gratification)
Is their own authority	Depends on external authority
Connected	Fragmented
Conscious being	Sleepwalker
Few	Many
Minority (for the time being)	Majority (until self-extinction)

CONDORIANS

Condorians exert honest effort to produce and create value for others. They earn self-esteem through creativity and integrated thinking, and do not need approval from anyone to create. They perceive time as finite and therefore precious. Self-motivated, responsible and self-authoritative, they pursue the truth through free and independent thinking.

Condorians act and possess genuine practical and creative power. As visionaries with uncompromising honesty, they are focused and conscious, mentally and physically alert and active. Nothing slips by.

Condorians do not sit idle and watch the world revolve away from them. They orbit in "**the constant now.**" They participate in the active motion of the world and integrate their bodies, minds and souls. Because of their characteristics, the Condorians experience super happiness, health, wealth and pure uncontaminated love. They are modest and their actions and movements are effective and productive. They exist in an exhilarating mode of being.

Condorians maintain these characteristics through a clear and lucid state of consciousness. Unfortunately they are few, but they are the natural future, shaping a new world based on the creative genius of humanity.

"To believe your own thought, to believe that what is true for you in your private heart is true for all men – that is genius"
– Ralph Waldo Emerson

TURTELIANS

Turtelians. The characteristics of Turtelians include bicameral[1] unconscious behavior, and being mentally dead, merely existing biologically. They are externally motivated, functioning through the automatic left/right brain functions without self-discipline. They have no concept of self, no concept of time, and a have a subservient attitude toward external or "higher" authority.

Turtelians are hypnotized by the follower's mode of thinking, being and living. They have no intellectual pursuit and are slavishly obedient to faith, and are therefore powerless and helpless. Their intrinsic motivation is mostly attached to survival issues, with procreation as their main objective rather than authentic and pure love. They are sleepwalkers pretending to be awake.

These characteristics lead the **Turtelians** to have self-doubt and a concept of infinite time. Time for them is devalued, and procrastination is rampant as they postpone the awakened intensity of living in the present.

They find left brain/right brain functions to be antagonistic and live in confusion and irresponsibility as they act in slavish obedience to dogmatic belief systems. Contradiction is the norm for them. Excessively non-productive and even counter-productive (nine to five superficiality), **Turtelians** are envious and lazy. They try, hope, and act from mostly existential subjective values. Even their death process is dependent on others. **Turtelians** are always in the transitional state of pursuing comfort and security or the illusion of personal freedom.

They are fragmented thinkers who use power games and victimize others to achieve a false sense of self-worth. The result is a lifetime of anxiety, poverty and envy. Regrettably, they are many, and probably will self-extinguish themselves with time.

"To be idle and to be poor have always been reproaches and therefore every man endeavors with his utmost care to hide his poverty from others and his idleness from himself." – Samuel Johnson.

Through bureaucracy and other types of bogus livelihood, Turtelians have prospered off of the Condorians' productivity. Turtelians wear many masks: "caring," "loving," "fatherly," "for the good of society," "for the security of our nation," and "protective," are a few common camouflages.

Masking their dishonesty with the age-old tools of mysticism, they create problems where none exist. They do so with the prolific use of **non-sequiturs** (Latin for "**it doesn't follow logically from the previous statement**"). In doing so, they distort people's way of thinking to believe things that aren't true, and make it commonplace to link a non-value to a value, and vice versa. See more about mysticism in the footnotes[2].

In order to soar as a Condorian, one must identify Turtelian characteristics in one's life and reverse destructive patterns, transforming them into productive ones. Through disciplined use of logic, integrated thinking, eliminating the disease of "personal mysticism," and through Totally Integrated Honesty, one can achieve the Condorian Factor in one's personal and professional life. The human may only walk on foot, but can soar with the mind, by simply shifting attention and awareness.

Until Roger Banister ran a mile in less than four minutes, it was thought to be an impossible feat. But once he broke that invisible barrier, many more promptly followed suit. Turtelians constantly meet invisible barriers. Most of the time, Turtelians simply ignore the metaphoric wall that prevents them from advancing and developing their true being as it was meant to be, and choose one of two options: 1. Turn around and retreat, or 2. Lie down and pretend the wall isn't there.

Unfortunately, most of humanity readily maintains these Turtelian characteristics by wasting precious and productive time living in confusion and contradiction—the perpetual state of Turtelian unconsciousness.

Only a few individuals dare to use the Condorian Factor to free themselves from the Turtelian traps of self-deception masked by "positive thinking" and the popular seminary of psycho babble—*pretending* to be happy and productive. As Shakespeare said in Hamlet, "To be honest in this world is to be one in a thousand." In our modern world, I believe it is to be "one in million."

When Gary Lee Christensen graduated from West Yellowstone High School in 1990, his salutatorian address raised the ire of some parents and classmates. He spoke of how he had "survived years of intolerance" because he "dared to be different."

"I was a good student when it was not popular to be a good student…an Eagle Scout when it was not popular to be a Scout." He also added that he had "played the piano when everyone else was playing football." He implicated intolerance as a threat to self-esteem.

"You can no longer cling to your friends. Know that by not following the crowd, you can succeed." Though parents complained and even wanted his scholarships revoked, Gary had enough honesty to deliver a "realistic" view of his experience. And for that, he soared far above the turtles waddling around him. (*The Denver Post*, June 5, 1990.)

My grandfather once taught me that "**Whenever the people go one direction, make sure to go the other direction**."

Because of daring individuals, human evolution continues. The dishonesty and self-deception of Turtelians has retarded our evolution, making the environment sluggish and tedious for the soaring Condorians. This dishonesty becomes the cause of wars, depression, violence, and the inhumanity of human history since the discovery of consciousness 3,000 years ago. **

THE FLYING TURTLE:
The Transformational Self-Evolution Shift

Here we dare to ask: Can the turtle learn to fly? Metaphorically and metaphysically the answer is yes. The obstacles are laziness and dishonesty and a dose of utter stupidity. We have to outsmart the "Amazing Stupidity Syndrome." As Einstein said, "**Only two things are infinite—the universe and human stupidity, and I'm not sure about the former.**"

A transitional stage does exist, a stage I call the "**Flying Turtle**," a conscious awakening to the next step of the individual's evolution. This is the point to which science and the arts have evolved. But the fact remains that the turtle is still a turtle and is only on the way to becoming a condor. This is the stage where artists continue to operate with the Right Brain while scientists lock themselves into the Left Brain. The step of integration that can catapult one into the flight of the condor is what the Flying Turtle wants to achieve.

Without inventing machines or superficial metaphors, the Turtle can fly. Whatever powers of invention are within reach of the Turtles, the key to unlocking the chains that bind them is within themselves—in their own hands and minds. To soar without ridicule may seem impossible in a world dominated by intolerant status quo Turtles. Jonathan Swift said,

"When a true genius appears in this world, you know him by this sign—that the dunces are all in confederacy against him."

It is human nature to be afraid of such greatness. In Shakespeare's *Twelfth Night*, he writes, "**Be not afraid of greatness. Some are born great, some achieve greatness, and some have greatness thrust upon them.**" Greatness is often misunderstood. Ralph Waldo Emerson pondered, "**Is it so bad then to be misunderstood? Pythagoras was misunderstood, and Socrates, and Copernicus, and Galileo, and Newton, and every pure and wise spirit that ever took flesh. To be great is to be misunderstood.**"

To cure the Turtelian mysticism disease requires discipline and Totally Integrated Honesty in all areas of life—to lead rather than follow, to act rather than react, to move forward rather than just try. There must be integrated thinking rather than non-conscious non-thinking. Independence must be exerted rather than dependence on others, especially dependence on the direction of external authority. Courage and initiative should override cowardice. The use of honest accurate facts should replace out-of-context traps or the "2-minute solution," the immediate results syndrome.

With this new attitude, one no longer fears the "unknown," but sees it as a place full of potential—the "not-yet-known." Rather than being unhappy and stagnant, the Condor strives to be happy, productive, and a producer and creator of values—soaring to unlimited use of consciousness.

When you develop and apply an integrated awareness of these daring principles, you can use your power of choice in your own life to become your true self—a Condor. All you need now, my friend, is simply to shift and focus your attention, in order to change your consciousness and move from the situation where you are now, to where you were intended to be—the state of perfect balance. Are you ready to take this step? To shift? It's up to you.

> **"There is no greater waste than potential unrealized."** – *Anonymous*
>
> **"An invasion of armies can be resisted but not an idea whose time has come."**
> *–Victor Hugo*

THE SHIFT, or the CURE

**Here are a few suggestions of how to shift
From Mediocrity to Excellence,
From Stagnancy to Productive and Creative Forward Movement,
From the Follower Mode to the Self-Leader Mode,
From the "Turtle State" to the "Condor State"**

The following nuggets are from the *BodySpeak™ Manual*...Notes de travail, titled: **Practical advice to myself from myself**

1. Organize yourself, your work, and your life. Guide your thoughts and actions toward enjoyable and profitable results.
2. Ask questions (Quest) with clear and focused attention. Develop your profound sense of listening. **Always listen carefully.**
3. Value your time and use it profitably with directed and disciplined attention.
4. Strive to understand fully and contextually before judging.
5. Maintain, cultivate and activate your honesty. Be loyal to it. And be fair regardless of near-term consequences.
6. Always see, explore and recognize facts **in full context.**
7. Avoid irrational reaction. Function from calm. Respond intelligently rather than react emotionally.
8. Think objectively, logically and rationally while constantly being aware of your inner self-guidance. This will help you to develop integrative thinking.
9. Be benevolent and passionate in your work, study and relations. Show **conscious innocence** toward all life.
10. In every situation, recognize and pursue the values of integrity and totally practiced honesty.
11. Focus on reality **AS IS. Do not escape WHAT IS**.
12. Do not create problems where they don't exist. Focus on solving the problems that do exist.
13. Remember that the whole must be grasped to understand each of its parts.
14. Value your solitude, privacy and your inner center of silence. Use contemplation to organize, clarify and define your own thoughts and actions.
15. Live 100% fully each and every precious moment of your life; **Be present**. This mode of thinking and being means that whatever you do now, it should be as if for the first time and the last time. This increases the intensity of living in the present. It will cause you to realize both your importance and insignificance in the same breath.
16. Speak only when necessary, what I call "**word economy.**" This is the source of daring to be yourself, a sovereign individual, enjoying your super happiness of life.
17. Finally, with practice, every suggestion here will lead you to:

> **Dare to constantly shift consciously**
> from **Thought** to **Action**,
> from **Idea** to **Product**,
> from **Chaos** to **Order**,
> from **Weakness** to **Power**,
> from **Limitation** to **Freedom**,
> from **Mediocrity** to **Excellence**,
> from **Pretense** and **Fake** to **Authentic** and **Real**,
> from **Sleepwalking** to **Conscious Awakening**,
> from **a Turtelian to a Condorian**
> from **a Drunken "Civilization"** to the
> **Lucid Civilization of the New Universe**

Consider these suggestions carefully and seriously. When you work each item until you master it, you will be surprised by the practical results you gain and by how little time it actually takes. **Dare, and you will find out how your new self and sense of being that has been buried and dormant inside you all these years will emerge, like a new power never known to you before.**

Another Personal Note:
Apply these three ways of learning to anything you aspire to know:

"When I was young, my grandfather told me that "**There are three 3 basic ways of living and learning."** Sitting there, on a small smooth rock in his yard, after rhythmically stomping grapes with my bare young feet in order to help him make wine, he told me this:

1. **The first** priority and the purpose of life is **live to learn,** absorbing like a sponge. Sharpen and use your intelligence to always increase curiosity and learn more with all of your ability.

2. **The second** priority and purpose of life is **living your learning,** mastering the practicality of your learning and perfecting it is as much as possible.

3. **The third** priority and purpose of life is to **tell your passionate story** of your experience, so others can also learn and benefit from your brief existence on this earth.

I will add that after applying these ways of learning and knowledge, only with great experience may you then someday dare to say the words: **"I DO NOT KNOW."**

Over the years, I reflected on my grandfather's profound and practical wisdom, with increasing curiosity. I wondered how long this process of learning would take. I adopted these three processes of learning in my activities, and experienced good practical results. In the process, I learned to always move quickly from thought to action, in applying the learning.

This personal note is appropriate here and now, to encourage you to **dare to take this step,** and shift from living in the herd-consciousness to becoming a self-leader. Think and apply these sound, proven and practical ways to be happy and fulfill the total potential of your being. Bon courage! Remember, Courage is a cloak you wear again and again until every cell in your body is named, "**Courage**."

> "Only those who attempt the absurd will achieve the impossible"
> - Albert Einstein

LE DESSERT — A FEW LAST TASTY WORDS

REMEMBER and REALIZE for Self-Guidance

A suggested philosophy for a balanced, happy and productive life:
"Identify and eliminate laziness and dishonesty in yourself and around you.

Live passionately without guilt. Be always ready, alert, creative
and responsive to the beautiful and vibrant life within you.

Happiness is your natural state of being and does not depend on anyone else.
but your own self. Enjoy 100% every present moment of your life.

Remember! Your life is your only moment in eternity, precious and full
with joie-de-vivre. Focus your energy with vitality to produce values
and earn your super happiness—your natural state of being.

Give more than you take. Produce more than consume."

"Vive La Vie, Vive L'Amour, Vive La Liberté, Vive La difference."

Samuel Avital. Sat, Nov 3rd. 1990.
in a public lecture on honesty and laziness,
Le Centre Du Silence Mime School, Boulder, Colorado.

Footnotes:

1 The Bicameral mind (two-chamber mind) is one that functions in an unconscious, two-step process. Automatic reactions and thoughts originate in the right hemisphere of the brain and are transmitted to the left hemisphere as instructions to be acted upon. Bicameral functioning is nature's automatic learned mode of response, without incorporating conscious thinking. The Bicameral mind was first identified by Dr. Julian Jaynes of Princeton University in his book, ***The Origin of Consciousness in the Breakdown of the Bicameral Mind***, 1976, Houghton Mifflin Co., Boston MA.

2 Mysticism. The definition of mysticism used here is any attempt to evade and contradict objective reality through dishonesty and deceit. Although the word "mysticism" may sometimes be used to refer to religions of the occult, this is not the context in which it is used in this article.

Mysticism is a rampant tendency which distorts human consciousness, promoting dishonesty and creating problems where they do not exist. It cleverly uses non-sequiters and other illogical statements to distort people's perception from seeing reality *as it is*.

Mysticism causes those who follow to it to react with the Bicameral Mentality. It encourages them to follow orders from an outside "higher" authority, to escape responsibility, and to behave automatically like robots following orders. In brief, it can be described as the most deadly, dangerous perversion and toxic disease of human consciousness.

The disciplines of the so-called new age since the 1960's, have been causing this regression back to bicameral mind mysticism. This is a contemporary and obvious example of the regression to bicameral mind behavior, encouraging the limited consciousness of the "**follower mode**", and inciting a state of **mass-hypnosis**. This way of thinking causes brain damage, and deeply harms the sanity and spiritual health of innocent practitioners. (See the article "The Spiritual Ratatouille of the New Age")

COSMIC ACCORDION

This expression, "**Cosmic Accordion**," was born out of necessity. Over the years, in working with my students, I found this natural law occurring over and over again in many varied situations. But, it had no name. We explored it together, and after some time, it finally distilled itself into these two words, which became part of our vocabulary. This was a form of condensed communication and helped shorten the space between thought and action in our class sessions. Thus, we are able to talk about it, see it, reflect upon it, and, BE it.

The Cosmic Accordion is the journey between the infinitely small and the infinitely big - back and forth, and back again. This process is inherent in the study of any art. By going deeply into the creative process and deeply into the self, one will eventually come upon the source of creativity — a source which is infinitely vast.

The artistic process begins with the artist's talent. Added to this is that which we call "inspiration." And then all remains is to manifest it, to actualize it, to physicalize it. This is the artist or the mystic's real work. Once the source of inspiration has been tapped (the infinitely large), the challenge is to bring it "down to earth," to materialize the realization for others to see, hear or feel, so that it can be communicated and absorbed.

In Hebrew, this funneling is called TZIMTZUM (צמצום), or condensation. The artist, or the mystic, becomes the vehicle, the vessel, the channel, through which the infinitely big (inspiration) is purified and gets molded by the artist's masterly actions. This renders it visible or audible or tactile as the case may be. In mime, it is the process of visibilizing the invisible.

For the mime, the body itself is the vessel. Through shape, form, gesture, rhythm and attitude, the body manifests that which is invisible and infinite. The mime must BECOME that which he wishes to portray. He is the medium itself, as well as its creator. He is the color, the musicality. He is the very thought made manifest.

In the actual exchange between artist and audience, the artist hopes to recreate the experience of the infinitely large so that it can be passed on to others. When the audience receives it, in its condensed physicalized, manifested form, it goes into the unconscious as an experience or perception, and it thus returned to its source — it has become, once again, infinitely vast. Thus, the circle is complete.

This same principle of the Cosmic Accordion is constantly active in the spiritual quest. In meditation and divine contemplation, we wish to experience, even for a brief moment, the freedom from the body and its physical limitations. In these moments, there is often an experience of being a part of the vast cosmic ocean. We are a mere speck — infinitely small in the cosmic scheme — but when we merge with this ocean, we feel that we have BECOME IT in all its vastness.

On the spiritual path, one learns to look within the self for many answers and to find all the expressions of the universe represented within the limits of the human body. There is a continual interplay between the large and the small. One is like a pendulum, swinging back and forth between the opposites ever seeking to find the balance, the middle pillar, where one can be in both "places" at once. One encounters here the paradox of that which is apparently insignificant on the one hand, but is tremendously significant on the other. All the great teachers throughout the course of history have presented their wisdom in this way—taking their spiritual knowledge and condensing it from the greater vision into the material world.

For the Kabbalist, the Cosmic Accordion is a ubiquitous principle, many variations of which can be found in every corner of the Kabbalistic literature. In one instance, it can be seen as the journey downward through the spectrum of the four worlds—Atzilut (אצילות), the world of emanation; Beriah (בריאה), the world of creation; Yetzirah (יצירה), the world of formation; Asiah (עשיה), the world of making of matter.

Through "inspiration" one may be graced with the ability to pull the idea from the world of Atzilut (the upper, big triangle), down through the world of creation and the world of formation, into the world of making. In other words, it is the process of creation itself, or the formula for bringing that which is hidden into the manifest world - From the invisible to the visible. This process allows for the possibility of communicating that specific idea or concept, for making manifest in the physical world that which seemed inaccessible to our ordinary lives before.

This experiential concept is also used by the Kabbalists to interpret the ladder of Jacob. In this case, it is the "angels" which descend and ascend, back and forth, in the eternal vertical process of manifesting the Essence of Being Within. It is participation in the great plan or scheme of human evolution, from matter to spirit, from spirit to matter - the grand cosmic theatre created to "entertain" the angels, humans, animals and all the kingdoms through which the Great One, the unnameable, manifests Himself.

DECLARATION OF PEACE – PERSONAL AND GLOBAL

I, this Being of Light, declare at this precious moment:

1. My sincere determination to see PEACE in every situation I encounter, with a positive attitude and the eagerness that emanates from my spiritual being,

2. That I am a being of PEACE, that PEACE begins within me, and that I radiate PEACE around me with every thought and action,

3. That by living in harmony with the laws of nature, I attract only that which is for PEACE,

4. That I am focused Light-energy with Divine intelligence, part of the whole Cosmic Universe, and so, I practice PEACE with all my mind, heart and might,

5. That as a spiritual and peaceful being, I do not dwell, in any way, on the negative aspect of life, focusing only on the positive so that I may teach PEACE simply by being in tune with my higher self here on earth,

6. That nothing can disturb the PEACE and cosmic harmony within, knowing that the Source of Life is always with me as a living flame of all that is,

7. That by keeping my heart free from hate and my mind from worry, by living simply and trusting the Creator of the Universe, I practice the art of PEACE and silence to the best of my abilities, and know that I am always guided toward PEACE profound,

8. That by planting the seed of PEACE in my thoughts every day, PEACE transforms me into a better being,

9. That by planting the seed of PEACE within, the world around me will transform into a place of harmony that radiates the Divinity within all beings. I know that all is working perfectly with universal order, and only by changing myself through PEACE, will the world change.

PEACE TO YOU. PEACE TO ME. PEACE TO ALL BEINGS HERE AND NOW.

HANDS — AN EXPRESSION OF THE SOUL

*The Inspiring Hand – "Thy hands have made me and fashioned me:
Give me understanding, that I may learn thy commandments."
Psalms 119:73*

Inspired by a visit to the *Museum of Rodin*, and by the work of this great artist in general, I was particularly inspired by *The Cathedral* - Rodin's famous work of hands joined in the fervor of prayer, their slow movement rising like a song of praise to the infinite Creator. In viewing this inspiring work of art, one is drawn in heart and mind to the inner realm to acknowledge and appreciate the simplicity of these hands that serve us.

Visualize for a moment the hands of Rodin, which shaped this beautiful sculpture, or the hands of Rembrandt while painting, or Michelangelo's hands while carving the stone to give it form. Visualize the hands of Arthur Rubenstein, or of Yehudi Menuhin, or Ravi Shankar performing on his sitar, and you will see how, through the hands of the great artists of all time, a human heart can come to appreciate and admire the work of God.

The creation of great paintings, calligraphy, and hieroglyphs by the hands of man has preserved the greatness of civilizations for us today. It can be noted, that nothing could be manifested without the touch of the human hand. In touching, one is touched — touched by the hands of the Creator, and blessed by The Infinite One.

In the language of the prophets of all times, we find this common expression: "And the hand of the Lord was upon me." This expression does not necessarily mean that God has physical hands, but it suggests that the power of God was upon him, upon his soul. The High Priest blessing the community with hands outstretched, the knowing hands of the healer, these examples suggest without a doubt, the wonderful power that is within each one of us, manifested through our hands.

We are made in the image of The Creator and express our gratefulness of being by giving with these hands, caressing the beloved. Hands hold the head to think, clap to express joy, and form attitudes of prayer. In all these actions, the hands do their work in a mighty and dignified silence.

If we, just for a moment, bring the human hand to the forefront of our awareness, and meditate on how it serves man in his quest for self-knowledge and practical life, we come to a greater acknowledgment and appreciation of the hand's importance.

Our hands may seem common because we all have hands. And yet, how often do we appreciate the sheer joy of having these hands at our service at any time to translate our thoughts into those beautiful creative actions of writing, drawing, and sewing? Look for a moment at your hands, and see how they live freely, listening to an unknown command to serve you, to scratch your face or to brush your teeth in the morning, or even to be still. It is observed that the hand is most natural and expressive when it is not doing anything specific. When at rest, the fingers, slightly bent, seem to surrender to the sheer joy of rest and relaxing.

And yet, when in action, they respond amazingly and immediately to our inspirational thoughts, in a beautiful, awesome silence.

In *Mime* and in *Dance*, hands design the space and sculpt the air into a moving illusion — creating a beautiful dimension of reality. From one's creative impulse, the air is given movement, the space takes shape. And when the hands grab the rock, we can climb the mountain. The silhouette of the hands is known to be an art form in the theatre of shadows. Hands become autonomously alive, imitating animals, human faces, and other objects. When the spirit works through the hands, allowing their creativity the freedom to move, hands can mysteriously move us to laughter and tears.

The Instrument

In French, the word human is spelled thus: *humain (hu-main)*. *Main* is the word for hand. *Hu*, is the divine sound, along with *Main* reads, "Being is hand." Is it a coincidence, or does it mean the He (God) is very near us through our hands?

In Hebrew, the word for hand is *Yad* (יד). *Yod* (יוד) is also the tenth letter of the Hebrew alphabet. *Yod* (יוד), the first letter of *Yad* (יד), designates the ten fingers, ten Sephiroth. It is with his ten fingers that man learns to count. His hands are the basis of geometry and mathematics.

Now, *Yad*, (יד) numerically in Hebrew comes to 14, designating the 14 phalanges of the human hand. We have two hands — 14 and 14 — which means in two hands we have 28 phalanges. This number, 28, creates the word *Koah* (כח) meaning power — the power that we possess in our hands or actions. Thus, is given to man the mighty power to create and expand and manifest.

And so, comes the discovery that we have two hands, the right and the left. When both are grasping or working at something, they are in the act of creating and producing. With a potter, for example — his two hands form the clay. Clay in the hands of the potter, and directed by his intelligence, might become a useful container for our very life. A cup, it is known, is an imitation of the human hand — one cups one's hand to drink, and this is coded in the Hebrew word of Kaf (כ).

The right hand without the left hand is not complete. One complements the other, and they represent the polarities of our being — the positive and the negative, the two hemispheres of the brain etc. It is the left hand of the violinist which holds the strings, and the right which draws the bow over the strings to create sound. Or, it is one hand which holds the paper, in order that the other hand can write upon it.

In prayer, these two hands resemble two branches on a tree of life, growing from the trunk's heart center and reaching toward heaven with their finger-leaves outstretched. In prayer, the hands and fingers reach out to master the ability to shape matter with their service, and by this, they cause the raising of the consciousness of man and unite it with the consciousness of the Cosmic through their work on this earth plane.

The Servant

What a miracle! The human hand is such a magnificent grouping of bones, formed in a truly beautiful way that allows us to touch all that is around us. This fact is taken for granted by so many: The ultimate goal of our hands is the very purpose of life – to serve.

We do not separate the hands from the body and the spirit. There is a simple relationship that has been emphasized here—namely, obedience and silent service. The spirit makes the hand, the hand makes the spirit. And the state of consciousness is revealed in every action in which the hand is involved—even that of stillness. The hand organizes the expression and the action directed from within.

The gentleness and innocence of the small hand of the newborn baby, closed and suggestive of holding a secret in its tiny fist, seems to say, "I have come to give; I have something in my hands." And the hands of a dying person are open, as if saying, "I have given; my soul can now soar to other dimensions."

In observing nature and its laws, the Creator in action, we discover something: The human is the tool of The Creator, and one's hands are the instruments through which creation is expressed. The human intelligence invents other tools, and a friendly relationship develops between man and these tools. They allow him to expand by mastering the gestures of the tool. The five fingers adapt to the shape of the tool to hold it, while the tool serves to create. Visualize for a moment the hands of the scribes of old and their magnificent work. Even in our very technologically developed society, which seems to take man away from his nature, we still need these hands to operate the machines, which are made in man's image.

The leader within man, one's will, has the ability to choose. He can direct his hands to do negative things, such as killing, or into positive channels such as hugging his beloved ones. If man is awakened to this gift and the realization of choice, then one will use his hands to serve, give, and work for the benefit of others as well as oneself. Just as the hands feed by bringing food to the mouth, so too, are they fed. Thus, the law of giving and taking is expressed in the same breath.

By constantly becoming aware of our hands and fingers, we come to the thought that they are actually transmitters of energy and knowledge, in which our fluid thoughts take form.

If we take this into consideration, we will see positive transformations in our lives. Every moment and gesture become of utmost importance to us. Poise is gained, and calm envelops all life within and without. We pray with these hands. We write our poems on the walls of history with these hands. And we build for mankind the continuity of our future being with ONE mighty hand.

Boulder, CO. August, 1978

HOMAGE TO MARCEL MARCEAU
Mon Maitre, Mon Ami, My Teacher, My Friend

It is with great respect and honor that I dedicate these words as Homage, a Kaddish, to Marcel Marceau. He was a teacher and friend over the years, since my studies with him in Paris of 1959.

This great French mime master popularized the beautiful Art of Mime to millions all over the world, and performed for almost seventy years, with mastery and excellence beyond definition. He was a genuine master of silence. He allowed us to encounter glimpses into our own lives with impeccable eloquence and captured the attention and the hearts of millions of people, without uttering a word.

Marcel Mangel, whose father was a kosher butcher, was born March 22, 1923, in Strasbourg, near the French-German border. The family moved to Lille and later to Limoges. He was 84 when he died Saturday, September 22, 2007 in Paris, exactly on Yom Kippur, the Great Day of Atonement in the Jewish tradition.

The inner meaning of leaving this world on Yom Kippur is very significant in the Hebrew Tradition, and an ominous sacred sign that his soul joins the assembly of the Just in the Garden of Eden. These are the ones who, by their simplicity of being and invisibility, sustain and brighten our world with hope, light, joy and genuine kindness. They assist us with a conscious intention to dare to transform our broken characters into a better, healthy and balanced way of being, and thus, to restore ourselves and the entire world.

The President of France, Nicolas Sarkozy said upon his death, "France loses one of its most eminent ambassadors." Indeed, he was a great artist and ambassadeur of poetry in action, with a human élan of sensitivity. His musicality of movement, and his silent eloquence spoke to all human hearts everywhere, beyond the limits of spoken language.

I used to see his performances every night in Theatre de L'Ambigu, not far from where I lived in Boulevard Magenta in Paris.

One day I had a great surprise when I passed by the back stage of that historical theatre. Marceau was leaning gently on the door, pensive, with those deep contemplative eyes and with his trickster smile. I stopped for a moment, and leaned by the same doorstep, as if saying silently, "I am here, to be, and to listen," including myself in his "private" contemplation.

We stayed still a while in silence, and then, from nowhere, he asked me with such a serious tone: "Samuel, where was God during the Holocaust?" I opened my two big eyes and looked at him. His gentle hand was still in the asking position as that question reverberated in the air. It was an unanswerable question. And he asks it to me? He asks that screaming question? Did he really expect an "answer" from me?

My first thought was to gently whisper, "Baruch Dayan Ha-emet" (Blessed be the Judge of Truth) — and to say to him that this mystery will be explored by many humans, and it is actually the kind of question that needs no answer! It is a great and wondrous human quest for justice and bewilderment. A sincere, innocent, defiant question, to consciousness itself, to the God who signed the contract with us at Sinai, when we accepted the Torah by saying "We will do and we will hear", and thus, agreed to be our guardian during our long and purifying exile among the nations of this earth.

He saw that I was touched by that wondrous question and immediately said, "Are you coming tonight to the performance?" "Yes," I said. And he went in for another Mime performance that night. That question haunted me for many years, and any pretentious "answer" would be an insult to human intelligence.

In our tradition, when we come to an impasse where we cannot answer any question, after exploring it from every angle possible, we say: TEIKU, meaning it has to wait for now, until the time when the Prophet Eliyahu will come to help us find the "answer." Maybe, when that time comes, we will evolve and use our consciousness and intelligence fully. We will be able to find that "answer." For now we say, TEIKU.

As far as I remember, I never had any conversation with Marceau on mundane matters, or gossip. We only spoke of lofty, meaningful and practical subjects that would rise up, things to explore when we had a time to dwell deeply into them. And we always ended with good humor, being seriously funny. He was a living question mark, probing and exploring the deeper dimensions of being, and discovering how to express that with our beautiful art of silence - mime. He was a great silent Lighthouse.

Prime Minister Francois Fillon praised Marcel Marceau as "the master," who possessed the rare gift of "being able to communicate with each and every person, beyond the barriers of language." Those who knew him a little more closely, his students, friends and colleagues, can testify to his generosity and patience in his relationship with them.

Annette Lust, the author of *"From the Greek Mimes to Marcel Marceau and Beyond,"* said that, Marceau's mentor, French mime master Etienne Decroux, "reinvented the art of mime to revive modern theater and the actor's art," whereas Mr. Marceau "popularized that art and brought it to the whole world."

When the Germans invaded France during World War II, Marceau's father was taken to Auschwitz, where he died in 1944. Marceau was 21.

In one of his performances, he introduced me to his older brother, Alain, who changed the family name to Marceau — after Francois Severin Marceau-Desgraviers, an 18th century French general. Both brothers became part of the French underground.

Marceau became talented at forging documents to help young Jewish men avoid the Nazi concentration camps, and he also helped many children across the border to neutral

Switzerland. Toward the end of the war, he joined the Free French Forces, fighting alongside U.S. troops under General George Patton.

Studying with Marceau was very intimidating in the beginning, until one began to understand the scope of this beautiful art of the essence of human expression. Dedication, devotion and a focused heart were the traits necessary to learn and master this artistic craft with Marceau. And it was essential to do all this without expecting any results. The way was just to practice, explore, and enjoy, and if the knees sometimes got tired, it was always a gift to rest and contemplate.

His endorsement of my first book *"Mime WorkBook"* on November 20, 1971 said:
"Somewhere in Colorado, in a beautiful town called Denver, there is a community of young people directed by the very talented Samuel Avital. I think that his work is important. He brings awareness to the soul of people, and gives the young dedicated artists who work under his direction the need, dedication, and love for the world of silence and the beautiful art of movement." Marcel Marceau, BIP. Nov 20, 1971

When he endorsed my second book *"Mime and Beyond: The Silent Outcry"* in March 22, 1980 at his birthday celebration together at the Brown Palace Hotel in Denver, Colorado, he wrote me in French:

"Mon cher Samuel, Les mots seront toujours pauvres a coté de notre silence, mais ils ouvrent les portes a notre esprit silencieux. De tout Coeur." *"My dear Samuel, words will be always poor besides our silence, but they will open doors…to our silent spirit. With all heart."*
Marcel Marceau, BIP. Denver, Colorado 1980

The last time I saw him perform was at The Denver Center for The Performing Arts, on Wednesday, April 9th, 2003. He was frail, but that evening, he gave a great performance that brought more than 15 minutes of ovations. There were many young people there from various schools. The audience was elated by his poetic humanity, and you forgot that he was in his 80's. He showed the same grace and mastery of eloquence, and the same energetic delivery as I knew in his performances in Paris when he was younger in age.

Once, in a performance I saw in the Theatre de Poche in Montparnasse in Paris, I was seated (by accident?) in a seat where Marcel Marceau's name was carved. He was amused and smiled when I related this anecdote to him.

"Mime, like music, knows neither borders nor nationalities," I remember he once said. "If laughter and tears are the characteristics of humanity, all cultures are steeped in our discipline."

From time to time, Marceau would ask me probing questions, on specific events of our tumultuous time, or on the Kabbalah. He knew I came from a Kabbalistic Sephardic lineage from Spain and Morocco, and he enjoyed lively conversations in this great body of knowledge and wisdom from our Hebrew tradition.

Samuel Avital

The truth is that I am both sad and happy while writing these reminiscences, knowing within myself that he left us a great legacy. He lives in our knowing and there is so much we learned from him while he was present here with us. My heart is full with respect and with good memories of him and his generous way of being and teaching. May his memory be blessed.

I remember when he performed "The Creation of the World," as an angel who descends on earth, and lands in a bar, with people drinking and loud music playing, and the angel must deal with the material entrapments, and the wicked ways of humans here. Now, he becomes that angel, returning back to the source of all souls, via the same ladder.

Rest well, Beloved Grand Maitre, your memory will live within me, and those beings you touched and entertained with such a great eloquence and gentle humanity.

May your soul rest in peace, in the source of all souls, within the sacred bundle of life.

Your humble student,
Samuel Avital

Weds, Sept 26, 2007. Boulder, Colorado

Marcel Marceau and Samuel Avital – 1974 Denver, Colorado

HUMAN, AWAKE FROM YOUR SLUMBER
בני האדם! התעוררו מהתרדמה העמוקה

Spirituality means awakening from the state of sleep, which is rampant in our world. Most people do not even know it, but they are born, live, marry, give birth and die within their sleep. They never understand the real joy of living and being, nor even have a clue of what human existence truly is.

Most streams of spirituality and religion can agree on one thing: that all is well, that the whole world is functioning well, and to keep a "positive mindset" — While they know very well that this world is not in order. They keep preaching that all is well, even when the world is continuously in a state of great disorder. This is a strange paradox indeed. But tragically, most humans on this earth have not succeeded in seeing that all is not in fact in order, because they are in the state of sleep and deep slumber. And in this, they have nightmares and they do not know why.

One must awake from this hypnotic slumber in order to see and sense this life in the Universe now. One must awake and stop playing the games that deepen this sleep.

That is why, for a wise Teacher, it is really futile to even try to awaken his students, because they are very comfortable in their sleep, and they continue to eat, drink, and walk all while sleepwalking, pretending they are awake. What a tragic reality! What a great insane asylum!

Even the great healers and therapy practitioners in all fields of human pain and suffering, tell us that people simply **Do not want to be healed**, because it is a "painful" process. All that they want is to ease the pain, not to **heal**. And so, the great pharmaceutical companies bathe in this ignorance and control the joy and pain of people by inventing new drugs to "**ease the pain**" of various states of disease. And with these placebos, they are successful at enslaving millions of people, deepening their sleep while earning billions each minute, all off of the misery of stubborn people who **Do not want to heal**, period.

Even if the teacher pleads to his students to **Awake**, they do not hear, because it is very comfortable to stay asleep. This, therefore, is the real cause of suffering. Once one is awakened, all the "troubles" and the "pains" and "suffering" of this world, disappear and **True Life** really begins. Those who have awakened know this reality. They live like you and me in "this" world, and they do not look any different from anyone else. Their great protection is the magic world of **Being Ordinary**.

The True teacher simply is. He lives life in an ordinary way. He does his dance of life openly and obviously, with the thought that if his students sense the benefits of this way of being, and know how to receive and learn beyond words, they will understand and gain knowledge. If not, there is a sadness that this obviousness cannot awake them to that great reality of being and becoming.

There is a wise teaching proverb about the rain. "The rain is the same rain, drops of waters falling from above. If it rains on rocky ground, it grows thorns, and if it rains on fertile ground, it grows blooming flowers."

So, go and ponder: Why all these words about awakening and sleep? Maybe in the process the "inner bells" will begin to signal you, and whisper silently, "Awake human from your slumber. Begin to listen to the voice of light and love."

That is why one first step toward this awakening is to begin to learn how to listen.

The following verses from the Psalms illustrate our current human situation:

ה. פֶּה־לָהֶם וְלֹא יְדַבֵּרוּ עֵינַיִם לָהֶם וְלֹא יִרְאוּ:

ו. אָזְנַיִם לָהֶם וְלֹא יִשְׁמָעוּ אַף לָהֶם וְלֹא יְרִיחוּן:

ז. יְדֵיהֶם | וְלֹא יְמִישׁוּן רַגְלֵיהֶם וְלֹא יְהַלֵּכוּ לֹא־יֶהְגּוּ בִּגְרוֹנָם:

תהלים קטו. ה, ו, ז.

    5. They have mouths, but they cannot speak;
       they have eyes, but they cannot see;
    6. They have ears, but they cannot hear;
       they have noses, but they cannot smell;
    7. They have hands, but they cannot feel;
       they have feet, but they cannot walk;
       and from their throat they cannot speak.
           Psalms 115. 5, 6, 7.

IF I AM BECAUSE I AM
By Rabbi Menahem Mendel from Kotzk

If I am I Because I am I
and you are you because you are you,
Then I am I and you are you.

But if I am I because you are you,
and you are you because I am I,
then I am not I and you are not you.

IN THE BEGINNING WAS THE DOT

"In the beginning there was the dot, and another dot and another one. They played and multiplied in space and time and became a **LINE**. And the line moved and became a **circle**. And the dot within the circle began to move, touching the walls of the circle, and bouncing strongly back and forth, from one wall of the circle to another; thus energy was created.

And with this mighty movement was created new forms that shaped into a triangle, cells, organs, hearts, kidneys, and a whole life became visible and manifested.

And finally, the human organism emerged and uttered the words, and worlds, and wrote them in symbols, lines, circles, diagonal shapes, letters. And the symbols became reality, and concealed within each letter were the "**secret**" codes of Creation.

From the **Original Dot**, we call **The Source of all Life** and beings, coming and emerging "**out of nothing**" (**Yesh Me'Ayin**), the whole universe comes into being, and contains all beings and all that is becoming. And they begin to "Breathe."

And the **CREATOR, DESIGNER** saw the "**Great Design**", and called it "**good**"= **Tov.**

So, our task now, as the created and creative human beings (as the **image, or Tzelem, of the Creator**), is to explore, decipher, recognize and use the **power** of the Creator. Our role is to align ourselves with that greater will. We call this **LIFE (Hayyim), LIGHT (Or Elion)**, and Good (Tov). Also we must use this "Power" (**Koah**), for the good and benefit of all living beings.

THE JOURNEY FROM THOUGHT TO ACTION

It is said that there are three kinds of people:
Those who ask what is happening, those who ask how it is happening, and those who make things happen.

The first two kinds of people are the same in the sense that these people are mostly unconscious of life—they just ask, without going further. They are curious but do not act. They are amazed at how things happen, but it stops there. They are mostly interested in the material level of living and therefore, are limited in their thoughts.

The third kind—the ones who make things happen—are more interesting. They have graduated from curiosity seeking. They know how to "ask" and "answer," and to act upon the results according to their level of evolution.

Among those who make things happen, there are two categories, the positive and the negative. The negative ones guide their know-how toward their own selfish and greedy ends. The others, who guide themselves toward the positive side of life, know the law of cause and effect, and use their knowledge for the benefit of mankind. They are called the "friends of humanity" and "men and women of good will." Both of these groups use the same law—one for the negative and the other for the positive. Since the law is impersonal, it works both ways. But one is lasting and eternal, and the other is just passing and ephemeral.

To make things happen—that is, to create—we must follow certain rules of the law diligently and faithfully. To make use of our creative abilities, we must fully explore the power of thought.

What is a thought? Thought is a force, a vibration, like light, heat, or sound, but, without any definite physical manifestation. Nothing is ever produced in life without first being a thought. As the Kabbalist would say, סוֹף מַעֲשֶׂה בְּמַחֲשָׁבָה תְּחִלָּה, "**sof ma'aseh be-ma'hashava tehilla**," meaning "**the accomplishment of an action or creation occurs first in the thought**."

The manifestation of the first act of creation was through the word—the Creator said "Let there be light," and there was light. And before the word was the original thought that arose before the Creator. So we can say, "in the beginning was the thought." It vibrates in the invisible, forms the image of the action (the verb), and then manifests it by creating it.

Therefore, thought is always creative. If it is not acted upon, it still exists in the invisible realm of being as potential until its time comes. If it is not expressed immediately, it may not be the right time, right place, or right people for its expression.

Thought is rarely personal, and when the unconscious registers it, even when we are unaware, it retains its influence until the time is ripe for its activation.

In spite of its immateriality, thought is a more lasting reality than material, tangible realizations. For example, let us take an architect who wishes to build a house. Before he can make it happen, he must use his thought to plan the exact design he perceives. Only after the image is clear, precise, and planned to the last detail, can he begin to realize it with material and form. Therefore, a finished house is the result of a thought. As the Buddhist master would say, "Man is the result of his thought."

According to mystical theories, when a human being emanates a thought, he creates an "entity," and according to the intensity of the cerebral action, this spiritual creature will have a long and lasting life.

We have positive and negative thoughts according to our degree of perception. Entities of the same nature will group themselves together by the law of attraction, and thus, bring about the creation of those thoughts focused together for a purpose. The Sufi wisdom describes this as: "Souls that recognize one another congregate together; those that do not, argue with one another."

The Use of Thought
The thoughts we carry within ourselves are living forces present in the auras around us, like little birds flying to find a fertile ground, to be manifested, and be born in action, as long as there is a conscious or unconscious being to bring them to the plane of realization.

According to our evolution, in whatever way we use thought, for positive or negative, the same law is at work. This illustrates the impersonality of thought. We have been given freedom of choice and according to that choice, we act, consciously using the process of thought to create reality.

As students of mystical work, guided by the aphorism "Know Thyself," we choose the positive side of work, while not denying the existence of the negative we encounter. Our choice is a result of experience and experiments. This is a genuine knowledge, based on sound and healthy perceptions.

To understand the proper use of thought, let us use the analogy of a seed planted in earth. The technique is the same. When we plant a seed in the earth, we must care for it in many ways: by maintaining it with a focused attention, by watering it, weeding the area around the seed, and nurturing it to its natural fruition.

The same is true for a thought. There is the intensity of focus of that thought. One must maintain that inner image, understanding the creative potential of its use. The purpose and conscious attention given to it matters, as does the intention to use it for the benefit of all. All of this allows it to grow into conscious realization. Thus, the journey from thought to action is fulfilled and realized. And once this journey has been mastered, we can go on and on in creating multiple projects for the purpose of being of service to others, thus, fulfilling our mission in this incarnation.

By using the above technique toward improving our well-being and health, we could actually replace medicine, since the source of illness is in the thought of the person, conscious or unconscious. It is sufficient to direct our thought in a relaxed way toward that area of illness, as it is known that the cells have their own consciousness to absorb thought and act upon it.

By nurturing the mental image of harmony and well-being in the whole organism, by feeling the creative light surround the body, and by perseverance and good faith, in time we will be awed and overwhelmed by the results of this magnificent law at work. For those who experiment with it, it is a fact, and the results are astonishing. Here, doubt is an enemy. Therefore, we need to be certain, in spite of all negative aspects we encounter during the practice of this law.

Thought as a Healing Power
The thought-force works by self-suggestion to heal. The unconscious adopts the suggestion very easily and acts upon it. If we do not interfere, the result is what we call the state of harmonium. This of course, could be effective in healing physical illness as well as mental illness. In brief, to use our thoughts properly, we must learn to control them patiently. That is, to be aware very consciously of the choices taken. Using positive thoughts, of course, is an asset for success, and thus, shortens the time involved between the thought and the action.

With experience, confidence, and a certain way of acting and thinking, this path is condensed. We have the sense of transcending time and space as a result of the focus of the work. This will occur only by cultivating the garden of our thoughts consciously and with a noble purpose of being happy and useful to humanity and ourselves.

This is emphasized here for the purpose of turning our attention to it: As thoughts are used and acted upon in the conscious level, so they are used and acted upon in the unconscious state. Here lies the difference between living consciously or living automatically.

We have the ability to choose to make things happen, or just to ask why and how...the choice is ours to make.

This is only one of many aspects for practicing the famous adage "Know Thyself." The practice of the laws mentioned here brings beneficial results to all concerned. Experience, perseverance, and silence will prove this to be a successful endeavor. The results are, one becomes an active being on the stage of individual and human evolution.

Another "trick" to success and self-transformation is that thoughts must be directed and guided toward the benefit of all humanity. The worker of light must have a keen and sincere attitude, total faith in the law at work (without any doubt), and above all a genuine love for humanity. This enables one to become a real friend for uplifting the human condition and caring for the "other" — thy neighbor.

Therefore, my friend, do not overlook the obvious situations. Be not fooled by appearances. Stay alert and awake, calm in the midst of tumult. Be silent and know the power of the Supreme Creator, whom we have in our being. That Creator has instilled in us, in our very cellular organism and our consciousness, the power of thought, so that we may create, in our turn, a constructive civilization for the great purpose of being and bringing good to all creation.

The thought is given to you to act upon. Now it is up to you friend. Work beyond personal gain—try this diligently for enough time, and you will be greatly surprised.

The following are a few thoughts from Kabbalistic and Sufi sources to ponder on in the privacy of the sanctuary of your heart:

רַבִּי טַרְפוֹן אוֹמֵר: הַיּוֹם קָצֵר וְהַמְּלָאכָה מְרֻבָּה וְהַפּוֹעֲלִים עֲצֵלִים וְהַשָּׂכָר הַרְבֵּה וּבַעַל הַבַּיִת דּוֹחֵק:
מסבת אבות פרק ב׳. כ

"The day is short, and the work is great. The workers are lazy,
and the reward is much. And the master is urgent."
Pirke Avoth 2:20.

הַכֹּל צָפוּי. וְהָרְשׁוּת נְתוּנָה. וּבְטוֹב הָעוֹלָם נִדּוֹן. וְהַכֹּל לְפִי רוֹב הַמַּעֲשֶׂה:
מסבת אבות פרק ג׳. ט״ו

"Everything is foreseen, yet freedom of choice is given;
for the world is judged by grace, and all is according to the amount of work."
Pirke Avoth 3:19.

"My existence is through you, and your appearance is through me;
but if I had not appeared, you would not have been."
Ibn-Arabi (A.D. 1165-1240)

"I was a hidden treasure, and I longed to be known.
So I created the world, that I might be known."
Ancient proverb

September, 1984

KEEP ME SANE IN THE MIDST OF MADNESS

Right now, no one can ignore the amount of insane and out of balance phenomena that we see in our world.

Our politicians have become professional liars. They push their way to the top, pretending to act "for the benefit of their citizens," while they pass laws for their own selfish purposes. They create a state of mass hypnosis that puts the whole society at war with one another.

In medicine, we once trusted our doctors for healing. Now, drug companies have mastered the way to sell us more pills, and keep us dependent for life. We see healthcare that has forgotten its true purpose and put financial gain above service to humanity.

We see it in religion too. Instead of sharing the truth of wisdom, we encounter corrupt religious leaders who care about controlling their followers. They wear masks of "good" and pray to God to help them win wars. This kind of behavior is a curse.

Unfortunately, on every level that we look, from the personal to the global, things seem to be completely out of balance. Everywhere we look, there is confusion, deceit, destruction, and humanity at war with themselves and one another.

What we need is a creative way to solve our collective human problems. The good news is, people in many different disciplines are now trail-blazing the path of the future. They are finding solutions that soar beyond the old limitations. Right in the mouth of the lion, new and intelligent organizations are acting successfully to correct the course of humanity, and prove that we can live harmoniously.

These groups are doing the exact opposite of today's corrupt way of living. Where there is noise, they relax and are silent. Where there is war, they practice peace. Where there is conflict, they produce harmony. Where there is disease, they create healing. Where there is irrational behavior, they rely on their intelligence and unique individual creativity. Where others follow, they lead. In all their endeavors, they set their way of thinking toward producing more and consuming less.

There is one essential thing that all these leaders recognize: **One has to change oneself first**. Starting by making the change themselves, these individuals then radiate and share that realization with others. When they find laziness in thinking, they become active and vigorous. In the presence of ignorance, they implant a thought of wisdom. Where there is a problem, they find a solution, with creative endeavors and fearless innovation.

This quiet cultural evolution is gradually being picked up by intelligent human beings. And as more people find a sane and clear way of thinking and living, it will eventually reach a tipping point. At that point, those who destroy value and manipulate others will simply be obsolete. This tipping point, or critical mass, can allow a new consciousness to come about in society. For example, when enough people are aware of the insanity of war, it motivates them to act in the name of sanity, and work for the continued evolution of the human species.

Even as the floods are rising, it is possible to keep one's head above water. The best way to do this is to return to healthy ways of being. We must be honest, even in the face of negative situations. We must increase the love of truth in our daily affairs, in spite of the widespread dishonesty and mass hypnosis we may encounter.

We can remain calm and serene, breathing naturally, so that our heartbeat becomes regulated with the rhythm of nature. We must be kind to the environment and help others without seeking anything in return, living in touch with the source of life, which is built into us all.

It is also good to develop one's intuition, without neglecting rational thinking. In this way, balance becomes a way of life. All of these things lead a person to be peaceful within. By reconciling the opposites and dualities we encounter, it is possible to realize harmony within the paradox. Then, a person does not just **HAVE peace**, they **BECOME peace**.

With time, as more and more people practice these balanced ways of being, the whole society can begin to shift to the healthy path of becoming peace. In turn, governments will come to change their ways, using their power towards creation of a better society.

And above all, each person must begin practicing unconditional love for all beings. This can come when we realize the connecting link between all humanity - that we are all one family of beings. We must reflect on the virtue of kindness and activate it with every breath we take and give. Especially in these perplexed times, we need to practice human kindness most of all. If we reflect on this deeply, we can begin to shift to sanity in the midst of madness.

Throughout life, let us remember the words of our ancient sages who said "**KEEP ME SANE IN THE MIDST OF MADNESS**." Remembering this, we can remain happy, productive, and wise, despite any imbalances we come to face in this world.

February 10, 2001. Boulder, CO

LISTENING

"We are not chosen to be illuminated;
We must choose to be illuminated."
— Anonymous

LISTENING IS AN ART that needs to be cultivated every moment. The sincere seeker must know the great value of silence in a practical way, so that they can delve deeply into the real source of listening.

One must be able to carry a quiet state of being in all situations. This quiet, is a path that needs to be walked constantly. Along the path, the individual becomes peaceful, learning to deal with all problems with clarity and balanced resolution.

With this practice, the practitioner comes to know about the act of conscious choice. He or she can think and act according to this acquired faculty of listening. Thus, they become illuminated by choice.

In the deep listening of the land of silence, one is led to the light of understanding, and becomes useful to oneself and to all concerned. Harmony of being is the result of this self-investment, made with efforts put in over time. It is like leaving a pot of water on the fire to warm or boil. The pot (body) must stay upon the fire (process of purification) so as to change the temperature of the water (the character).

Harmony is a welcome change for the person who is a conscious worker in the process of self-transformation, a process, which will bring more light and clearer understanding of this natural law. As a natural consequence, the listener becomes more appreciative of their gifts, more reverent to all life, and more tolerant towards others.

After mastering the art of listening, one can listen to what is going on in their own mind. The listener begins to sort out what is truly needed at the time, and to discern the quality of their thoughts. In turn, this leads to proficiency in the control of one's thoughts, which become a guiding force in life.

This guiding force, discovered through patience and perseverance, is known by many names — the Inner Voice, Intuition, Inner Guide, etc. But the name is not of great importance. The results and the effects of this guidance are what cause the changes that the person is truly seeking. This is the road to harmony with one's self and the universe.

So, this triangle of transformation — listening, silence, and illumination, culminates in a state of harmony, and the person can be "sane in the midst of madness" — a quality much needed in our perplexed and troubled times.

Constant practice and activation of these three principles brings happy results to the listener. They add to an individual's self-evolution within the whole, thus creating light in a dark world of matter-worship, disharmony, conflict and war.

So, the choice is ours. We must follow the course of our hearts and be guided toward the light of understanding, in order to become complete beings, in tune with the heartbeat of the universe. This is the service we are called upon to fulfill, while we are passing through this life from matter to spirit. And we do this, knowing that the spirit is actually our real home, and the source from which we all spring.

May we all discover that inner guidance, to be the beam of light we are meant to be, and to emanate that to all.

March 1984. Boulder, CO

MADNESS AND SANITY ON BROADWAY
Encountering America's State of Mind in the Mid-Sixties

The event 30 years ago that gave me the first clue of what America was all about, remains vivid in my mind today. It was a first encounter that prepared me for America's state of mind then, as well as now. It was only later, through great effort and much struggle, that I came to understand the meaning of this event.

I remembered a few years earlier in Paris, watching the assassination of JFK on French television. With the astonishment of that momentary emotion, I wondered, why would a great and rich country kill its president? I developed a keen sense of observation while living in America during the turbulent '60s.

I arrived in New York City via Montréal from Paris in June of 1964, as a visitor of my friends Moni & Mina Yakim, who I resided with until I found my own apartment.

As an innocent immigrant, not yet knowing English, American history or culture, I just dived in. New York was a jungle of confusion for me. I focused on learning the language fast, so I could catch up with my self-education and face the realities of my new adventure: the discovery of my America.

In 1965, I had my first American performance at the theatre of La Mama, downtown in the neighborhood of Second Ave. I offered classes in different schools, spoke enough English to get by, and read a lot.

Some of my performances depicted in silence and movement those personal observations, made through the artist's eyes. These were my own efforts to "understand" the western culture in which I chose to learn and develop my artistic career.

Then one day, a street encounter gave me a real clue of the diseased symptoms in the way of thinking of America in its un-united "state".

I was walking on Broadway between 82nd and 84th streets, happy but contemplative about the strangeness of being here. I considered myself to be a physically and mentally fit and healthy individual, and I was simply glad to be in this country.

I met a friend, actually an acquaintance, whom I had known some time ago, and as we greeted each other, I asked him where he was going. He said, "I am going to see my Psychiatrist." I thought to myself that to see a psychiatrist one must be mentally unbalanced or unable to cope with reality. So, I said with honesty, "Is something wrong?" He then reacted very defensively. "No," he shouted, "If you don't have a Psychiatrist then something is wrong with **you**!" he said and disappeared into the crowd.

I was transfixed, planted firm on the ground, as dumbfounded as if I had just been struck by lightning on that beautiful and sunny day. My mind went blank.

Shocked to the core, I thought about the irrationality of this person's behavior, his twisted logic, and his distorted perception of reality. I couldn't understand then how such a mentally disturbed individual could jump to a false conclusion about me, and dare to judge me as abnormal because I did not have a Psychiatrist. I found it to be utterly outrageous and insulting to my intelligence.

My thoughts raced for a conclusion or resolution as I woke up out of my stupor. Smiling to myself, I processed and absorbed this event. I identified and analyzed what had just occurred using my natural sense of objectivity, in order to make sense of it without being mentally injured by the distortion I had just witnessed. I found myself greatly amused, with a deeper smile.

I realized and told myself, "My dear Samuel, you have just witnessed a glimpse of insanity and twisted reality. Now, you know that you have come to an immense insane asylum. This asylum is caught in a trap of false identities and distorted realities that have become the norm, and now relies on psychiatrists and external authorities, using them as an escape from facing the truth as it is."

This innocent nouveau immigrant suddenly understood the scope of his survival: that one has to be mentally strong and healthy to face the irrationalities of the majority - irrationalities which are considered a norm in this society. I developed a safety valve called **"KEEP MYSELF SANE IN THE MIDST OF MADNESS."** This valve of thinking objectively with common sense kept the flame of sanity alive in me, in spite of the imbalances that I had to deal with. I sharpened my intellect more to work creatively in carrying out my artistic work.

I developed a keen sense of observation, and an ability to identify irrationalities and reject them in order to keep my sanity alive. I used my objectivity to stay logical and practice honesty in spite of the popular belief that it does not pay. I identified reality as it was, in regard to my emotions, the cheating and lying that were commonplace, and the "mystical" ideas that create problems where none exist. My experiences and involvement in my newly adopted and discovered country made it possible for me to practice freedom of thought and action.

So my motto was, and is, to actively repeat to myself **"KEEP ME SANE IN THE MIDST OF MADNESS"**. This allows me to stay alert and consciously awake to any winds of change, and be armed with a healthy sense of life and determination to be creatively happy, and above all, increasing kindness to all. That event—an immigrant's encounter with madness and sanity on Broadway, New York City of 1965, gave me a shining glimpse of what was going to be my American Experience and a great lesson in my life.

THE NEW ARTIST AS A PLANETARY HEALER
(TIKKUN MAKER)

I believe that every person is a special kind of artist, rather than the common belief that artists are special kinds of people.

What kind of a person is the artist? The artist is someone who observes his/her surroundings, knows his/her feelings about a situation, applies the tools to express these feelings and observations and thus transforms them into something unique. In order to do this, the artist must work from the heart.

When I speak of art, it is an art that has to reach all. Since everyone is a potential artist, everyone has to put forth his own effort for the betterment of this perplexed world in which we live. That is an important point because that is the ultimate purpose of being an artist. The purpose of art is to heal.

The artist uses his tools to express the inner self for the benefit of all humanity, not just for himself. At the same time, the artist must be on guard against being taken advantage of commercially. Of course, there are practical considerations; one has to eat. But the artist must find a creative solution to that problem. That is why painters are banding together to exhibit their own works so as not to deal with the profit-makers and those who pander to commercialism. This is a creative and practical solution.

To be an artist, one who has a vision, is to be consciously mad and to get paid for it. Those who are locked in mental hospitals are potential creators. And the society that locks them up, locks up its own truth and its own humanity and its own love. I have worked with the mentally ill, and I have proved with my art that they are potential creators who could learn to serve their fellows.

The root of mankind is brotherhood. We have forgotten that we have only one father and only one mother. The purpose of the microcosmic family is to teach us that there is a physical father, and we must learn that there is an invisible father with whom we have to get in touch. If we did that, we would not spend our time and our energy to belittle one another, but rather we would encourage and inform and share with one another.

Before we are ready to share, however, we must learn to understand ourselves. This is the proverbial "spiritual quest." But today, even in this worthy search, everyone is jumping from group to group to find out where to fit in. By jumping from stream to stream, our energy is scattered; it is not focused. That is because we are not using all our abilities. Intuition is a tool which could help us to focalize our quest.

In the west, it is very important to develop intuition. Intellect and intuition are separated five hundred thousand miles from each other in the west, but they can be united through art.

Our ancestors were physicists, mathematicians, and alchemists all in one person. But today, we are specialists, compartmentalized. The technology now underway will create many victims of this fragmented, linear way of thinking.

The true artist must know how to utilize both hemispheres of the brain, to think by way of the spiral rather than the line. When we make that connection between right and left, one of the joyful results is laughter. Laughter is Mr. High Kind of Self-Healing. When we laugh, it is because a thought or situation makes us vibrate in a certain way. If we don't have humor, our day of death, self-extinction is very near. If we are laughing beings, we prolong our lives all the time. Why? Because when we laugh, the whole system vibrates—a dancing diaphragm, dancing cells. All the cells are happy, and when we are happy, we have longer life. If we don't furnish our cells with this vibration of dancing, which we intellectually call "laughing," we are robbing them of life. Laughter is a potent transformer.

The artist has been transformed by his art and his inner being. Yet, that's not enough. If he wants to live, he must transform others, which he can do only through some form of communication.

This is how I perceive the role of an artist, and this is why I went into a non-speaking art, mime. Beyond words, there is the infinite potential to express ourselves and to communicate in a universal language. Mime is now undergoing a renaissance in the world. It has a fantastic potential for development of human consciousness that has not yet been fully explored or unfolded. It is a potent means of self-transformation. I see it as an art capable of expanding the consciousness of the average person, and of developing a new kind of audience. The audience today is conditioned to verbal communication. As a visionary artist, I see that through this art form—through the silence, the movement, mime will add its contribution to the evolution of humankind.

Every human being is a soul that is full and ready to express itself as a born artist. The new mime, the new artist, will be required to use his total being to consciously express and translate the tremendous potential which he pulls down from "upstairs," the "heavens." The new artist will have to have a planetary vision. The new art will have to come out of necessity, from inner spiritual necessity. If it doesn't, it will not be valid, and it will not last.

In my vision, we will soon experience a tremendous leap in human evolution, in consciousness, that we have not yet dreamed of today. The challenges we will encounter in the future will probably help eliminate the old decadent institutions—institutions that are probably what has brought man to his near self-destruction at this very critical moment in time.

Historically, art has always expressed that which is invisible, that which is subjective, and shared it with the many. The artist is actually the healer, who will bring about the restoration needed now, as it is dictated from the heart. The artist will express the seed thought-forms to be planted here, so that we can leap that giant step into the New Age—the age of actively working for Peace, for the benefit of humanity, and in harmony with the universe.

THE "OTHER": THE GREAT KEY FOR PERSONAL AND GLOBAL PEACE

"Whenever love depends upon some material cause,
with the passing of that cause,
the love too passes away.
But if it is not dependent upon such a cause,
it will not pass away forever."
Sayings of the Fathers 5. 19

כָּל אַהֲבָה שֶׁהִיא תְלוּיָה בְדָבָר, בָּטֵל דָּבָר בְּטֵלָה אַהֲבָה,
וְשֶׁאֵינָהּ תְּלוּיָה בְדָבָר, אֵינָהּ בְּטֵלָה לְעוֹלָם.
אֵיזוֹ הִיא אַהֲבָה שֶׁהִיא תְלוּיָה בְדָבָר, זוֹ אַהֲבַת אַמְנוֹן וְתָמָר,
וְשֶׁאֵינָהּ תְּלוּיָה בְדָבָר זוֹ אַהֲבַת דָּוִד וִיהוֹנָתָן:
פרקי אבות פרק ה. יט

One of the greatest problems in all human history is finding the natural way to be at peace with oneself, with one another, and with different groups of people of various traditions and beliefs. That is the source of genuine prosperity and human evolution.

Loving one another does not have to have a reason or a "**because**." It is a pure and noble love. When there is a "**because**," when there is something we want out of it, the value of that love diminishes. It does not last, and can even lead to hate, the exact opposite of love.

When one embraces **the ALL**, without any reason, with no "**because**" and with no self-interest or gain, one can realize the state of peace and completion. For the **great key for individual and eternal peace** is to <u>LOVE THE OTHER MORE THAN YOUR SELF</u>.

Not every person in history, or even now, easily accepts this natural law, let alone practices it often, as the **GREAT HARMONIOUS RULE of the Universe**.

This natural practice and way of living is very difficult for many, yet it is the easiest route to acquire genuine knowledge of oneself and all creation. As we live it, we can come to know where we come from, who we are, where we go from here, what our purpose is living on earth, and what is the meaning of all life.

The "**difficulty**" (or human escape) to understanding this natural law is because of so much clogging in the tubes of our communication—the deep conditioning and habits we built unconsciously and consciously. Because of this, there is a constant struggle to **free** ourselves from the "**chains**" that bind us like slaves, from the "prison" we built through our habits and by hardening our hearts toward the other.

Go and study the history of mankind since its beginning and you will find this Key of Peace reveals to us the source of all conflicts, wars and turbulence among humans, individually and collectively. It is utterly the most important principle of life.

This **conflict** is rampant in humanity throughout history, and so obvious that almost no one is aware of it. This conflict is the cursed habit of saying one thing and doing another. This constant self-lying deepens the conflict until it becomes very difficult to distinguish the true cause of our "misery" and "suffering."

This is what the Kabbalists call the "**END OF THE DAYS**," where the state of peace and justice will be the norm in human life everywhere. This State of Peace will come about either when the face of the generation is totally pure and just, or totally corrupt and evil. Indeed, we witness this situation today, where we call light, dark and night, day. And above all, the words are abused to a such a high degree that they have no meaning at all, except those that are used in the language of the law.

At "**that time**," as our time was called by the ancients, humans will understand this principle **from their own volition**. They will begin to practice it, out of a great necessity to be kind and harmonious with one another, until it actually becomes a question of life and death. Humans will be convinced to practice it through evens of upheaval that will make them **Live** this principle naturally. In other words: be kind and gentle, act cooperatively and peacefully, just and loving with the other — or perish.

When this principle is practiced fully and honestly by all humans, the state of peace and authentic prosperity will be the norm everywhere. The ancient wise beings called that state, "**That Day**." What one thinks and does will become sacred and of utmost importance, and the way of living will be always new, creative, and highly productive and abundant.

At "**that time**," **creativity** will be the most natural state and apparent to all. **Education** will be totally changed and will be oriented and guided toward learning and being in this state of peace, within and without, from childhood. Children will grow up with these natural laws, and will develop a just and honest generation that will change the whole way of human thinking very radically.

As long as the humans on this planet are still settling matters between individuals and nations with war and violence, it is shameful to be called by the noble name of human beings. As long as as scientific and philosophical pretense dominates, and society wears **masks** "**to protect the people**" and "**for the good of the people**," when actually the intention is the opposite, we do not merit that name. As long as this is upheld by the corrupt speech of various charlatans, politicians, lawyers and other "do-gooders" and hypocrites, this "civilization" is not worthy of that name. As long as people harm the other, humanity does not deserve to be called by that name of **BEING HUMAN**.

I am uttering this simple truth today, because when there are people that teach their children to kill from an early age in school, to blow up themselves for their crooked agenda, for a cause devised by twisted and sick minds — all the while pretending to be "evolved" and "just" humans — When this happens, it is a shame to be called "human." These are people who do not want the "other" to exist. They encourage a culture of death.

The simple answer and the **Only** healthy voice of sanity, understanding the depths of this madness, is to begin <u>**With Oneself**</u>: One can practice this simple principle to "<u>**Love the OTHER more than yourself,**</u>" and not wait until times of upheaval force us to change. It is better to change from within now, and avoid the times when one will be forced to practice justice and kindness by the forces of cataclysmic events and the evil inclinations of humans on the planet.

When the **IMPORTANCE of the OTHER** is more than oneself, in any situation or emotion, many gates of light and love will open widely, and it will be easier to enter and be in the state of being we call the "**Garden of Eden.**"

So, my friend, those who make a directed and focused effort to understand the utter simplicity of this law, will be on their way to **REALLY know** the "**Mystery of our BEING,**" which is **TO BE ONE** with all creation. Remember always to activate your wisdom valve: "**ONE and NOT TWO.**"

So, go forth and develop the attitude of this great order of the universe in every aspect of your life. And practice every day the nugget of active wisdom to "<u>**KEEP ME SANE IN THE MIDST OF MADNESS**</u>."

THE PUZZLE OF "THE HIDDEN OBVIOUS"

THE PUZZLE of the "HIDDEN OBVIOUS" explores the amazing "invisible" links of "relationship." These "invisible links" reveal our connection to each other in this world and this universe, yet they are so obvious that we tend to overlook them. We take these things so completely for granted that they disappear from our window of awareness, and as a result, they become a "puzzle" to us, that we do not know how to solve.

Let us observe a few obvious phenomena to demonstrate how this utter simplicity escapes our immediate awareness. I find that this is the source of confusion and misunderstanding of ourselves, and our relationship to our greater environment.

These examples are so obvious that they may seem completely irrelevant. This is because we are used to the superficial way of living and looking at the reality of our being here. We take the obviousness of life for granted until we become completely unaware of it. We sense and feel the positive space rather than the negative space.

However, it is possible to make a shift and begin to observe the obvious appearance and the hidden essence of the things around us, by simply being present totally at every moment.

OBVIOUS APPEARANCE

THE TABLE. Observe a table. The table holds many different objects. On first glimpse they may appear to us as separate objects that do not relate to each other. But actually, their relationship is that they are all there for a common purpose, to be used by us when we need them. That is their role to play and their essence and necessity of being. By being on the table together, they are linked with each other, and their common denominator is the TABLE that holds them and links them together as one. Many objects but one table.

THE BODY. Observe our human BODY, which contains many organs that all function independently of each other. Each organ and system within us has its own autonomy to fulfill the perfect function it was given for the purpose of existence. All these separate systems are very contrary to each other. Yet all of them work together harmoniously, as if orchestrated by an "invisible" power, to produce our very existence and life itself.

THE ROOM. A room can contain people, objects, a bed, a desk, many things in it, all connected in one unit container—the room.

THE CHAIR. I sit on a chair. The chair sits on the floor. The floor extends to the outside, sitting on the earth floor. That earth floor extends out and connects to everything that sits, on all the face the earth. All is connected.

THE PERFORMING STAGE. The director sets up the stage. He or she places various objects for the purpose of serving the play. Each object is in its right place, for a specific purpose. All these "separate" objects are there, connected with each other, in an order that an outsider cannot understand, but which functions perfectly for the unfolding of the play.

THE AIR WE BREATHE. We breathe the same air everywhere on this earth. That air energy is the **obvious connector** we all take for granted. This is something most of us do not even recognize consciously. We simply don't notice it in this present moment.

THE OCEAN. The immensity of the oceans connects all the pieces of the earth and its continents as one whole world. On it, we all live and walk, and do not recognize the constant connection that is obvious and always holding us together on one round planet that is traveling through space so fast we seem to be completely still…!

HIDDEN ESSENCE

All the simple examples above are easily recognizable by every human being, revealing to that we are all deeply connected to the whole world we live in. But we often do not acknowledge this simple and obvious fact. If from time to time, we do so, we may be kinder and gentler to one another, while traveling smoothly through the universe, on this one small ship of earth.

In reality, we are all relatives with each other, and are continuous companions in this obvious linking, which is such a puzzle to us. When we realize this simple fact of our connection and relationship, we will cease to feel lonely or alone in life, and we will begin to see the "otherness" and the "differences" are not other and not that different than our own being, breathing the same air, and swimming in the same waters.

To live and be with this Hidden Obvious that surrounds us every breath of our lives does not take any effort from us. The conscious awareness of these simple realizations that are present all the time can inspire us to know our place in this life. It illuminates our role to play in this life, in order to BE that Link and that Connection with everyone—even those who are unaware of this Hidden Obvious that surrounds us all the time and everywhere that we are.

Lafayette, Colorado. Jan 2, 2006

SPIRITUAL ARCHAEOLOGY:
BODYSPEAK and the HIDDEN OBVIOUS

The BodySpeak™ movement training method is a process I call "Spiritual Archeology." In it, we dig down to find that which is not yet known. What we find is that what is "not yet known" is actually pleading to be known, and we will in fact discover it in the very next moment. I prefer to use the words "**Not yet known**" instead of the word "**Unknown.**" Because when you say "unknown," it sounds as if all possibilities are closed. It is unknown, period. When we use the words "Not Yet Known", we leave the doors of infinite possibility wide open to make new discoveries. In this, we find a new way to appreciate life and all creation.

Spiritual Archeology teaches us to be an agent, to spy on ourselves and to discover how to restore and correct the mistakes we make every second.

The secrets of life are revealed when we know **where** and **how** to look. **Our body intelligence** hints every second at the great "miracle of being," which gives us the ability to move and think. And with even more subtlety, that intelligence can guide us to become the "mystery itself," right here and now.

The "Cell", the most intelligent and exceptional dot, thinks in such an amazing way. It is the manifestation of the Hebrew Letter YOD. We humans do not yet even have a clue of the higher intelligence contained in it.

All the billions of cells, which actually are the multiplication of that original YOD, build and maintain what we call "life," right within our bodies. They animate us and give us the ability to BE. All this is done with such utter simplicity that we take it all for granted. We do not appreciate the amazing systems that allow us to walk, talk, eat, etc.

By observing the intelligence of our body, this great vessel of life, we find one common denominator, that from the level of the cell's consciousness and built-in intelligence, there is **No Because**. All our cells are at the service of the whole purpose of being, growing and producing life and happiness all around us with **No Because**. It is for the sake of **Life Itself**! This simple thing yearns and pleads in silence within you and me, to be discovered and Lived 100,000% - To assist all creation, as you and I were created. What a noble thought this is! To assist life without asking for anything!

Let us look next at the nature of water, which as we know, makes up more than 70% of those harmonious cells, and which flows through the earth just as the blood flows through our bodies.

In nature, when the rains fall on the earth, we see that they flow by their own nature into streams and rivers. But the question is — when does the river-bed guide the path of the water flow, and when does the water guide the path of the river?

We see that the water and the river are very close to one another. They are inter-relating all the time, mutual and dependent on one another. The river and its waters are ONE and not two. It appears to us to be two, but in reality, they are one.

The life energy that flows through us is similar to the situation of the river and the water. The question is: who is the one who passes through, and who is the one who carves the path? This is worth considering.

Water also takes the shape and color of any container that holds it. With a white bottle, the water inside will appear white and bottle-shaped. Blue, large, tall, short—the water will adapt to every object and color. Yet the water stays the same water. Only the form, the shape and color change. There is the container and the contained. This principle also applies to us human beings whose bodies are made of over 70% water. We are also containers. But do we pay attention to our container? And do we know what it contains?

As we see, the water always takes the shape of its container, and it does this without any reason or agenda, totally ego-less. It does not have any "because." It is the nature of water to BE the way of what it is placed in. That is the natural character and intelligence of the water.

I say and repeat this to my students during the Mime Workshop. Whenever we do any Mime exercises, I suggest they move as if we are in water. Even though we move through air, we move slow and flowing, going with the breath, and just doing it to learn, as if we are moving in the water. This moving like water helps us breathe calmly, and as a result we learn the lessons very fast. (By the way MAYIM—in Hebrew is Water, MIME—MAYIM; the words sound the same).

But if you are thirsty in the desert and shout, "Water! Water!", sadly enough, this will not keep you alive, not until this precious fluid, the alchemical solvent of water, actually flows inside your body. So, I emphasize this obvious simplicity to my students, that Water is most precious. Water is the life itself that our body needs in order to exist. Period.

This observation can assist us in changing our character. We can move and flow like water in our daily life, using our unique will to receive in order to give. Using these suggestions from the great body of practical knowledge of the Kabbalah, it allows us to begin our Tikkun, Restoration. This way, we transform ourselves from living "To receive just for myself" to "Receiving in order to give," imitating the water qualities, bettering our subtle view of our reality, and living creatively.

Let's go back for a moment to the YOD, the original cell that manifests life itself. It exists in our physical bodies as a conscious cell that multiplies itself until it becomes the miraculous manifestation of beings like you and me. This is what allows us to be here now in this very moment, in which you are reading these characters which we call letters and words. And somehow, marvelously, you are able to understand these same symbols that "I" wrote earlier, in order for you to be able to read them now. This perfect communication is quite remarkable, and yet, sadly, we all take it for granted.

Observe for a moment that you live now. Close your eyes to this world and focus through the breath. Just observe the inhaling and the exhaling of the breath, and just enjoy it. It introduces a calm, so we can begin to observe and feel the inside activities of our bodies. HEAR the flow of the blood in the veins, the beat of the heart, and just listen quietly and get to **know** at least this physical aspect of your being. Allow yourself to wonder also **Who is doing all these activities** that actually **Give you Life itself**. Just wonder.

It is said that there are three partners in giving a person life—the body, the soul and the Creator*.

---

*Three Partners in the Creation of a Human Being
Talmud Bavli, Nidda 31. 1.

Our masters taught: There are three partners in man—the Holy One, his father, and his mother. His father inseminates the white substance, out of which are formed the child's bones, sinews, and nails, the brain in his head, and the white of his eye. His mother inseminates the red substance, out of which are formed the child's skin, flesh, and hair, and the black of his eye. The Holy One implants in him spirit, soul, beauty of countenance, eyesight, the capacity to hear, the capacity to speak, and the capacity to walk, as well as knowledge, understanding, and intelligence.

When a man's time comes to die, the Holy One takes His part and leaves the parts contributed by the father and mother before them, and they weep. The Holy One asks them, "Why do you weep? Have I taken anything of yours? I have only taken what belongs to Me!" They reply, "Master of the universe, so long as Your part was mingled with ours, our part was preserved from worms and maggots. But now that You have taken away Your part, behold, our part is exposed and laid open to worms and maggots."

*שְׁלשָׁה שׁוּתָּפִין יֵשׁ בָּאָדָם.

תָּנוּ רַבָּנָן: בִּזְמַן שֶׁהַוָּלָד נוֹצָר בִּמְעֵי אִמּוֹ שְׁלשָׁה הֵם שׁוּתָּפִין בּוֹ הַקָּדוֹשׁ-בָּרוּךְ-הוּא וְאָבִיו וְאִמּוֹ, אָבִיו מַזְרִיעַ בּוֹ לוֹבֶן, שֶׁמִּמֶּנּוּ הַלּוֹבָנִים וְהַמּוֹחַ וְהַצִּפָּרְנַיִם וְלוֹבֶן שֶׁבָּעַיִן וְהַגִּידִין, אִמּוֹ מַזְרַעַת אוֹדֶם, שֶׁמִּמֶּנּוּ הַדָּמִים וְהָעוֹר וְהַבָּשָׂר וְשֵׂעָר וְשָׁחוֹר שֶׁבָּעֵינַיִם, וְהַקָּדוֹשׁ-בָּרוּךְ-הוּא יִתְבָּרַךְ שְׁמוֹ וְיִתְרוֹמַם זִכְרוֹ נוֹתֵן בּוֹ עֲשָׂרָה דְבָרִים וְאֵלוּ הֵן: רוּחַ וּנְשָׁמָה וְקַלְסְתֵּר פָּנִים, וּמַרְאִית עֵינַיִם וּשְׁמִיעַת אָזְנַיִם וְדִבּוּר שְׂפָתַיִם וּנְשִׂיאוּת יָדַיִם וְהִלּוּךְ-רַגְלַיִם, וְחָכְמָה וּבִינָה וְעֵצָה וְדַעַת וּגְבוּרָה וּכְשֶׁבָּא שְׁעַת פְּטִירָתוֹ הַקָּדוֹשׁ-בָּרוּךְ-הוּא נוֹטֵל חֶלְקוֹ וּמַנִּיחַ חֵלֶק אָבִיו וְאִמּוֹ לִפְנֵיהֶם וְאָבִיו וְאִמּוֹ בּוֹכִין, אָמַר לָהֶם הַקָּדוֹשׁ-בָּרוּךְ-הוּא מָה לָכֶם בּוֹכִין כְּלוּם נָטַלְתִּי מִשֶּׁלָּכֶם? לֹא נָטַלְתִּי אֶלָּא שֶׁלִּי, אוֹמְרִים לְפָנָיו רִבּוֹנוֹ-שֶׁל-עוֹלָם כָּל זְמַן שֶׁהָיָה חֶלְקֵךְ מְעוֹרָב בְּחֶלְקֵנוּ הָיָה חֶלְקֵנוּ שָׁמוּר מִן רִמָּה וְתוֹלֵעָה וְעַכְשָׁיו שֶׁנָּטַלְתָּ חֶלְקֵךְ מִתּוֹךְ חֶלְקֵנוּ הֲרֵי חֶלְקֵנוּ מוּשְׁלָךְ וְנָתוּן לְרִמָּה וְתוֹלֵעָה.

תלמוד בבלי נדה, דף ל"א. א.

THE SPIRITUAL RATATOUILLE OF THE "NEW AGE"

I call this article **The Spiritual Ratatouille of the "New Age,"** after seeing the symptoms from the growth of the so-called "New Age "movement in this country over the past 49 years. This movement is actually composed of a mish-mash of hundreds of different streams of thought and philosophy. From my own observation, I find that the streams of the New Age movement have no true foundation. It can be hard for people distinguish when what they teach is helpful, or actually harmful. I have noticed over the years many flaws in the way of thinking, and observed some dangerous practices that have caused harm to many.

I warned my students about how these various streams of New Age can affect them very negatively. The spiritual supermarket movement has influenced mainstream life greatly. I have observed these spiritual wounds in some of my students. I am not a scholar, and I have no intentions of being a scholar, but I feel compelled to share these practical observations, after seeing the growing popularity of this movement.

Many of the ideas and philosophies of the "New Age" are borrowed randomly from various sources like astrology, alchemy, magical tendencies, distorted Kabbalistic ideas, numerology, tarot cards, UFO literature, numerology, Zen Buddhism, and Chinese medicine, many of which have then been adapted to fit Western Psychology and Carl Jung's stream of Psychotherapy. These scattered and misunderstood streams of information have been thrown together in a sort of "spiritual ratatouille" — disconnected from their original intention and taken totally out of context.

Some of the main characteristics of the New Age belief system are as follows: There is no root, foundation, logic or coherence. Topics are only partly examined and pseudo-explored. In fact, this movement mostly defies and rejects any critical thinking. Illogical statements and non-sequiturs are used to escape any direct exploration. It relies on superficial content and no subject is examined in depth or with honest exploration. In short, it is based on half-chewed information.

Abuse of Words

A key characteristic of the so-called New Age movement is the abuse of words. It relies on half-truths, and incomplete or false information. Simple direct information is made complicated and overly conceptual by leaders in order to confuse people. The result is that the truth is masked, which leads to confusion and perplexity for their followers.

Words abused by the New Age movement include: spirituality, new, self, truth, love, space, time, energy, consciousness, good, evil, enlightenment, darkness, environment, ecology, green, therapy, happiness, obsession, extremes, and sexuality. Actually, almost every word in the dictionary is being abused, because there is no effort to define them. Because all the information is made overly complicated and abstract, the so-called leader or guru is able to impose authority over others, making it difficult for them to verify and question what they are told, or examine it from their own understanding and experience.

To observe this, stop any one of the New Agers in one of their conferences, and simply ask them to define the words they are using. You will be encountered with silence and stupor. Try insisting on being told the meaning of their words, and they will treat you as if you are totally ignorant, and do anything to remove themselves from your presence. They will do anything in order to avoid a simple clear definition of their own words.

The New Age is also full of very "positive" and "spiritual-sounding" language, which makes it attractive to many. These are nice sounding words like "positive thinking," "feeling good," "going with the flow," "being in the now," often used as a sophisticated way to escape reality. In fact, these words are often used to cover up negativities. This is obvious in the rampant fake kindness, with its dishonest and exaggerated expressions of caring. We are "full of light," "we are all one," "we care for you," etc. Yet if you need any actual help, that person will be nowhere in sight.

And so, the words are based on superficiality, banality, and chewed clichés. In essence, they are non-substantial, meaningless, and empty.

These "post-modern" clichés delivered daily through the mainstream media, have created widespread cynicism, fear and doubt. This is mixed with narcissism and lack of respect for "the other." Everything is done with the attitude of "me first," and "after me, let there be flood."

Superficiality becomes the new norm, which is quite comical and tragic at the same time. The ego competition is what is important. The evolution of Social Media has also further distorted the use of language, and increased obsessive and addictive behavior, and this is greatly affecting the human psyche.

The "spiritual supermarket" pretends to guide its followers to "achieve enlightenment," but all these deceptions just camouflage and obscure the truth with nice sounding phrases. It is an attractive way to hide the lies. I call that endarkenment. I witnessed this influence on some of my students and warned them against these dangerous and distorted ways of thinking, which unfortunately, are very popular and can appear very attractive.

Information Versus Knowledge

The root of all this confusion is the failure to distinguish between information and knowledge. In this superficial culture, information is confused with knowledge. But for information to become knowledge, it must be tested, verified, and realized with one's own knowing. Otherwise, this is just "pretending to know." Once we learn to distinguish between information and knowledge, we can prevent accidents and avoid the unnecessary suffering that pollutes our consciousness. Authentic knowledge helps us avoid confusion and maintain our sanity and balance in life.

Knowledge requires deep exploration. As King Solomon said, "All the rivers run to the sea" (Ecclesiastes 1:7). But, instead of aiming towards deeper waters of understanding, the unconscious followers of the new age constantly "**Jump from stream to stream,**" so they

never reach the ocean. They jump from one path to another, without truly understanding any of them. So, they miss the opportunity to follow and explore one, unique chosen stream which could lead them to the ocean of wisdom.

Magical Thinking and Harmful Effects

The New Age movement has also adopted many imaginative ideas from science fiction films and TV programs. In this way, real reality is confused with virtual reality. There is no doubt that imagination is a positive force activated by our neurons and is a great source for creativity and innovation in our life. But when the use of imagination is misdirected into fantasy by those with hidden, negative agendas, it harms the followers. Suffering follows as a result of the distorted thinking and false messages that are implanted. For example, a person could be led to believe that they only need to look at a picture of a mansion to get a mansion. When of course, the reality is that one must plan and take purposeful action toward what they want to achieve in life.

These things are now skillfully marketed, with great pretense and empty promises. But this "magical" New Age way of thinking becomes the root of so many physical, mental and spiritual problems. The result of these unhealthy ways of thinking is "**creating problems where none exist**!" These false beliefs act as the very obstacle to true realization, success, and happiness. This "**Grand Valley of confusion and mediocrity**," has now come to be accepted as "**The New Norm**." (See *The Fish Story*)

External Authorities and Ego-Driven Leaders – The Grand Theater of the Absurd

I must say that it is painful and sad for me to point out these lies that are presented as truth.... They are imposed upon people by external authorities and self-appointed individuals lacking true knowledge, conscience, or self-respect. They act from their own egoistic agenda, while at the same time, lining their pockets. They wear masks of deception, illusion and smiles — parroting empty words, which are devoid of experience, while camouflaging reality with positive words. I wonder how many innocent souls have become casualties to these distortions.

As I said before, these "spiritual" movements have become very dangerous, absurd and comical. The leaders of these "movements" are trapped in "God" complexes and peddle many distorted ideologies. And many innocent people become lost from these destructive ideologies. This is what I call "Le grand theatre de l'absurde." I really find myself in the situation, to quote one of my spiritual teachers, "**I am in trouble if I say it as it is, and I am in trouble if I do not say it as it is**." But the good news is, if we pay attention to the obvious, there are simple ways to outsmart them and maintain a healthy way of thinking and being.

Practical and Applicable Suggestions

On the next page are a few suggestions to apply, for those who have resonated with these words. By practicing some of these sixteen suggestions, I am confident you will discover that great and hidden talent of learning how to learn, and you will find the way to self-govern your being. From this, you can escape intelligently from the "**Land Of Fools**" and live as a sane and healthy human being. In essence, this means becoming the being you were meant to be in the first place.

Bon courage! Have COURAGE and DARE to be yourself against all odds. It is worth it.

1. Begin to observe every word you speak and every thought that passes through you. Decide whether it is necessary to speak it. Try to speak less and do more. Examine profoundly by verifying the actual value of every thought, idea, and belief.

2. Learn to be silent within and without, so, you can function from calm in the midst of activity. This will help you to verify and sort out the good from the bad. **Speak less and do more. Train yourself to speak only when it is necessary.**

3. Ask yourself "Who is leading your life?" and "Who is writing your script?" Be the author, and play the lead actor in your life, now! Exercise this principle to unleash the fearless creative powers within you. Make sure you write the script of your life.

4. Stop seeking support outside of yourself, so that you can find your own living truth. Once you have done this, you will probably find that those who gravitate toward you are the type of people who can be true and lasting friends.

5. No matter what your actual situation is in life, search and find a true and authentic teacher to assist you. This is someone who will point out the true path toward yourself, without wanting you to become dependent on his or her person.

6. Trust your intuition to communicate to you the difference between what we call good and bad.

7. Produce and create more. Consume only what you need for your safety and well-being.

8. Avoid gullibility and trust your guts and your inner practical wisdom. This will allow you to transform the negative to positive, and the bad to good. Become aware of the memes, the thought viruses that are introduced to us every moment, day and night, without our awareness. Once you are aware of them, you can choose between positive thoughts that are constructive, and negative ones that are misleading and harmful.

9. Always ask if an emotion, idea or thought is from your own personal experience, or if someone told you. Take the time to examine your thoughts and ideas from all angles.

10. The most abused verb in many cultures and languages is the verb to "KNOW", so, examine well if you really KNOW, or if this is just information.

11. Never make any decision from an emotional state, or from outside pressure, or inner pressure.

12. Beware of greed, pretense and the masks people wear in order to be accepted and loved. Especially, notice the words people "**do not**" say.

13. Watch out for delusion. Our minds have an incredible capacity for imagination, and that imagination can make things seem to be what they are not.

14. Remember, anger can destroy a good heart and shorten your life.

15. In order to activate these suggestions, you need great inner courage and strength in order to finally arrive at that place of being who you were meant to be.

16. Be present every moment and appreciate the present moment always. Be aware of your breathing. Many "problems" will disappear. You will have many conscious moments of this now, to create and enjoy every breath in your precious life.

Conclusion

As I said previously, I am not a scholar, nor do I want to be a scholar. I have learned simply through living experience, here in this school of life, not through academia. I am a man mostly of silence, who has focused all my life on the silent Art of Mime. I consider Mime to be an essential language of expression, moving the mind and body, without overusing and abusing words. Making this statement leaves me free to present some of my views about this "Spiritual Ratatouille" I experienced and observed in this country since coming to America in the mid 1960's. (See my article *Madness and Sanity on Broadway*).

In my teachings, I differentiate between Information and Knowledge. Most information is mistaken for knowledge. This is because the left-brain is dominant in this society (intellect, logic, analysis, etc.) Everything is intellectualized and dissected down into particles, but reuniting the particles back into their original wholeness is forgotten. The right side of the brain is neglected (creativity, intuition, abstraction, arts, etc). As a result, innate intelligence is neglected and reactive behavior is widespread in our culture.

We have to graduate the so-called "paradox*" and begin to integrate intellect with intelligence. As a result, we will abuse words less. A critical mass of abusing words can ultimately bring the downfall of civilizations. Words become meaningless when the fake is seen as real, and, the real is seen as fake. Describing reality with non-meaningful words simply leads to confusion and avoiding reality.

Because of the abuse of language, we talk about life rather than live it. We neglect the present moment, missing life that is occurring and allowing us to be. Abuse of language camouflages reality with "positive thinking" memes, which keep us from the true reality of being. Language has become a clever tool of simply lying, calling the truth a lie, and the lie the truth, thus reversing the order of life. Please consider this nugget of profound practical wisdom:

כָּל־הַנְּחָלִים הֹלְכִים אֶל־הַיָּם וְהַיָּם אֵינֶנּוּ מָלֵא אֶל־מְקוֹם שֶׁהַנְּחָלִים
הֹלְכִים שָׁם הֵם שָׁבִים לָלָכֶת: קהלת פרק א. ז

"All the rivers flow into the sea; yet the sea is not full.
To the place where the rivers come, there they return again"
Ecclesiastes 1. 7.

Rather than **jumping from stream to stream**, try to make a conscious effort to honestly follow 100% that "one stream" that your heart yearns toward. Maintain focus, consistency and practice, and sooner or later, you will reach that which you aspire for—that which will be your ocean.

And when you finally "arrive" to that "ocean," you will realize that there are no more questions, that there is nowhere to arrive. You have finally discovered your authentic, veritable, and essential being. Then, it is up to you to manifest your journey to nowhere.

So, when I say that "New Age meditation" and "fake compassion" are hazardous for your spiritual, mental and physical health, perhaps that can mean something to you now. From experience we know now, and I will repeat again, that "Words that come **BEFORE realization and experience** are not valid and meaningful at all. Words that are uttered **AFTER one's own realization and experience** are very meaningful and truthful."

Over the years, I have suggested many exercises to restore these distortions of reality, using an artistic approach. In this way, we can shift our attention and awareness to really enjoy life through both tears and joy. In the same breath, we can learn to be both significant and insignificant, as we pass through this ephemeral life on this planet. We can finally overcome all seeming "difficulties" and "problems," that really have nothing to do with our true reality beyond words and descriptions…

There are some practical exercises from my book *The BodySpeak Manual*, which can be helpful in grounding one's awareness. These include: The Impermeable, The View from the Boat and the Helicopter, Stop and Consider, Motion and Stillness, The Edge, The Cosmic Accordion, The Hidden Obvious, and, Conscious Innocence. Also, see the Defintuitions section of this book, which contains short versions of some of these exercises.

And in conclusion, please remember, the more one is aware and present to every moment, and maintains a creative way of being rather than "talking about it," there is a real hope to stay sane in the midst of madness, living in a true integrative way. If one chooses to apply practical changes to their life, they will enjoy calm, serenity and sanity, even in the midst of the madness or confusion of this world. We can leap beyond creating problems where none exist…

And here's a final thought for your contemplation, please:

"Inhale IMPORTANCE and exhale INSIGNIFICANCE."

*For an understanding of Paradox, see the Defintuitions section

יח. רַבִּי עֲקִיבָא אוֹמֵר: הַכֹּל צָפוּי, וְהָרְשׁוּת נְתוּנָה, וּבְטוֹב הָעוֹלָם נִדּוֹן, וְהַכֹּל לְפִי רוֹב הַמַּעֲשֶׂה:

יט. הוּא הָיָה אוֹמֵר: הַכֹּל נָתוּן בָּעֵרָבוֹן, וּמְצוּדָה פְרוּסָה עַל כָּל הַחַיִּים, הֶחָנוּת פְּתוּחָה, וְהַחֶנְוָנִי מַקִּיף, וְהַפִּנְקָס פָּתוּחַ, וְהַיָּד כּוֹתֶבֶת, וְכָל הָרוֹצֶה לִלְווֹת יָבוֹא וְיִלְוֶה, וְהַגַּבָּאִים מַחֲזִירִין תָּדִיר בְּכָל יוֹם, וְנִפְרָעִין מִן הָאָדָם מִדַּעְתּוֹ וְשֶׁלֹּא מִדַּעְתּוֹ, וְיֵשׁ לָהֶם עַל מַה שֶׁיִּסְמוֹכוּ, וְהַדִּין דִּין אֱמֶת, וְהַכֹּל מְתֻקָּן לִסְעוּדָה:
פרקי אבות פרק ג. יח, יט.

18. Rabbi Akiva said: All is foreseen, but freedom of choice is given. The world is judged in goodness, yet all is proportioned to one's work.

19. He used to say: All is given against a pledge, and the net is cast over all the living. The shop stands open and the shopkeeper gives credit. The account book lies open, and the hand writes. Everyone that wishes to borrow, let him come and borrow. But the collectors go on their daily rounds and exact payment from man with or without his consent. For the collectors have that on which they can rely, and the judgment is a judgment of truth. And all is made ready for a feast.

The Ethics of the Fathers, Chapter 3, 19, 20

WORDS, WEB OF NOISE

**"So shall it be, with the words that go forth from my mouth;
They shall not return to me void,
but they shall accomplish that which I please,
and cause the thing for which I sent them." Isaiah 55:11**

These days, we see that language is being abused in an alarming way. When words are no longer a source of living wisdom, but a source of confusion, we find ourselves in a web of noise. It is a verbal prison that seems to have no exit. This noise seems to surround us everywhere. Words are spoken constantly without meaning or awareness. Lying, distortion, and "spin" become "normal," painting the good as bad and the bad as good. How often do we see a politician or public figure do something wrong, followed by a beautiful speech that sounds completely just and good?

In this way, language has lost its spiritual reality. Words have become nonsense, not true communication. This can make us long for a quiet place within, to restore both personal and collective sanity.

At the edge of noise, one can find a quiet space, and can experience, in serenity and calm, a center of silence from whence word and sound are born.

Man invented the word out of fear of silence. The more we abuse words, the more we become alienated from the true nature of our being. Words become a "rational" escape from the true reality of one's self.

Now, we find ourselves in a crucial crossroads of time. With rapid change and increasing noise in all aspects of life, we search for a way to sanity and happiness. Words cannot cover up a reality which has gone out of balance. So, how do we return to harmony and true creativity, to the original way of balance with nature and ourselves?

To find this sanity and balance, we must re-evaluate the way we use words, sound, and color in this civilization, find the way of balance, and work toward a reconciliation of all "opposites." This means finding what Walter de la Mare called "The use of living words" and finding out what words and language truly are. When we do this, we will no longer parrot the words of others, knowing there is no life or power in words just repeated and not deeply known, examined, and lived.

The purpose of words is to express thought. Words are like an envelope. They make visible the invisible thought. They assist us in establishing order in communication with one another, with nature, and with the higher self within.

But one must choose carefully the kind of words to use—and the less the better! Words are the outer form of the inner reality, like clothing is to the body. With inspiration and intuition, one can express thoughts through essential words only, and thus, keep communication clear, simple and precise. As the Kabbalistic sages would say, **"Say little and do much."** (Sayings of the Fathers, 1:15)

The Kabbalists would say that we are what we think. We are what we speak. One should not pollute the air with unnecessary talk, because through one's speech, one invokes the presence within - and the quality of thoughts translated into words becomes the expression of the inner truth, the reality of becoming.

An increased awareness of the power of the silence between words is essential. The attentive use of the word assists us to be productive. And by conserving the energy of speech through silence, we increase our potentiality to live harmoniously, and to use this power for the benefit of ourselves and humanity.

I remember an event from my childhood that illustrates the necessity of conserving the energy of words. My grandfather's way of imparting this potent lesson to me has been of great significance throughout my life. I call this:

"Word Economy"

"Before one is born," he said, "one is given a certain amount of words to use in one's lifetime—like a Cosmic word bank, a word account. You must be very careful in using words properly, and with great measure, in how you express yourself. Every word you use is out of your Cosmic account. That is why you should turn your tongue seven times within your mouth before uttering a word. Otherwise, you may finish your quota early in life, and you will find yourself mute."

This had a very great impression on me as a young being. It was engraved in my consciousness as a positive power. This probably affected me so much that unconsciously I chose my artistic life work to be in the Theater of Silence.

Now let us examine and observe together the question of—what is a word? In the Hebrew language, the word for "word" is name, **DAVAR**. According to tradition, the "**word**" is an agent of the inner realms of the Essence, a communication device to connect with the creative potential. The "word" symbolizes the creative force of consciousness. It is the creative idea that brings order and form to matter, a bridge between heaven and earth. It is the creative mediator between God and humanity, between humans, between man and woman, between the "master within" and the "soul personality," between spirit and matter.

Now, **DAVAR** (ד ב ר) is formed of three letters. **Dalleth (4)** (ד), **Beith (2)** (ב) and **Reish (200)** (ר). Each letter contains a certain spiritual and cosmic power of great significance. This word **DAVAR,** through the Kabbalistic code of letters, will mean this: "The balance and harmony of the Universe is contained in the Cosmic container, funneled through the particular container of the human vehicle, the body of creation, and through sound and the utterances of creative forces. Once in the human container, there is the choice to use or abuse this power, and the results will follow accordingly."

Another word in Hebrew for "word" is AMOR (א מ ר), spelled Aleph (א) Mem (מ) and Reish (ר), AMARIM in plural (א מ ר י ם). The Kabbalistic interpretation of this word is: "The power of life and death, the nameless, timeless and spaceless, is invigorating and impregnating and filling this container with the Cosmic waters of life, through the sound, and it intelligently fashions thoughts through the envelope of the human organism."

A third word for "word" in Aramaic is **MEMRA** (מ י מ ר א), spelled **Mem** (מ) **Yod** (י) **Mem** (מ) **Reish** (ר) **Aleph** (א). Here it is formed of the same root verb as the word **AMOR**, but with the double letter of **Mem** (מ). This accentuation is to double the element of the waters of life for emphasis. Since the letter **Mem** (מ) is the basic sound of all humanity, this is very significant.

MEMRA also connotes the "**DIVINE WORD**," which in Hebrew is manifested in the word **HOKHMAH** (ח כ מ ה), the **DIVINE WISDOM** that guides the mouth and heart to utter the truth of being. **HOKHMAH** is the right side of the upper triangle in the holy tree of life of the Kabbalah, the masculine creative force of the universe.

MEMRA means "uttering" or "saying" and connotes the manifestation of God's power in creating the world by "uttering" through sound. It acts as a "messenger" and is analogous to the **SKEKHINAH** (ש כ י נ ה), the **DIVINE PRESENCE** and wisdom in all creation.

Here are a few contemplations from the Kabbalistic and Sufi traditions:

There is a proverb, which says, that every word should pass through three gates before being uttered:
At the first gate, the gatekeeper asks, "Is it true?"
At the second he asks, "Is it necessary?"
And at the third he asks, "Is it kind?"
If you answer in the positive, go ahead and utter it.

"If what you are going to say is not more beautiful than silence, do not say it."

"A word is like an arrow; in a hurry."

"One word can start a war; one word can make peace."

"Words are like medicine. They should be measured with care,
for an overdose may hurt."

"Words are like bodies; meanings are like souls."

"A learned being spares words; fools love to use words."

The great Rabbi Shelomo Ibn Gabirol adds:
"Guard your tongue as your treasure, your wealth."
He also said: "If I do not utter a word, I am its master.
Once I utter it, I am its slave."

"Life and death are contained within the power of the tongue." - Proverbs 18:12.

To conclude this sharing/offering are some words of Lao Tsu, which might appear very contradictory to some, but with an unconditional observation and reflection, they penetrate the real essence of understanding.

"Truthful words are not beautiful.
Beautiful words are not truthful.
Good men do not argue.
Those who argue are not good.
Those who know are not learned.
The learned do not know."
Lao Tsu

FIFTY GATES TO PRACTICAL WISDOM

FIFTY GATES TO PRACTICAL WISDOM: CREATIVE LIVING PRINCIPLES

Or a Spiritual Guide to the Perplexed: A Possible User Manual to Live By

These Creative Living Principles (CLP) have been collected over the years to help simplify the confusion of these perplexed times. They have been condensed into a workable, comprehensive reference guide in order to assist you with the quest for self-realization. I am confident that these CLP's can assist the honest, sincere, genuine person who desires change for self-transformation and enlightenment.

Consider these "Lucid Memos." They are one way to working towards REMEMBERING who you really are in essence. After reading these steps carefully and thoughtfully, simply decide to practice the ones that you feel you are ready to study in an orderly fashion.

As you practice these creative principles, always be PRESENT in the MOMENT at hand. Become aware of your thoughts and actions throughout the course of the day, weeks or months. Note the changes in life and in your sense of well-being while working towards mastery of the principles you have chosen. Do not look for results. You will be able to sense definite changes, and a new sense of well-being. You may discover new dimensions in your experience, as you shift toward a NEW way of LIVING.

These principles will allow you to become your own guide in life, walking with confidence. Keep it simple, enjoy life with humor, and Bon courage, mes amis! And remember, "**that which you are looking for, is looking for you....**"

FIVE SECTIONS:
- VIRTUES
- OVERCOMING DIFFICULTIES
- TRANSFORMATION
- ULTIMATE BEHAVIOR
- BEING AND BECOMING

VIRTUES

WE ARE GODS
1. Know that WE ARE GODS, CREATORS of the UNIVERSE. The ultimate problem is that we have forgotten HOW we created ourselves and the Universe in which we live. So, our main purpose is to direct our effort and focus towards remembering. We must remember WHO and WHY we are here, taking the path back to the SOURCE of BEING, RETURNIN to our TRUE SELVES. This is what we call the state of Homeostasis. This is living with dignity, honor and the greatness of BEING and BECOMING.

TRUTH
2. Truth is not relative. It is not something we create. It is something to be found, realized and lived. Attention, awareness and self-observation are measured by how much you allow yourself to know your own truth.

GOODNESS
3. The concepts of "right" and "wrong," moral and immoral have been based on the premise that "the root of human nature is bad," therefore, they are not valid to live by. If one would shift to the concept that "the basic root of human nature is good," one's life could be transformed to a healthy and balanced way of living as the result of authentic positive thinking.

LOVE
4. Whatever you deny to others will be denied to you. Love others as you would love yourself. Touch the world the way you would want to be touched. Accept and treasure the uniqueness of others as they are, and the doors will be open for genuine love.

PATIENCE
5. Patience is a compassionate virtue. Always accept and give kindness as a genuine sense of caring about others, life and yourself. Also, when you give and express the attributes of attention, mercy, grace and love, you will receive plenty in return. Remember, if you want something in life, always GIVE IT FIRST.

KNOWING
6. We all have a built in, innate intelligence which is instinctual and intuitive. If we would take the time to listen to the **"small still voice within,"** we would know the right thing to do in every given moment. Most of us fail to trust this inner voice. We deny our own body intelligence and understanding of knowing. Learn to trust that knowing. Listen...

HONOR
7. Do not ever think or do anything that causes you to lose your honor, self-esteem, or, your deep sense of life. Maintain your integrity by doing what you know is right and honest. There is great strength when you are just.

BEING
8. When you value being who you really are, more than being accepted, you will live in the peaceful current of life.

AWARENESS
9. Everything we think, say or do has a great ripple effect, similar to when a stone is dropped into a calm lake. We are totally responsible for everything that happens to us or will happen. This is the basis of all reality. So, we have to be 100% aware of what we are doing every single moment. This means focused awareness.

SILENCE
10. This is a great value to observe and exercise to find out how powerful it can be. Being silent inside with quietness generates an immense force of energy. It is not only wise, but also a practical necessity to use silence in a world full of noise. This is a state of being I call, **Le Centre du Silence**, the Center of Silence. "Speak less and Do more." Speak ONLY when it is necessary. And even then, speak only that which is 100% honest from you. Do not feel any pressure to talk. Small talk is a sign of emptiness. Silence enables you to increase the ability to listen and respond with only the amount of words necessary for expressing yourself. When you practice this value of using silence, you will realize the power of being happy and productive—A sense of Super Happiness.

OVERCOMING DIFFICULTIES

FALSE PROPHETS
11. Avoid self-appointed "gurus" and organized religions. They are bad for your mental health, and they want your money. Unfortunately, pretense and denial are the norm in the thinking of this society. Society has twisted all possible healthy ways of thinking. Therefore, learn to recognize the True Teachers from the fake.

EXPECTATIONS
12. Do not expect anything, and expect everything. Be comfortable with whatever comes your way, whatever the results may be, and in whatever form. Maintaining this balance will give you a deep sense of being, and can help you to navigate calmly in the "midst of madness."

CONFLICT

13. Living in conflict is a rampant state in our society. Conflict is when you say one thing and do another. Not until you practice without compromise Total Integrated Honesty, will you function from calm and peace and flow with the "current" of life.

CONTROL

14. When you no longer attempt control the outcome of any project or image, you use your ability to be detached from the chaos in life. This is also true when interacting or relating with other people in any given situation. Look at the situation from all possible angles. Be open to new possibilities, and leave the doors open wide for the manifestation of your heart's desires without the "control factor."

RESISTANCE

15. Anything that is easy is not interesting. In life, it appears we are presented with "seeming difficulties" (in the form of people, situations or events). These seeming difficulties can provide us with the opportunity to respond in new, positive and innovative ways to the "what is." The more you resist learning how to respond to these "seeming difficulties," the more you will find yourself attracting the situation back, in order to resolve it. So, respond rather than react. Be kind to yourself and others.

NEEDS/WANTS

16. Most of the time we do not know what we want or need. Some do not even know the difference between wants and needs. We try to "fill" ourselves from the outer world, rather than from the inner world. This is one of the reasons most people are unhappy and walking around spiritually unfulfilled. Learn why you are here, know where you are going, know what you want. Find a true teacher to guide you, or you may remain lost....

FEAR

17. Never use fear to justify avoiding life. Ponder on this deeply and discover a treasure of your being.

SUFFERING

18. Use suffering as a source for self-transformation, self-evolution and awakening.

FORGIVENESS

19. Forgiving others is a great release for new energy and new events to enter your life. Forgiveness is a selfless act you do for yourself and others to evolve and walk ahead in practical knowledge and active wisdom.

ECSTASY TO LUNCH

20. Ecstasy to Lunch is the power to SHIFT your attention from this to that, from thought to action, from this action to the next, while always being present. This will make you more mentally and physically agile. When you learn to remain focused from moment to moment. it will become natural to shift easily from here to there, without awkwardness or accidents.

TRANSFORMATION

OBSERVATION

21. Observation can be a powerful tool. When conflict arises in life, we have two ways we can look at the situation. One is from the boat, our personal view, which is very subjective. The other is the view from the helicopter, in which you have a more objective perspective of the situation, the detachment of an observer. Practice this consciously by first observing any situation from your personal vantage point. Then, take a few minutes to close your eyes, relax your body, and see your situation from high above, as if you are on the ceiling, or up in a helicopter. See what new things you see clearly from this observer awareness.

INSIGHT

22. Take the time to practice "quiet moments" alone, totally relaxed, reflecting and keeping the focus steady on a thought or object in order to cultivate insight. Quiet moments can provide you with the opportunity to see things more clearly, while realizing the essence of all things.

SIMPLICITY

23. Simplicity in life is one of the world's greatest and most well-kept secrets. At times, life can seem complicated and complex. We have to overcome many obstacles and much conditioning in order to be able to find the simpleness in life's pleasures. This means going back to our original, natural state, which is happiness, well-being and constant joy in life.

IMAGINATION

24. Imagination is one of our most powerful tools in living and being creative. It is more powerful than will power. Visualize. Form the image. Tend to the intention of that which you see. Form, mold, and condense from the invisible, to create that which you truly believe in. Meaningful and lasting change begins and ends with imagination.

VISION

25. Dare to be a visionary with every thought and action. Think big. See beyond your own little world. Expand your vision to include the plight of humanity. The size of your vision is the key to your success and practical happiness.

MANIFESTATION
26. Anything you want to manifest begins with an idea or thought. The journey from thought to action begins with a "seed" idea. Ideas and experiences create our beliefs, which in turn, create our perceived reality. If you desire to change your reality, you have to change your beliefs. Remember, beliefs ARE NOT reality.

LAUGHTER
27. Laugh out of existence all thoughts, emotions and situations that are not good for you, and block your way. One minute of good daily laughter in front of the mirror will release all body and mind tensions, introducing you to a joyous state.

IMPERMEABLE
28. Visualize that you are wearing an invisible raincoat. Like a real raincoat that protects you from the drops of rain, this invisible one allows outside circumstances, events and energies, to simply slide off. As you make a mental practice of "wearing" the impermeable, you will find that daily events no longer affect your state of balance and harmony. Learn to become calmly detached to worldly affairs, but not indifferent.

UNE CHOSE A LA FOIS (One Thing at a Time)
29. Focus on one thing at a time, as if it is done for the first and last time. Break the components of the task or project down into small movements or actions, to finish in less time than a scattered mind would take. Attend to the action at the time of the action

FIRST THOUGHT, LAST THOUGHT
30. Become aware of your first thought when you awake in the morning and your last thought before you sleep. Before you sleep, do a daily review of your thoughts and experiences of the day, and resolve to sleep well with a clean conscience of having lived that day with awareness and honesty.

ULTIMATE BEHAVIOR

SMILE
31. Always smile. Smiling reverberates ALL the systems of your being and relaxes the whole body. The smile is not only in the face, but a natural reflection of happiness.

BREATHE
32. In every situation, observe the way you breathe. Be conscious of your breathing. Whenever you feel tension in any area of your body during any activity, remember to breathe. Breathing oxygenates the whole organism.

RELAXATION

33. Observe tension in your jaw, neck, shoulders and pelvis. As soon as you become aware of tension in a specific area, remember to breathe and release. The more you practice this relatively simple technique, the better your body will learn by doing.

FOCUS

34. Focus your attention by listening openly to your breathing. Respond rather than react. As you learn to focus on this present moment, it will reveal to you how every situation is an opportunity to learn something new about yourself and how you function. Practicing this will make you discover the precious intimacy of this very moment of relating to yourself and others.

FLOW

35. Where we place our attention, energy flows. What we focus on expands. So where your attention goes, your energy flows. Any resistance to the flow of "what is" and "who we really are, as we are," in life is the main cause of suffering. Therefore, the "easy" application is accepting and seeing things AS THEY ARE and CAN BE.

NOWNESS

36. Stay here now. Keep a constant attentiveness to this precious moment of being present. Feel and seize the full life power of this moment. Feel how the life force breathes and activates your being, always making you fully conscious of every moment. This is the only moment where you become aware of change, realizing who you are, keeping your visions and goals in mind, and acting to realize them. This ability of NOWNESS assists you to integrate past with future into a potent and constant presence.

CALM

37. Function always from an inner and outer state of calm and poise. Find yourself relaxed physically, calm emotionally, focused mentally, and keenly spiritually aware.

POSTURE

38. When walking, sitting or while doing any other activity, imagine seeing yourself in a mirror. LOOK at your posture. KEEP THE SPINE STRAIGHT. Ease the pressure from your abdominal area. Posture is the reflection of that which you are. Emotions condition our posture. Changing posture can change your emotions.

MENTAL CONTROL

39. Observing reality AS IT IS. Become aware of your thoughts as an observer, and the one who is being observed. Develop your mentality in a healthy, balanced way using your faculties of thinking creatively with no limitation. **SEEING THINGS AS THEY ARE** will become natural.

ACTING CONSCIOUSLY

40. Never make a choice based upon emotions or from the expectations of others. Instead, act consciously and clearly in ways consistent with your own intended true purpose.

BEING AND BECOMING

ACCEPTANCE

41. Let the basis of your relationships begin with total, unconditional acceptance of the other **AS THEY ARE**. Practice genuine humanity refraining from judgment, blame and expectations. People you meet and relate to are reflecting a mirror for you. The way you respond to others is an indication of recognition of that which is in yourself.

CHOICE

42. The greatest power you have is the **POWER of CHOICE**. You are totally free to choose how you will respond to any given situation. It is not what is happening to you, but how you respond to what is happening. The power of choice provides you with the opportunity to respond rather than react. When you respond, what others say and do will not affect you. Do not ever make a choice based upon emotions or the expectations of others. Instead, act consciously and clearly in ways consistent with your intended purpose.

THE CHALLENGE

43. It is a real challenge in these times to be a genuine, authentic person. This is the one who dares to explore beyond the superficial and outer appearances in the world. It is the one who practices aliveness and integrates challenge until courage resides in every living cell of the body. Through creative, challenging living, one's life can be more interesting, productive and worry-free.

CHANGE

44. Change is good. It can break us out of the stagnant, static, routine of everyday living. Anything that the mind has created, the mind can also change. The problem is, we become comfortable within the routine and the familiar. Dare to leap into the unknown and accept the change, and you will be very creative in many fields of human endeavor.

SUPPORT

45. The unnamable Source of Life is always supporting you, whether you are aware of it or not. You increase the quality of life if you become aware of this supportive power. All your clearest desires will be manifested as you live by this attitude. So, pursue all your desires with focus and awareness, and eventually you will receive what you need and want.

BECOMING

46. It is of utmost importance to NOT to RESIST BECOMING. The more you resist becoming, the more you postpone your chosen destiny and knowing the purpose of your life.

COMPLETENESS

47. Any thought, action, project or event, which is incomplete, will have to be repeated until you learn how to complete it. That which you totally conceive and believe, you can achieve. There is no doubt about this as long as your desires are realistic and do not conflict with the free will of others.

SELFNESS

48. Who are you? What are you here for? What is this journey called life? What have you come here to do? Attitudes, values and beliefs are shaped and formed by our surrounding environment. The way that we have learned to think is how we act in life. So, we are the mirrors of our own thoughts. Happiness and success are self-imposed, and unhappiness and failure are self-inflicted.

TRUE SELF

49. Dare to be your true and authentic self. A peaceful, creative existence is one of the most difficult things to practice in this world. Being yourself is the greatest gift you can offer to another human being.

CONSERVE YOUR WORDS

50. Finally, speak only when necessary, observe and watch diligently what you say and talk about. Here is a personal story I call **"Word Economy"** that helped me practice this valuable and practical wisdom:

WORD ECONOMY

"My grandfather once told me that we are born with a certain number of words in our "**word bank**." If one uses too many words, it is like over-spending. It empties our word bank account, and we become overdrawn, or we become mute. So, when we use words only when necessary, we practice word economy.

"Words are only one of the ways to communicate; 99% of our real communication, however, occurs in silence, through our body language.

"I highly recommend to practice one day of silence a week to achieve the ability to **speak less and do more** and **produce more and consume less**—practicing consistently the practical wisdom of the **Word Economy**."

PRACTICAL EXERCISES

First Thought, Last Thought

Ten Gates of Wisdom

Use Your Time Wisely

28 Daily Practices

Eleven Principles for Teachers and Students

Learning from a Child and a Thief

Eight Gates to Become an Authentic Being

FIRST THOUGHT AND LAST THOUGHT – CONSCIOUSLY

Practice and Master the
First Thought and Last Thought Exercise (FTLT) – Consciously

Practice First Thought, Last Thought every day, becoming aware of the FIRST THOUGHT that comes to you in the morning, and the LAST THOUGHT that you think before going to sleep.

When you master this technique, you can consciously use the following statements, making a clear decision to live and be grateful for the gift of life.

MORNING FIRST THOUGHT

When you awake from sleep in the morning, repeat this thought loudly
to yourself 3 times before getting out of bed, giving meaning to each word, and setting out
to carry this attitude all day long.

**I am grateful for the gift of life.
I consciously decide to live today fully awake and ready.**

EVENING LAST THOUGHT

At night before you go to sleep, as you place your head on your pillow,
read and repeat this last thought consciously,
carrying it with you into sleep.

**I am fully grateful that I have lived today to
the best of my ability and potential. I love life
and I will wake up tomorrow to greater possibilities.**

"Souls that recognize another…Congregate. Those who don't…argue"

TEN GATES OF WISDOM

Practices for Personal Success and Happiness
Suggested to Dedicated Students of Life

The Importance of the Creative Individual and Integrated Being to Exist in This World:

The most important and essential value in the universe is the individual human being, capable of creative genius to manifest events and invent unexpected values to benefit humanity.

The future belongs to the triumph of the visionary individual, the artist, the creator of new ways of thinking and being. It is for the individual who is a self-leader - the one who dares to think for themselves, who has a fearless attitude towards shaping the future with utter simplicity. It is for the one who ignores consciously the ways of the herd, and dares to be oneself, unique and with humility and happiness.

All these characteristics will always be essentially present in the healthy sense of being of the creative artist within. Most artists know and aspire to these values, to shape the unshapeable, to dare to say the unsaid, doing the "impossible" through various artistic fields with color, movement and sound. The future is shaped by such beings that soar while others crawl.

Strive to develop these characteristics and you will be a most happy being. You will find yourself alive and well, always ready to help others see the sun. You will discover the light of the one who dares to look within and to express without fear the murmurs of the heart, and the élan of balance, justice, honesty, self-responsibility and self-reliance."
 —**Samuel Avital**, in a class session 1972, Boulder, CO

The ten gates exercises may at first glance appear simple and insignificant. Don't underestimate these simple practices. This simplicity is one of the ways to activate and apply wisdom, and enjoy your success and happiness. Practice these "musical notes" of being and becoming. In doing so, you will become a symphony of living an ecstatic life, rich with creativity and joie de vivre.

1. Genuine kindness and success **is not what you do, it is what you are. By simply knowing and being** this fact deeply, you will experience the genuine state of happiness constantly.

2. Wherever you are, you have chosen to be there, consciously or not. Observe how consciously you choose to think or do something. **By using your will to Choose, you choose yourself.** The most powerful force in life is the power of choice, when used consciously and knowingly. Use this power and experience the genuine and intense happiness of being alive.

3. Look around you, observe how you breathe. Increase the ability to be fully 100% awake and aware to this very precious moment of life. This simple awareness has more infinite value than years of absence of mind and heart — the state where most humans sadly dwell daily.

4. Make sure you laugh. You don't need a reason to laugh. In our times you laugh not only to release tension, but also to protect yourself from crying. Have you noticed that laughing and crying are expressed with the same movements? Every night, lucidly dream all your aspirations, desires and visualizations vividly. See yourself **in** the image, realizing all your goals.

   Remember: <u>Your thoughts determine what you want, and your actions determine what you get. Thought affects muscle.</u>

5. **Decisions, decisions**! When you decide, make sure to be conscious, and after you have done the "circle thinking" exercise, to align your decision with your heart center. Make definite decisions to be and become what in your heart you so desire to be and become. Dare to be creative in your "<u>**circle thinking**</u>," and follow those decisions with a focused mind and heart. Stick to it, until all is realized as you have pictured it.

6. You have an innate ability to think, and to be, and are capable of focusing without fear toward achieving your goals.

7. Set goals in writing. Write detailed visions. Make sure this is really what you want. Determine the price, pay it and go with certainty towards it. It is yours. Always give more than what you take. Be generous in helping others help themselves. This is another simple and powerful fact for achieving success and happiness.

8. Reflect on your journey from thought to action. Observe your way of thinking. Shift from traditional thinking to Creative and Innovative thinking. **Dare a little, NO, dare a lot**.

   How long does it take for you to act after you first think about doing something? Minimize the time gap between your thought and action. By doing this, you will achieve what I call "<u>**Minimum Movement, Maximum Expression**</u>." Successful people do it. You can also do it, right now. It is in your immediate power. You were just told otherwise during your "**public education.**" **When you change your way of thinking, your actions will change for your benefit.**

   In the Western education, we learn <u>**WHAT**</u> to think, not <u>**HOW**</u> to think. <u>**External authority dictates "WHAT" you think**</u>. They teach you what to think according to their hidden agenda, to be like the mass, the group, the collective.

   You must discover for yourself "**How to think**" in order to express your unique individual creativity. It is very exciting and attractive to be your own thinker, and not be like the herd. <u>**DARE**</u> to think by yourself, for yourself, to yourself.

9. <u>**THINK**</u> of a person who has contributed to your life in any way. It could be someone who has enriched your life, who has helped you at one time or another to make an important step in your way of being. Perhaps they have given you a gift or a value, or awakened you to your deep sense of self, and increased your creativity in your life.

Now, **FOCUS** on that person. See him or her vividly, with a deep gratitude in your heart and silently feel good and remember only the good.

Find a creative way to express your gratitude to that person. Create a beautiful surprise, and cause that person to feel the unexpected by your thoughtful action. This practice will make you remember and give more than what was given to you, to **Produce More Than You Consume.**

10. Establish and schedule a regular rendezvous, a dedicated time with yourself, to simply practice Self-Attention and Silent Awareness. Simply dedicate this quiet space and time for reflection within yourself, without the noises of this hectic world. This will clear your mind and heart, so you can function harmoniously through the changes occurring in your life.

One of my mottos that has helped me to overcome many irrationalities in this world is: "**KEEP ME SANE IN THE MIDST OF MADNESS**." Make it yours.

Simply sit quietly in a comfortable place. Tense each part of your body individually, then the whole body at once. As you tense, take one deep breath: Inhale with the count of 5 for each part of the body, and hold it while tensing that part to the count of 5. Then exhale and release the tension with the count of 10.

Do this short cycle of tense-release 3 times. Then sit still quietly and reflect on just being able to breathe, to recharge your cells and become more energetic in your thoughts and actions. The more you practice this simple exercise, the more you will feel its power.

I repeat, please do not underestimate the power of these of these exercises in their simplicity. **Practice, see,** and **feel** the **results** for yourself.

Finally, recognize and realize this knowledge:

In essence, all you really need to succeed in anything are **3 basic factors**—The **desire**, the **vision,** and the **courage** to navigate and be the author of your life.

**From experience, I suggest that you develop
within yourself these qualities of being:**

1. **BE TEACHABLE**, and use your ability to sculpt and re-shape your character, in order to know who you really are, by knowing that you do not know.

2. **BE ORIENTED TO SUCCEED,** always expecting with certainty the outcome as you visualize it to be.

3. **BE READY TO CAUSE A CHANGE**. Use your state of readiness at all times. Be always on your toes, **"alert and agile like a cat."** Develop your creative edge for "new" experiences, by using your ability to think, act, and do, with vivid desire, vision and courage, of course!

Bon courage, Mon ami(e)....... Samuel.

USE YOUR TIME WISELY
Dedicate a Conscious Moment to Practice

1. **USE a TIME** to sit quiet in a restful moment, and feel the Great Force of Life within you. Listen to your breath and heartbeat. Make this a steady practice when possible, and **JUST BE**.

2. **USE a TIME** to ponder about the miracle of being alive here and now. Contemplate your whole existence and be profoundly grateful that you are here at this time.

3. **USE a TIME** to practice goodness and kindness to yourself and others. Focus on a specific person and send them a mental note, a thought for their good health and spiritual evolution. Know that those who think and activate the good with profound intention, always find good everywhere, within and without.

4. **USE a TIME** to discover the sacred connection you have between yourself and the Creator, **_The ESSENTIAL BEING_**. Staying and resting in this state allows you to realize the existence of the Creator within yourself, **_THE UNIQUE ONE_**.

5. **USE a TIME** to be with yourself, and explore your full existence, on this visible material plane, and on the other invisible dimensions of living and being.

6. **USE a TIME** to contemplate a thought to surprise a friend. Then act on it, in a way so they will never guess that you are the one who caused them to feel elated, happy and surprised. This is a good activity to practice the **_Journey from Thought to Action_**.

7. **USE a TIME** to make a new friend. Share your good thoughts and learning with them, in a genuine way that will deepen your relationship, both spiritually and materially.

8. **USE a TIME** to be ONE with yourself. Realize that the source of everything is ONE, SILENT, STILL and RESTING. Find a unique way to UNITE and BE THAT ONENESS. Know the way to UNITE all that is separated, and practice applying it in a creative way.

9. **USE a TIME** to read inspired books of wisdom that are elevating and provide insight. Find ways to go beyond the story. What are you are learning, and HOW will you apply it creatively in your life **NOW**?

10. **USE a TIME** to find creative ways to laugh and play in an unexpected way with your friends and children. Use music, drawing, clowning and other creative playful ways to improve happiness through laughter in your life. Discover **_the music of your soul_**.

11. **USE a TIME** to explore your spontaneity and enthusiasm, to activate your **_conscious innocence_**. Develop the lost art of **_Self Dialogue_**. This is the well-kept secret of your longevity, and of **_BEING SANE in The MIDST OF MADNESS_**.

28 DAILY PRACTICES

We know that we create our world through the thoughts we choose to focus on. When we focus our thoughts with constant gratitude, we become gentle beings. This constant gratitude fills our lives with great joy and good feeling. The focus upon the great goodness of the Creator and the understanding and certainty that the Creator is always within us, and with us, uplifts us. It strengthens our spirituality and the quality of our lives. Reading and focusing daily on this list of 28 practices can have a great and profound influence on our lives.

1. The Creator is with me at all times.
2. Nothing can exist besides the Creator.
3. I love my Creator, my king, who renews the world constantly.
4. The Creator loves us more than we love ourselves.
5. I am constantly grateful for all the good that I have in my life.
6. I will make sure to always communicate positively with myself.
7. I am constantly grateful for every second of my life.
8. I am constantly grateful for every breath that I breathe.
9. I am constantly grateful that I am able to see.
10. I am constantly grateful that I am able to hear.
11. I am constantly grateful that I am able to speak.
12. I am constantly grateful that I am able to walk.
13. I will practice diligently to grow through every event and situation in my life.
14. I will practice diligently to always find the positive angle in every situation.
15. The human being was born in the likeness of the Creator and I respect every human being, everywhere.
16. I will love humanity without condition.
17. I love to act with gentleness to the best of my ability.
18. I will see the good in every person that I meet.
19. I will say and do everything to bring about the good in every being that I meet.

20. I will always encourage and support people to the best of my ability. I will speak words of encouragement to whomever I meet.

21. I will always feel and experience a strong sense of power and courage.

22. I will remember all of the strong and courageous people that have ever lived. I will learn from their thoughts and from their deeds to be very courageous and very powerful.

23. I will learn from every human being that I meet.

24. Everything I experience enriches the knowledge of myself.

25. I will always remember my accomplishments, merit, and virtue, and will apply them in every situation possible.

26. I will always imagine myself as I want to be.

27. I will always bless everyone with peace and happiness.

28. I will see myself all the time happy, gentle, brave and courageous, patient, tolerant, calm, relaxed, serene, and enthusiastic. Every time I live these qualities, they will become ever stronger in me.

Adapted from Various Hebrew Spiritual Sources by Samuel Avital

Sunday, October 16, 2011. Lafayette, Colorado.

11 PRINCIPLES FOR TEACHERS and STUDENTS

These are eleven (11) suggestions to teachers and students who are sincerely dedicated to learn and teach. The true teacher is ready to emphasize by example the subject of exploration, and consider the obvious and that which is taken for granted. The true student dares to examine through experience, with a manifestation of a joyous heart, and not just through words and theories.

1. **You will integrate education and learning as first priority.**

2. **You will not glorify mediocrity.**

3. **You will not denigrate the power of reason and shall allow the intuitive to be expressed. And do not shame the student in public.**

4. **Remember the creative potential in each human being.**

5. **Always honor excellence.**

6. **You will not repress curiosity.**

7. **You shall not confuse innovation with progress. Adopt the motto "KEEP ME SANE IN THE MIDST OF MADNESS" in all situations.**

8. **You will not rob the student of dignity.**

9. **You will not pretend that learning is painful. Actually it is joyous. Direct your teaching efforts with humor and stories, so it is easy to understand.**

10. **You will not court popularity, self-approval, nor self-aggrandizement.**

11. **In any situation in life, adopt this attitude that will simplify life complexities: "THIS TOO SHALL PASS" and "THIS ALSO IS FOR THE GOOD."**

LEARNING FROM A CHILD AND A THIEF

From various sources and from Samuel Ben-Or Avital

מִכָּל מְלַמְּדַי הִשְׂכַּלְתִּי כִּי עֵדְוֹתֶיךָ שִׂיחָה לִי: תהלים קיט. צט

From all my teachers I have gained understanding,
for your testimonials are my meditations. Psalms 110:99

From a child you can learn
1. Always to be happy,
2. Never to sit idle, and
3. To cry for everything one wants.

From a thief you can learn:
1. To work at night.
2. If one cannot gain what one wants, try again the next night.
3. To love one's co-workers just as thieves love each other.
4. To be willing to risk one's life even for a little thing.
5. Not to attach too much value to things even though one has risked one's life for them.
6. To withstand all kinds of beatings and tortures, but to remain what you are.
7. To believe that your work is worthwhile and not be willing to change it.

And I humbly add: Samuel Ben-Or Avital
8. Work quietly without bothering others.
9. Plan without telling anyone.

Another Kabbalistic Sage once said that what you can learn from something from everything—even from a train, a telephone and a telegram:

From a train, you can learn that in a second, one can miss everything.

From a telephone, you can learn that what you say here is heard over there.

From a telegram, you can learn that all words are counted and charged with the "MasterCard."

In that same tradition, I humbly add: Samuel Ben-Or Avital.

From a television, you can learn: The all-knowing eye watches what you do, say or think within your inner chamber.

From the computer, you can learn: Direct communication and intention. What you command it to do it does, but it may not be what you intended it to be.

From the Internet, you can learn: That "here" is "there" and "there" is "here," always present and absent, visible and invisible.

From Email, you can learn: That in communication there is no privacy. Many can read your thoughts. All is known even though you do not know it. Fast is slow and slow is fast.

EIGHT GATES TO BECOME AN AUTHENTIC BEING
The 8 Basic Principles of Conscious Integrated Being and Self-Harmony

Here are eight simple and important principles to practice for self-guidance and practical insight. Keep them in your mind and heart, taking each one as a daily exercise to focus on. Reflect and apply these principles and witness the changes unfold in your life, as a result of the efforts you have invested and your self-dedication to the practice.

1. SMILE

Always smile. Smiling reverberates ALL the systems in your being and relaxes the whole body. The smile is not only in the face, but a natural reflection of happiness.

2. BREATHE

In every situation, observe the way you breathe. Be conscious of your breathing. Whenever you feel tension in any area of your body, during any activity, remember to breathe. Breathing oxygenates the whole organism.

3. RELAXATION

Observe tensions in your jaw, neck, shoulders and pelvis. As soon as you become aware of tension in a specific area, remember to breathe and release. The more you practice this relatively simple technique, the better your body will learn by doing.

4. POSTURE

When walking, sitting or while doing any other activity, imagine seeing yourself in a mirror. LOOK at your posture. KEEP THE SPINE STRAIGHT. Ease the pressure from your abdominal area. Posture is the reflection of that which you are. Emotions condition our posture. Changing posture can change your emotions.

5. FOCUS

Focus your attention by listening openly to your breathing. Respond rather than react. As you learn to focus on this present moment, it will reveal to you how every situation is an opportunity to learn something new about yourself and how you function. Practicing this will make you discover the precious intimacy of this very moment of relating to yourself and others.

6. MENTAL CONTROL

Observing reality **AS IT IS**, become aware of your thoughts as an observer, and the one who is being observed. Develop your mentality in a healthy, balanced way, using your faculties of thinking creatively with no limitation. **SEEING THINGS AS THEY ARE** will become natural.

7. NOWNESS

Stay here now. Keep a constant attentiveness to this precious moment of being present. Feel and seize the full life power of this moment. Feel how the life force breathes and activates your being, by always making you feel fully conscious of every moment. This is the only moment where you become aware of change, realizing who you are, keeping your visions and goals in mind, and acting to realize them. This ability of NOWNESS assists you to integrate past with future, into a potent and constant presence.

8. SILENCE

This is a great value to observe and exercise. You will find how powerful it can be. Being silent inside with quietness generates an immense force of energy. It is not only wise, but also a practical necessity, to use silence in a world full of noise.

This is a state of being I call, Le Centre du Silence, the Center of Silence. Speak less and Do more. Speak ONLY when it is necessary. And even then, speak only that which is 100% honest from you. Do not feel any pressure to talk. Small talk is a sign of emptiness. Silence enables you to increase the ability to listen and respond with only the amount of words necessary for expressing yourself. When you practice this value of using silence, you will realize the power of being happy and productive—A sense of Super Happiness.

"Si ce que tu vas dire n'est pas plus beau que le silence ne le dis pas."
"**If what you are going to say is not more beautiful than silence, do not say it.**"

REFLECTIONS

Always the NOW
Love the Paradox
All Moments are Holy
The Silence Within
The Director of the Heart
Guidance from Within
Whispers of the Master Within
Guided by the Breath
The Great Flame
From the Center of Calm
In the Center of Silence
The Mother Whispers
Meeting the Divine Mother
The Riches of the Universe
Becoming
The Gift of Consciousness
It Is In Your Hand To Do It
The Flame of the Creator
One
As a Tree
The Dance of Being
A Circle Without A Center
In the Center of the Circle

REFLECTIONS, CONTINUED

A Vertical Line

My Bones Sing

Without Name

The Spirit of Love

Harmonious Will

The Fact that I Was Born

Friendship

Only Peace

Light

At This Quiet Place and Hour

The Song

No Heaven, No Earth

Beyond Appearances

Keep Me Sane in the Midst of Madness

With Eyes to See

May We Be Delivered

The Great Plan

You are the Path and the Destination

A Being of Light

Whisper to My Ear, Oh Beloved

I Am Confident About the Future

From My Heart

REFLECTIONS

Always the NOW

There is a magical way to appreciate this very moment, no matter what is happening or is not happening. When we know the sheer fact that life is eternal and all is ever changing, being totally in this moment becomes a sacred breath. It is ordinary; it is Sacred. Always the NOW. Breathe this moment now. And the next moment will become NOW again, and again, and again, until the infinite is expressed in you. Say to yourself, "This is the moment of my life, and I live it to the best of my ability." There is nothing happening, yet all is happening now, just as it happened one moment before—which is again this very moment.

Love the Paradox

To be enlightened is to realize the truth of being, which is the living of this precious present moment. Only in stillness and silence do we enter that state, in which we contact our higher being, the One in all. Until we really love this mighty paradox of being and becoming, we will never meet this GREAT SELF. The more we live simply, with constant appreciation of all life, the more all "mysteries" will be revealed and discovered. So, the inner quest of being is within each of us. And the more we realize our being, the more we will be able to become that which we aspire for. The door to that is simply to LOVE THE PARADOX of being this and becoming that, at one and the same time.

All Moments are Holy

All moments are holy, whole and full of the Presence Divine. This is true at work, at any time, at any place. Knowing this within one's heart, one can be the right person at the right time, with the right people, manifesting the right plan and right work. At all times, at all places, one exists for a purpose. Be in tune SIMPLY with the SOURCE OF BEING everywhere. Cultivate this Presence, and all doors will open before you. You will be a friend of the Right time, Right place, and Right work.

The Silence Within

Inspired by calm and serenity, I sit before my Creator, listening to the silence within. I am filled with confidence and patience to work all things for the good of humanity. Still and silent, I work in the small theatre within.

The Director of the Heart

In nourishment and warmth, I respond to the "call" of my "Director," who resides within my heart. Free from all conditioning, I soar on high, while my feet are planted on earth, responding to every need, and to all who come to me. My response is service and love for all the workers of light everywhere.

Guidance from Within

In the presence of my "Director Within," I see the light, and the purpose of my Life's evolution on earth. I am open to this sacred guidance from The Source of my inner being. It speaks to me in silence and lucidity, guiding me to see clearly with my oneness with all.

Whispers of the Master Within

All my aspirations are towards Light. The name of God instilled in my name is my banner of protection and certainty. It breathes through all my bones and cells. In the Silence beyond time and space, the whispers of the Master Within are like pearls, shining and guiding me in all my thoughts and actions.

Guided by the Breath

Sitting quiet, still and calm, the crystal clear breath guides me to the inner eye that sees all. This is an inner place where the Divine Essence speaks, acts and thinks through this vessel of service and devotion, guiding me to BE HERE.

The Great Flame

I am aware that the One who lives in me, thinks through me, acts through me, and breathes through me is the Great Flame of life in the Universe. That is the one who beats in my heart, the Resident within this "me." This is the the "Master" of my heart.

From the Center of Calm

From the Center of Calm, I radiate a silence through which I see clearly that I am One with all: A unit-spark of Light, living within the envelope of this harmonious cell-organism of being.

In the Center of Silence

In the Centre of Silence, I meet and become one with the Divine Presence within me and within all nature. I remember always that I am made of matter earth, and guided by the spirit above. I am a bridge between heaven and earth. I am the blessings of my Creator, and all who come in touch with me are blessed.

The Mother Whispers

The Earthly Mother within me whispers to me every moment to remind me that I am made of her substance. She is Me and I am her. I am her becoming; I am the earth and the fruit. She nurtures me with her love and constant breath. Through her waters and her air, I am alive in my beloved Earthly Mother—life, life and life in all. I know this and am blessed.

Meeting the Divine Mother

In the Goddess Divine Mother of all, I dwell with strength, nurturing all that is Created with her power. I meet her by swimming in her beloved ocean of love, in drinking the elixir of her kiss. I join her. My heart runs with joy to be ONE with her, in her becoming, in ONE BREATH. In the Goddess's breasts, I find the source of my being, my whole being. The Goddess smiles, and blesses me. I am whole, perfect and beautiful in the Goddess.

The Riches of the Universe

I am the vessel of Peace, I am the channel of Light, Life and Love. I am the abundance of all in One. All the riches of the Universe are mine to enjoy and become that which I am.

Becoming

I am the experience itself of becoming. I am here to share and to shine light, to be light, a luminous crystal of nature. To be Light, to be Life, to be Love. I am here to radiate the Soul's light, from the Source of being. I am in Him-Her.... I am in Her-Him with my every breath. I am the experience of Joy in all.

The Gift of Consciousness

The gift of consciousness, which I have been given to use in this life, is a precious jewel beyond compare. The use of this gift gives me a clear and noble purpose. Through it, I know that the Light of the ancient echo vibrates within me as a celestial song to all the Cosmos. I am complete in this way. I know be the roots of my eternal being, to return to the source of all that is and that is not. All my cells and my heart rejoice in this realization. I am the Precious Jewel, shining every day, working in harmony with all.

It Is In Your Hand To Do It

The mystery of self-discovery is really no mystery at all. Simple selflessness is the actual key to realize this ancient truth. When one realizes the self, one becomes selfless. It is as simple as that. But in the process, one passes through many purifying and trying experiences which lead to this beautiful realization. Be open, then, to this possibility of attainment, because it is within your grasp every moment of your life.

The Flame of the Creator

As I allow myself to grow to Higher dimensions of consciousness, to "KNOW" MY "PLACE" in the evolution of the Universe and the betterment of mankind, I walk the path of those who serve and grow. As I walk, all becomes illumined in "The Flame of the Creator." As I grow and become confident, my thanks grow, hoping that all the containers be filled with "THE FLAME." My heart wings thanks to the Supreme Being in all.

One

I am invisible and One with all in the source of Being. I soar in my thoughts toward the ultimate Reality of light in all the universe. With a happy heart and mind in harmony, I am happy to be here at this time. All that is good I attract. All that is beautiful I am at One with. Joy to all. All is the joy of becoming.

As a Tree

As a tree, I grow to express the strength of the roots of my being. As a trunk, I grow to express the straightness of walking with God, honestly and purely. As the leaves and branches, I grow to multiply the oneness in me, which stems from the One who is my Maker and Creator. As the fruits, I come to receive the good I planted, and share with all my kind the joy and the elixir of life eternal.

The Dance of Being

At this very moment, here and now, I AM dancing the dance of being and becoming in every living thing. I am one with the infinite intelligence, and receive the abundance present in all creation. With my awakened heart, I am being and becoming THY presence, wherever I am, wherever I go, and whatever I do. Always being, and not being, in Thee.

A Circle Without A Center

I am a circle without a center; I am a center without a circle. I fly without wings; I am wings of being. I am an invisible Dot soaring in Eternal space. I bring the message of continuous life to All beings and non-beings.

In the Center of the Circle

From the central point in the midst of the holy circle I dwell. It is the source of all my being everywhere. Day and night, it brings healing to all who need it. I am weary of being in the periphery of the circle. I become that very dot, the Center of the center, that is present in all things.

A Vertical Line

I am the vertical line. I am made of the Atomic Dust of matter, infused with the spirit in one organism. I am the vertical line connecting up and down, heaven and earth. Reaching to the sun, becoming light, I am made from the earth, and I drink from the sun. I am the bridge between up and down, a connecting channel of all the particles of light, from here to everywhere. Wherever I go and whatever I say, beams forth from that supernal Light of becoming.

My Bones Sing

All my bones and cells are singing the song of Heaven. I live every breath, every word, every action, with this consciousness of oneness with all. Health and prosperity are my birthright, expressing the inexpressible, being the non-being, and living the eternal here and now. I am ONE.

Without Name

How could I dare to name you, beloved ONE in all? The naming of the ONE is just for the little self to realize this paradox. Many names were given, but realization of the unnameable ONE is the becoming of that ONE within one. And this is the same ONE within me. The Fana, Samadhi, the enlightened one, the Ein-Sof, the realized One, the Ultimate Tao, the Mystic Rose - these are some of the names humanity has given to the ONE WITHOUT SECOND. But, when realization or enlightenment is the natural state from which we begin to function in everyday life, one does not need words to describe that. Because ONE ALREADY IS THAT. The words are no longer necessary. Therefore, SILENCE IS THE DOOR, to enter the Palace of the ONE WITHIN ALL.

The Spirit of Love

As the Creator, the source of all life, lives in me, I live in that being of being. Consciously, I know I am light, and all my cells are an expression of light eternal. I am the source of the Great Self, in the living form of a human being. The spirit of Love is the road to this Divine realization. And I feel this love every moment within me and all around me. Peace and Love to all beings. The spirit of this source of love permeates and guides all the affairs of my life.

Harmonious Will

Happy is the one who knows to trust in the Creator of all things, to make the will of Him-Her manifest, and to work in harmony. This is the way to connect all the fragments into one whole. Breathe joy and light. Become whole, being creative and useful in all works.

The Fact that I Was Born

The fact that I was born in this world, is the sign that the Creator gives to me Enlightenment of heart and mind. The fact that I breathe the air of life, is the sign that the Goddess relates to me her love. In relating this to "others," I continue the Work of Light. I walk in the path of knowing and becoming that which I breathe. I align my small being with the Great Being. This is my heritage from Above, to channel to Below, and become the bridge of heaven and earth. In this, I take that which was given to me, and give in return to all around me, knowing the joy of relating.

Friendship

The most high and noble human expression of Love is true friendship. Ponder on the meaning of the word FRIEND, and you will hear an ancient echo beyond time and space. Be that Love, that Friend, with yourself first. And then you can be it with others, which are none other than yourself. Victor Hugo wrote: "The supreme happiness of life is the conviction that we are loved."

Only Peace

Peace is in me. I am in peace. I see, hear, feel, and speak only peace. Peace is in all beings. Peace is seeing, feeling me in all. I am peace, I am all, all is I am. I resonate the sound of peace in all my being.

Light

In the Light of my Creator, I bask and bathe. Then, from that center of Light, I radiate thoughts of Peace to all creation.

At This Quiet Place and Hour

My hands stretched toward the Supreme Being of Light, reaching high to the realms of wonder and joy, the feeling of confidence envelops me at this quiet place and hour. I know that with this confidence in my heart, my work is guided for the benefit of mankind in many ways. I elevate my consciousness to the invisible, renewing my everyday consciousness for the purpose of serving, in love and wisdom.

The Song

The Joy of Being envelops me. The breath vibrating in me sings the Glory of God, my Creator, my friend, my sustainer, my protector and my beloved. The Joy of Being sings the song of fresh Morning, with early blessings of the Creation. I patiently await the guidance from the Dweller of all hearts. May Peace and Joy of being be with all worlds.

No Heaven, No Earth

The Psalmist sings: "With His word all the heavens are made, and with the spirit of His Mouth all His workers." "Heaven" is only a convenient term for human understanding, so that one may see the symbol and what it represents. In reality, there is NO heaven, and NO earth. Ponder on this.

Beyond Appearances

See beyond appearances that deceive. There is more than our physical organism. When you meet someone, see the inner person in him or in her. The ancient sage says, "Do not look at the container, only what it contains." Both container and content are important, each in its right time and place. To see only one aspect is to be blind to the all.

Keep Me Sane in the Midst of Madness

Beloved One, beyond form and name, my maker and my Divine One - I ask that you keep me sane in the midst of madness. In strife and difficulties, keep me still in the midst of turmoil. In tumultuous times, Beloved One, keep me silent in the midst of noise. Keep me whole in the midst of parts. Keep me sane in the midst of madness. Keep me joyous in chaos and sadness. And, may sanity be with us all.

With Eyes to See

This world is in essence full of love and order, for those who have eyes to see. Only a limited way of thinking blinds one from seeing this true reality. From the Divine Order-Mind-Truth, I see this vehicle where I reside in this time-space continuum. This body-temple is the instrument of seeing this Divine Order at work on all planes.

May We Be Delivered

May we be delivered from personal and material slavery. May the blinders be removed so we can begin to see who we really are, as we really are. May we enlarge our view of ourselves and the Universe, so that we may work in attunement with the Order of nature, which is the Book of Life. May we read and live this Book.

The Great Plan

Every person has the ability to become more and more aware of their part to play in this world, according to the Great Cosmic Plan. This opens new doors for the unfolding of human consciousness. This is something still unknown to many here on earth. Discover that role through self-observation without condition. Become the eye itself, that sees to be seen. Radiate conscious awareness. Speak consciously to all you meet. Use discretion, and know that the "Director Within" is always guiding you. Go, Be and Do.

You are the Traveler, the Path and the Destination

The illusion of matter is the obstacle to realizing that you are the path and the destination. You are the one that you are looking for. Comprehending the union of God and humanity is the state of all states. It is a condition of all conditions, a realization that transcends the whole of the cosmos. And yet, it is as close as the marrow in our bones. Merging the personal self with the self of all is both the path and the destination. It is a oneness beyond compare—

beyond time and space and all causes, beyond the little ego and all the conditioned senses of the "I."

This divine understanding will ease all the seeming difficulties of daily life. It is available to all who seek earnestly, beyond curiosity; only for them is the door open wide. Only for them is the realization that the Path and the Destination are one.

A Being of Light

At this state of evolution, what humanity needs most of all is a genuine practice of being kind to oneself, and to the "other," which is none other than one's own self. In reality, you are a being of light, already perfect. It is the little self that sidetracks you from your true being. Your body is a vessel of great importance, an instrument capable of generating the light within, and radiating it to all without.

So, bless your eyes that see. Bless the feet that allow you to walk without fear. Bless the mouth that utters the truth of your inner being. Mentally, bless all you see. Mentally, give from your light to all that surrounds you and to all beings.

Whisper to My Ear, Oh Beloved

Whisper to my ear, oh beloved one, the words I write today. They are addressed to you who read them now. May you realize this truth and be of true service to all humankind. And, as you bless "others," so you are blessed a hundred-fold.

I Am Confident About the Future

I am very confident today and every day about the future. The "Divine Presence" acts and directs my thoughts through this "me." It is a gift to know this. This is the source of my strength in daily living. For this, I praise and give thanks, to my Rock and my Redeemer, my Creator and Maker, my Eternal friend here and now.

From My Heart

Great Being of Light, I stand in humility, still before you, knowing you sense the Presence that seeks to unite with itself. My head bends down, focusing on my heart. In self collection, my hands sense the beat of my heart, my king. In this holy moment of peace and tranquility, and with constant yearning and supplication, I pledge my birthright to be among you, Invisible Assembly of the Holy Light. I bear in "me" the Key of 9, the great symbol of 3 x 3, triple triangle. In silence, my prayers soar into Infinity, to the Whole "MEETING."

Beloved Invisible One, in my heart's sanctuary, the LEV, the 32 paths, lead to the mighty and awesome Place of silence, mercy and total Light. Open to me the door of Thyself, Beloved One, invisible to the blind. Into Thee I enter, and am purified by the "Fire" of purification.

Let me approach, be, and become united with you in ONE Flame, Invisible One of light. I come to serve and restore myself and the entire universe, as thou has ordained it to be. In thy will, all is done.

SACRED POEMS AND STORIES

Gratitude for the Gift of Life

Emet Mandala

Le Centre Du Silence Mandala

Shekhinat-Or

Singing Thy Name

The Horizon – Aleph

The Radiant Letters

Thus Saith the Aleph

Tree of Life Meditation

Waiting for the Messiah

The Song of Samuel, Son of Hannah

GRATITUDE FOR THE GIFT OF LIFE

These words are an expression
of profound gratitude to
The Giver of Life, The Empty Space,
The Unnamable, and Infinite Source of Life,
The One without Two, that cannot be counted,
The Creator of the Whole Universe
and The Most Hidden "Mystery" of all life.
Adonai HaEhad, Hayahid ve-Hameyuhad
The One, the Unique and the most singular ONE.

אֲדֹנָי הָאֶחָד, הַיָחִיד וְהַמְיוּחָד

Please Be with me when I breathe
Please Be with me when I think
Please Be with my mouth when I speak
Please Be with my hands when I touch
Please Be with my feet when I walk
Please Be with me when I hear
Please Be with me in my silence when I meditate
Please Be with me in my stillness when I listen
Please Be with my voice when I sing
Please Be with me when I bend my knees to bow before you.
Please Be with me when I am that which I need to Be
Please BE with me when I honor my feet and remove myself
from the forces of darkness, and move toward the forces of light.
Please OPEN my eyes to experience the emanation of the
Concealed light of Eden
Please OPEN my ears to hear the proclamation song of
your Oneness in all creation, now and always.

אָנָא אֵלִי ! שְׁמוֹר לִי אֶת שְׁפִיּוּת דַעְתִּי בְּעוֹלָם מְטֹרָף זֶה

Please, Keep me sane in the midst of the madness of "this world."

יִהְיוּ לְרָצוֹן ׀ אִמְרֵי־פִי וְהֶגְיוֹן לִבִּי לְפָנֶיךָ יְהוָה צוּרִי וְגֹאֲלִי: תהלים י״ט. טו.

May the WORDS of my mouth, and the prayer of my HEART,
Be acceptable before YOU. Psalms 19:15

EMET MANDALA

EMET אמת in Hebrew means to reflect. In the language of man, it is translated as TRUTH. It is formed with three stones (letters). These three letters build the concept of beginning, middle and end, with regard to the way man measures time on the physical plane.

ALEPH א and MEM מ form the concept of Motherhood, source of all life. MEM מ and TAV ת form the concept of "death," which the Zohar refers to as "the transition from room to room".

Thus, we can say that Birth, Life, and Death are connected on all levels. It also depicts the concept of TAV ת and MEM מ, meaning purity, simplicity, and completion. It has the stamp of perfection. We call this "Holy Innocence." The root letters of TAV ת and ALEPH א are the cells we are made of. This is the original cell of creation, as the truth of being and becoming.

All the web of the universe is connected by the design of the triangle, which is the symbol of perfection and simplicity. The computation of the holy name is woven into each of the six small triangles, inside the large triangles. Wheels into wheels, lines and circles, coming into the harmony of the truth in each cell that makes the whole.

The letters, visible but invisible in the same breath, aid us to try to comprehend this concept, and live it in our own cellular organism. They guide us in the way of "Holy Innocence," and the completion of the work that we came to this world to accomplish.

The Center is the "Great Name," surrounded by all the letters, in the embrace of the one in all, and the all in one, and it expands in all directions to reach all who need to drink from the "Holy Fountain." The circular movement of the design suggests that this oneness is here, and all we need to do is to open our hearts to the OBVIOUSNESS of TRUTH in every level of our lives.

> "Turn it, and turn it, and turn it over again, for everything is in it.
> Contemplate and look deep into it, and wax gray and grow old over it,
> and stir not from it, for you cannot have no better rule than it."
> Ben Bag Bag – Pirkei Avot - Sayings of the Fathers 5.25

From Ecstasy to Lunch

EMET MANDALA

LE CENTRE DU SILENCE MANDALA

This Mandala was created through an inspiration from the TREE OF LIFE, integrated with the MA'ASEH BERESHIT (מעשה בראשית), and the idea of the MERKAVA (מרכבה), the Chariot.

Star of DAVID (Beloved of God), symbol of total perfection, thou art.
Balanced between Male and Female aspects of the Creator,
Propelled from your center by the 22 holy letters/elements of Cosmic forces.
Into an orbit of Merkabic energy you sail, wheels activated and turning,
Surging onward to the Great Palaces of the THRONE.

As above, so Below;
Upper wheel and lower wheel depicting the
GREAT NAME OF "EHIEH ASHER EHIEH"
אהיה אשר אהיה—I AM THAT I AM,
PERPETUAL BEING, ETERNAL, IMMORTAL
in all spheres of the life/death continuum.

The 22 central letters sit on the petals of our HOLY ROSE –
symbol of TRUE ISRAEL (YASHAR with EL),
straight with EL, name of all names.

Four wheels hold the Circle.
These are the four worlds of the Kabbalistic system:
Atzilut, Beriah, Yetzirah, Assiah
They stand as Guardians of the influx of LIGHT from EIN SOF (אין סוף) the Infinite,
filtering through all levels of life in all matter.

The Kabbalistic adage says,
"ALEPH IS IN ALL LETTERS, AND YOU ALSO ARE IN ALL OF THEM."
Thus, the idea of wheel into wheel into wheel.

All this activity, dynamic in its own ALEPH energy, supports and nourishes the letters in their paths to manifest visibly into one's Neshama (Soul נשמה). Thus, when one utters a WORD, formed and created from this activity, one enters the Sacred GROUND, upon which the TREE is rooted, and basks in the LIGHT of the FIRST ORIGINAL SPARK.

Please see this from the multi-dimensional perception of yourself and allow the seemingly non-existent movement to move you. Thus, with intention and persistence, one can see the inner movement of this mandala, which is called, the **CENTER OF SILENCE** (MERKAZ HA-DEMAMA מרכז הדממה).

SHEKHINAT-OR

I am the vessel in which you dwell
With your Great Infinite Light.

I am the cup, the grail that contains you.
Your castle is the very cup of the wine of life.

You are the source of all things,
The womb from which all is becoming.

With my first breath, I inhaled your Divinity.
You are the unending spiral of life and death.

I know you have many names, and remain unnamable.
And the name I learned to call you is
The Beloved SHEKHINAH.

Within my breast and all nature
You are constantly present within all.

The light of joy within me is your light,
A light that is and was, before all things.

You are the wheel of life, the soul of the circle
Manifested within all beings and me.

You dwell within all life in many aspects
Of becoming, with many faces,
But you are one and unique.

I know you intimately in my dreams,
And you reveal yourself to those who
Have eyes to see and ears to hear.

You are the very soul of nature,
The voice of all voices.

You are the invisible connecting link
Of all that is, seen and unseen.
Your celestial circle is everywhere,
Whirling and dancing the eternal ecstasy of being.

Many seek your presence, but are blind to the obvious.
You are elusive, yet, so vibrant in my heart.

I know this to be my truth, beyond name,
Beyond form, beyond any human description.
And I call you the Land of Youth and Bliss.

Oh SHEKHINA! Universal life force,
The hidden female essence of my being.

You are my cosmic lover, my muse,
Forever my eternal desire.

You are known among the wise to be
The bride and the beloved.

You make me aware of my inner being,
For you are the voice of my female being.

I know and feel your inner murmurs
When you show me yourself in all my thoughts
And actions, and I am guided by your spark of light.

You are the Divine mirror, ungraspable,
Playing hide and seek with all life.

I read you in the Hebrew letters, in
The streams of waters, in the leaf and the rose.

Your name contains all breaths and forests.
Your circle is within the heart of all
I know your voice, and am filled with your light.
You are inclusive, merciful, and when I have
A glimpse of you, I become drunk from your elixir.

To you, I raise the voice you fashioned in me.
The eye's joyous tear is your sign of fire.

Wherever I go, whomever I meet, I see you.
It is you in the eyes of my mother, my lover, and daughter.
You are my constant neighbor.

Samuel Avital

In ecstatic love of the Tao, you are me.
In the darkest place, you are my light.

The subtle movement of Divine energy
Is your holy sphere of being and non-being.

I hear your love, and my heart trembles.
I walk the earth, and you warm me with your caress.
I know you, yet you make me humble before you.

From you I come, to you I will go,
And my path here is to know you more and more.

Until I become one with you, in the One Light.
Until I merge with you in one ecstatic love.

In all my relationships, I decipher your presence.
And when you are absent, I cry like a leaf in a storm.

To you, this song is written with your own word.
To you, this voice is dedicated in the wheel of my soul.

OH SHEKHINAT-OR, Source of my being:
Me, you, no you, ONE LIGHT.
One source of all sources, to you I sing.

Boulder, Colorado. February, 1985

SINGING THY NAME

Breathing the sound of my heart,
I sing Thy name.
Facing the sunrise and sunset,
Thy name sings me.

Hearing the Echo of Divine Voice,
I sing Thy name.
Leaning on the oak tree, resting,
Thy name sings me.

Watching the eagle's flight in the sky,
I sing Thy name.
Sitting on the summit of the mountain,
Thy name sings me.

In my sleep and in my awakening,
I utter Thy name.
In walking, sitting and talking,
Thy name utters me.

Floating in the river of life,
I sing Thy name.
Soaring within my inner being,
Thy name sings me.

Facing the East, stretching out my arms,
I breathe Thy name.
Drinking the waters from the source,
I inhale Thy name.

In light and in darkness,
Thy name is with me.
In heights and depths,
I sing Thy name within me.

Samuel Avital

In my sorrow and in my intense joy,
I breathe Thy name.
Being a woman or a man, one or two,
Thy name breathes through me.

In my body and within my soul,
Thy name is me.
In my heart and in the gaze of my eye,
I AM THY NAME OF THE ONE.

Boulder, Colorado. February, 1985

THE HORIZON — ALEPH

When I was a child, I was fascinated by my first encounter with the horizon.

One day after school, I found myself walking unconsciously in some unfamiliar direction, and suddenly I realized, consciously, that I had gone far away into the fields. Looking to the horizon, with those majestic mountains of my birth city of Morocco on my left, like a flute calling, I asked myself, "What am I doing here? I should be home by now. My family is going to worry about me." But under those blue skies, the landscape hypnotized all of my being. I stood there like a statue, immobilized with great awe, with the thought, "I want to visit the horizon. I want to go to the horizon. I want to be the horizon."

And my legs walked, and walked, and walked. The only focal point ahead of me was a single beautiful tree alone on the horizon line. One tree. That accelerated my fascination. I walked, and walked, and walked, while saying, "I'm going to meet this tree. This is probably the tree of life I learned about in school." I could think no other thought. I could see only the tree.

The afternoon sun warmed me, and, I was not tired of walking. I just wanted to meet the horizon, and rest under the tree, and praise the grandeur of creation. I walked, and walked, and walked. When a child does something, he does it wholeheartedly, with all his might, and so I walked with complete dedication.

And then, I was under the tree, looking up at its outstretched branches. I had reached my goal, my destination. I sat under the tree and read Psalm 104, and I understood, or pretended to understand, its Kabbalistic meaning.

The blurry afternoon sky made me realize that it was sundown. I stood up and looked beyond the trees, and there, amazingly, was another horizon. I made a few attempts to walk toward it, but I soon realized I had to turn back toward home. But first, I turned right, left, to every side of me, and I found the horizon embracing me, calling me from everywhere. And then, while returning to my home, under the stars, already the horizon had become me, and me the horizon.

It was only at that focused moment as a child, that I began to understand what ALEPH is, without needing words.

As one sage said, "I wandered in pursuit of my own self. I was the traveler and I am the destination."

And today, I am still fascinated by the horizon. It has no beginning and no end. If you try to look at the beginning or at the end you'll never find it. The horizon is in you. The horizon surrounds you like water in the ocean. You are the horizon. You are that ever-receding destination, the traveler, and the way.

THE RADIANT LETTERS

1.

In the midst of the storm that penetrates "me,"
To the center of my consciousness, my hidden soul whispered.
She murmured to me in silence, the secret of existence of the cells
That are working with faithfulness
The GREAT WORK of the heart.

2.

And like waking/sleep, I reflected in the endless space,
Between the sacred forests, between the huge mountains,
That hug the majesty of the horizon in which I dwell now.

3.

And Lo — The letters appeared with a glow of splendor
Dancing before me with a mighty light,
Enticing me to EAT and be satisfied from their wisdom.
And all of me was transmuted to be one letter, and another letter.
I am the letter, the cell, the verb,
I am the letters of LIGHT.
THE RADIANT LETTERS

4.

My eyes hear, my ears see,
My mouth walks, and my hands speak the light,
And I swim in the smooth, great light,
That unveils and guides me, to the
WAY TO BE.

Boulder, Colorado. August, 1973

THUS SAITH THE ALEPH

I am an ancient echo
who beats in the heart-bell
and awakens the flame to soar higher than air.

I am the echo of a message unwritten, untold,
Buried in the cell primordial, original,
The Yod that multiplies into eternal letters.

I am the echo of a forgotten song.
An unseen leaf reaching to the sun
In remembrance of mother-soul
that generates me to BE who I am.

I am a thought that has been transformed
into a dot, into lines, into circles,
into cells, into organs, into heart, into brain.
Briefly, my friend, into this "pen" that
scrambles these letter-words onto this white paper.

I am the place of justice, balance and tranquility.
I am the time into which all beings become.
I am the light that attracts all flames unto me.
I am the living word that comes through every mouth,
every cell in this eternal universe.

Briefly, my friend, I am Thou.

Boulder, Colorado. September, 1981

TREE OF LIFE MEDITATION

Please sit quietly and close your eyes to this world. We are going to go to an inner dimension, to visualize a few things to help us overcome any of the difficulties we experience in life.

See yourself in a great field of green grass. Green is a symbol of healing. On the horizon, you can see a large lone tree. You walk toward it. Count your steps, and be aware of each one, until you arrive and stand before the tree. When you stand before the tree, lift your right hand into the air and catch a golden key. Hold it.

There is a door in the trunk of this big tree. Open that door and go inside. Close the door behind you and you find you are in an elevator. Push the button 7 down. The elevator goes down and you can watch the light that says Aleph 1, Beyt 2, Ghimel 3, Dallet 4, Hey 5, Vav 6, Zayin, 7. Open the elevator door, and go inside.

There is a big hall and in it there are 600,000 people dancing. And they chant a beautiful tune, that nobody knows but you. I would like you to record that song in your memory. Let every cell in the body learn that song—a niggun, a beautiful song.

After that, you want to approach them to dance with them. So, you join them and you dance together. But then, suddenly, you are transported back to the elevator.

Standing in the elevator, now push button 7 going up. Look at the light that says what level you are on: 1, 2 ,3, 4, 5, 6, 7. Open the gate of the elevator, open the door of the tree, and go out. Close the door of the tree behind you and lock it with your key. And when you are in the green field, throw that key into the air and say shalom, goodbye.

Now lie on the grass that is near the tree and rest. Rest until you don't feel your body anymore.

And then, there comes a mysterious bird to wake you up, and she begins to tweet. You realize you know what this little bird is telling you. She is telling you her secret. But be careful, don't tell it to any human being. Keep that secret there. And stay on the grass, until the raindrops begin to fall and splash on your face. Then you open your eyes and say, "Aha, I'm awake."

WAITING FOR THE MESSIAH

Torn between the real and the imaginary,
between being and becoming,
between lucidity and madness,

TALIEL wants to catch a cloud to reach
the state of the Messiah.

TALIEL is a living symbol—the image of Israel—
waiting over all the centuries;
Waiting, waiting,
waiting for the deliverer,
the restorer,
Waiting for the Messiah.

TALIEL personifies the collective consciousness
of the Hebrew people, and by the same token
he is the interrelation of all the Hebrew letters
in their eternal effort to return to the dot, the source,
To return to the Messiah.

TALIEL demonstrates the passage through
waiting, hope, youth, old age,
jumping from cloud to cloud,
But each time he awakens with a shock—
History has taken another turn:
The Temple destroyed, the destruction of Masada,
the expulsion from Spain, the Holocaust,
Exile after exile.

And yet—TALIEL waits, ever reaching for
the ephemeral cloud.

He knows that the restoration of a being
can happen in the blink of an eye.

And then—suddenly, finally,
Is it true? Can it be?

From Ecstasy to Lunch

TALIEL has captured that cloud and rides atop it
like the true King of Israel.
He rides high above the earth's growing pains,
a struggling planet in its effort to become.
He looks down.
Behold!
TALIEL rides the holy cloud over
the celestial City of Peace.

Boulder, Colorado. January, 1980

THE SONG OF SAMUEL, SON OF HANNAH
A Praise to my Creator

By Samuel Ben-Or Avital

The Lord shall keep and guard him. Amen.

So may it be Your Will.

Sun, 30 March 1975 = 18th of Nisan, 5735

יום א, י"ח ניסן ה.תשל"ה –פרשת שמיני. חול המועד, ל"ג בעומר

<u>Parashat Shmini</u> - <u>Pesach Pesach – Hol Hamo'ed,</u> 4th
<u>Third day of the Omer</u>

אֲדֹנָי שְׂפָתַי תִּפְתָּח, וּפִי יַגִּיד תְּהִלָּתֶךָ תהלים נא. יז.

My Master, open my lips and my mouth will utter your praises.

Psalm: 51:17

This sacred poem was written originally in Hebrew

38 years ago, and it was translated recently

by a hidden Kabbalist who asked me to keep

his name anonymous.

If you speak Hebrew fluently,

the Hebrew version may be found on page 344.

Thank you,

Samuel

From Ecstasy to Lunch

I sing to the supreme G-d the song of my heart
and the murmur of my soul to unify You forever.

You chose me to be created,
in order to do Your Will with a complete heart,
my Creator and my provider of goodness.

You are great, beyond the ability to investigate
Or comprehend Your greatness,
Your strength always stands firmly
in the keyhole of my heart.

You have implanted and impressed
Primordial knowledge into the essence
of my soul, to feel and sense Your creation in all.

Lead me and guide me in the ways
of Your wisdom, and show me your wonders
in the worlds that are hidden from our eyes.

And emanate from Your hidden light
upon all of creation, so that they will know
and understand the greatness of Your creation.

Recall for us the earliest love,
and may the merit of our fathers always support us,
in any time of trouble and difficulty.

Show grace and mercy upon all of Israel and all of the creation,
and shine upon us Your glory every single day and hour.

Purify my heart and mind to focus
upon the repair of my soul
and to serve Your Will with awe and love.

Unify my being, which is always directed to You,
and do not conceal Your face from me
nor from Your nation Israel.

Samuel Avital

All of my existence gives You praise continuously,
and all of my breaths praise Your name forever.

Forever I will exalt You and make You great,
my king, from the radiance of my soul,
which You have guided in the ways of the eternal.

From generation to generation,
my soul longs to return to its supernal source,
the source of emanation and blessing.
Place me upon the straight path, to hear the small silent voice,
and to be a fitting vessel for the repair of the world.

Support me with Your providence in all my heart & mind,
to find favor and good thought,
in the eyes of the Creator and the created.

Help me, my G-d, everywhere that I go,
and set my steps to come
close to You always, with every breath

I will proudly extol Your great Name,
which is known and concealed,
and your Supernal Light
shall reveal to me all your treasures.

Your image and form is a help to me,
since the days of the beginning,
to do my repair and the repair of this world with love.

Bring my heart close to the Infinite Light
of Your Indwelling Presence,
and take me out from the darkness, into the light of Torah.

Have mercy upon Your nation Israel,
wherever they are,
and prepare their heart to serve You,
with a pure heart and a proper soul and spirit.

Place Your peace and kindness in the essence of my soul
and in all of the pure souls of Your nation Israel.

Repair my heart and my soul with the eternal existence
of all of the holy souls of the nation of Israel,

And send us the Messiah, the Deliverer,
very soon in our days,
for the auspicious time has come,
Amen and Amen.

שִׁירַת שְׁמוּאֵל בֶּן חַנָּה –
שֶׁבַ"ח לַבּוֹרֵא לְפִי סֵדֶר הָאָלֶף בֵּית.
ע"ה שְׁמוּאֵל בֶּן-אוֹר אֲבִיטַל הי"ו אכי"ר

אֲדֹנָי שְׂפָתַי תִּפְתָּח וּפִי יַגִּיד תְּהִלָּתֶךָ : תהלים נא. יז.

אָשִׁירָה לְאֵל עֶלְיוֹן אֶת שִׁירַת לִבִּי וְהֶמְיַת נִשְׁמָתִי לְיַחֶדְךָ לְעוֹלָם.
בְּחַרְתָּנִי לִהְיוֹת נִבְרָא, כְּדֵי לַעֲשׂוֹת רְצוֹנְךָ בְּלֵבָב שָׁלֵם, בּוֹרְאִי וּמֵטִיבִי.
גָּדוֹל אַתָּה וְאֵין חֵקֶר לִגְדֻלָּתֶךָ, גְּבוּרָתְךָ תָּמִיד עוֹמֶדֶת אֵיתָן בְּמִפְתַּן לִבִּי.
דַּעַת קְדוּמִים שֶׁתַּלְתָּ וְרָשַׁמְתָּ בְּמַהוּת נִשְׁמָתִי לְהַרְגִּישׁ וְלָחוּשׁ בְּרִיאָתְךָ בַּכֹּל.
הַדְרִיכֵנִי וְהוֹרֵנִי דַּרְכֵי חָכְמָתְךָ וְהַרְאֵנִי נִפְלְאוֹתֶיךָ בָּעוֹלָמוֹת הַנֶּעְלָמִים מֵעֵינֵינוּ.
וְעַל כָּל הַבְּרִיאָה הַשֶּׁפַע מְאוֹרְךָ הַגָּנוּז לְמַעַן יֵדְעוּ וְיָבִינוּ אֶת גְּדוּלַת יְצִירָתֶךָ.
זְכוֹר לָנוּ אַהֲבַת קְדוּמִים, וּזְכוּת אֲבוֹתֵינוּ תַּעֲמוֹד לָנוּ תָּמִיד בְּכָל עֵת צָרָה וְצוּקָה.
חוֹן וְרַחֵם עַל כָּל יִשְׂרָאֵל וְהַבְּרִיאָה כֻּלָּהּ וְהָאֵר לָנוּ הוֹדְךָ בְּכָל יוֹם וָיוֹם וְשָׁעָה שָׁעָה.
טַהֵר לִבִּי וּמַחְשַׁבְתִּי לְכַוֵּן אֶת תִּיקוּן נִשְׁמָתִי וּלְשָׁרֵת אֶת רְצוֹנְךָ בְּיִרְאָה וְאַהֲבָה.
יַחֵד אֶת הֲוָיָתִי הַמְכֻוֶּנֶת אֵלֶיךָ תָּמִיד וְאַל תַּסְתִּיר פָּנֶיךָ מִמֶּנִּי וּמִכָּל עַמְּךָ יִשְׂרָאֵל.
כָּל יְשׁוּתִי נוֹתֶנֶת לְךָ תִּשְׁבָּחוֹת תָּמִיד, וְכָל נְשִׁימוֹתַי מְהַלְלוֹת אֶת שִׁמְךָ לָעַד.
לְעוֹלָם אֲרוֹמִמְךָ וַאֲגַדֶּלְךָ מַלְכִּי עַל זוֹהַר נִשְׁמָתִי אֲשֶׁר הִנְהַגְתַּנִי בְּחַיֵּי הַנֶּצַח.
מָדוֹר לְדוֹר נַפְשִׁי נִכְסְפָה לַחֲזוֹר אֶל מְקוֹרָהּ הָעֶלְיוֹן מְקוֹר הַשֶּׁפַע וְהַבְּרָכָה.
נְחֵנִי בְּדֶרֶךְ יְשָׁרָה לִשְׁמוֹעַ אֶת קוֹל דְּמָמָה דַּקָּה וְלִהְיוֹת כְּלִי רָאוּי לְתִיקּוּן הָעוֹלָם.
סָמְכֵנִי בְּהַשְׁגָּחָתְךָ בְּכָל לִבִּי וּמַחְשְׁבַי לִמְצוֹא חֵן וְשֵׂכֶל טוֹב בְּעֵינֵי הַבּוֹרֵא וְהַנִּבְרָא.
עָזְרֵנִי אֵלִי בְּכָל אֲשֶׁר אֵלֵךְ וְכוֹנֵן אֶת דְּרָכַי לְהִתְקָרֵב אֵלֶיךָ תָּמִיד עִם כָּל נְשִׁימָה.
פָּאֵר אֲפָאֵר אֶת שִׁמְךָ הַגָּדוֹל הַיָּדוּעַ וְהַנֶּעְלָם וְאוֹרְךָ הָעֶלְיוֹן יְגַלֶּה לִי כָּל צְפוּנוֹתֶיךָ.
צֶלֶם דְּמוּתְךָ עֵזֶר לִי מִימֵי בְּרֵאשִׁית לַעֲשׂוֹת אֶת תִּיקּוּנִי וְתִיקּוּן עוֹלָם זֶה בְּאַהֲבָה.
קָרֵב לְבָבִי לָאוֹר הָאֵין סוֹף שֶׁל שְׁכִינָתְךָ וְהוֹצִיאֵנִי מֵאֲפֵילָה לְאוֹרָה שֶׁל תּוֹרָה.
רַחֵם עַל עַמְּךָ יִשְׂרָאֵל בַּאֲשֶׁר הֵם וְהָכֵן לִבָּם לְעָבְדְּךָ בְּלֵב טָהוֹר וּנְשָׁמָה וְרוּחַ נְכוֹנִים.
שִׂים שְׁלוֹמְךָ וְחַסְדְּךָ בְּמַהוּת נִשְׁמָתִי וּבְכָל הַנְּשָׁמוֹת הַטְּהוֹרוֹת שֶׁל עַמְּךָ יִשְׂרָאֵל.
תַּקֵּן לִבִּי וְנִשְׁמָתִי עִם הַנֶּצַח שֶׁל כָּל הַנְּשָׁמוֹת הַקְּדוֹשׁוֹת שֶׁל עַם יִשְׂרָאֵל,
וּשְׁלַח לָנוּ יִנּוֹן הַגּוֹאֵל, בְּקָרוֹב מְאוֹד מְאוֹד בְּיָמֵינוּ, כִּי בָא מוֹעֵד, אָמֵן וְאָמֵן.

WHAT ARE THEY SAYING ABOUT SAMUEL AVITAL?

Marcel Marceau

Maximilien Decroux

David Passig

Melissa Michaels

Rav Zalman

Moni Yakim

Mark Olson

TESTIMONIALS

"I think that Samuel's work is important. He brings awareness to the soul of people and gives the young dedicated artists who work under his direction the need, dedication, and love for the world of silence and the beautiful art of movement."

"Mon cher Samuel, Les mots seront toujours pauvres a coté de notre silence, mais ils ouvrent les portes a notre esprit silencieux. De tous Coeur."

"To my dear Samuel, The words will be always poor besides our silence, but they will open doors…to our silent spirit."
Marcel Marceau, BIP, Paris, France.,
November 20, 1971 and Denver, Colorado, 1980

"Samuel Avital—whom I have known since his first years with my company in Paris—I suspected would become one of the great mimes. He has fulfilled that promise. He was among the first to reveal to me what creative interpretation could be, surpassing the creativity of the art of mime in order to become a human being who dares to be different. This great artist has discovered an extraordinary relationship between being an artist and becoming a true teacher of his own method. Our acquaintance has brought the greatest joy and surprise to my life and art."
Maximilien Decroux
École Internationale de Mimodrame de Paris
Paris, France, 1961

"Rabbeynu Shemouel Ben-Or Avital, descendant and disciple of Moroccan kabbalists, has opened access to the language and content of the sacred kabbalah and the very studies of the sacred letters for those who have not yet overcome the barrier of Hebrew writing and language. He not only addresses the mind, but also the soul.

Being the master of Le Centre du Silence Mime School, he views the body as the "Merkaba," "chariot" of the spirit, and as a generous soul, readies you for the ride. May the letters connect you, the reader, to the Great Word."

"Shemouel Avital teaches a Kabbalistic Tai-Chi in which God and Man are fused in Mime. If only my teachers could have Mimed the world of Yetzirah, how much more I would know of the light today. Shemouel is a Kabbalist's Kabbalist."
Rabbi Zalman Meshullam Schachter-Shalomi
Emeritus Temple University,
Founder of Aleph: Alliance for Jewish Renewal.
Boulder, Colorado, USA.
April 10, 2001 and June 11, 1975

"I think Samuel has created simple tools that absolutely awaken the spirit and ground the body. Each learner is initiated into the reality that coded in the physical body are key principles for living a creative and purposeful life. He is a grandfather in this field of using conscious movement for one's inner practice."
Melissa Michaels, Movement Educator

"Shemuel has found an original way to deeply touch the eternity of our physical and spiritual existence…an authentic way to express Kabbalistic and Cosmic ideas with the medium of the human body. With the soul's means, he has pierced many ways to The Great Wisdom."
Dr. David Passig,
Futurist, Bar Ilan University, Israel, 2003
Author of "The FutureCode: Israel's Future Test", published 2008
and "2048", published 2010

"Mr. Avital is a remarkable man of astonishing depth and an artist of great magnitude and achievement. His profound knowledge of physical expression, teaching and performing is vast, rich and highly creative; his artistic fervor is contagious and his mastery is impeccable and practical… If you seek some truth or direction in life or art, stay close to Samuel for he might just then crawl out of his shell and give you of his soul."
Moni Yakim,
Movement Theatre Director,
Juilliard Drama Division NYC, NY

"Samuel Avital is an artist of conscious life, conscious theatre and cosmic laughter. When the madness of the world starts to get me down, I am lifted by the knowledge that men like Samuel exist. He remains unique, elusive, profound, demanding, dedicated, theatrical, passionate, and one of the most vibrant teachers I have encountered."

"Samuel's teaching goes directly to the heart of each person, challenging them to formulate their vision with unflinching honesty, chart their action with verve, take responsibility for their choices with relish, and then to free their imaginative powers from conditioned self-imposed restrictions."
Mark Olson, Professor
Juilliard Drama Division NYC, NY
March 17, 1999

DEFINTUITIONS

(A GLOSSARY OF EXPERIENCE)

DEFINTUITIONS

**Consider these terms, words, expressions and
suggestions, from various sections of the book,
defined via intuition, and experience working with students.**

"ALEPH" HIGHWAY.	The highway a person travels on to reach a specific destination. Sometimes we get hungry and take a side exit to a restaurant to eat and rest, assuming that, obviously, we will then return to the Aleph highway. But unfortunately, often we are on our way and stop to consider something temporarily, and we tend to stay on the sideway, forgetting to go back to the highway and our true destination.
APPLICATION.	The situation or an occasion where one manifests the learning, thus making the abstract concrete. Understanding by doing and being the learning.
ARTISTIC ZERO.	Natural posture. Physically, standing as a perfect vertical line. Being focused and totally present mentally and spiritually in all living situations. A state of being 100% totally in the present moment, as a preparation to be in the inner Artistic Zero.
BENESTROPHE.	Expect benestrophes rather than catastrophes. Bene is Latin for "good." Strophe means "to turn." <u>Thus, to turn everything for the good</u>. We can say that as we focus our imagination constantly on generating benestrophic events in the future, so it will be — by our positive attitude in action. By overcoming the negative with the positive, by filling the darkness with light, by finding balance and peace within, one can indeed remain sane, happy, and calm, while sailing one's ship amidst madness and turbulent waters.
BILL OF DUTIES.	We have the **BILL OF HUMAN RIGHTS**, which are now more important than the "Human." This connotes the rights to have, to receive, and NOT to give.
	It is about time now that the **BILL OF HUMAN DUTIES** must be written, to balance the giving and receiving in our consciousness. It is not just to receive but to give. This

is a very important principle for balanced and just living for all.

I am daring to hope that some intelligent and consciously awakened humans on this planet are busy writing this very important <u>DOCUMENT OF DUTIES</u>. It will likely appear when most humans evolve and awake from the unconscious slumber of "these days."

LE CENTRE DU SILENCE. A neutral space/time in absolute silence and stillness, from which clarity of sight can be manifested on all planes, with an amazing simplicity. The **Center of Silence** is an invisible dot in an infinite circle. It is a good place/time to function from, in total calm and poise, in any situation you are in. Teach yourself to always respond to life from a **center of silence**.

COMPULSIVE THINKING AND DOING.

We know that most of our tendencies lead us to be compulsive consumers, and to engage in compulsive thinking and compulsive doing. From that state, we tend to react rather than respond, thus creating problems where they do not exist.

CONDORIANS AND TURTELIANS.

Condorian—One with an unlimited view of reality, perceiving the whole picture from the Condor's expanded view. Because of this, Condorians are able to make healthy decisions both artistically and in life. They are their own authority, leaping ahead of the masses and creating true value for all.

Turtelian—The opposite of the Condorian. One who is lazy and perceives reality from a small limited view, lacking vision and courage to act.
See the article on the Condor and the Turtle.

CONSCIOUS INNOCENCE. A living state and a natural quality of being, where one is totally at one with their child innocence, and is consciously aware of it. A Paradox, yes. But, when one knows with "certainty" that paradox does not exist, then this state of conscious innocence can be totally understood, experienced, and lived with every breath, thought and action.

Clowns, genuine artists, musicians, painters, writers, actors, and yes, mimes, also have this beautiful quality of being, which is a great source of true and potent creativity. It is a kind of innocence, but aware. Einstein and some other scientists had it. It is known that the gaze of a consciously innocent being is the most powerful in the world. It can be, what people call a "**miraculous**" event.

If you did not lose your innocence after childhood, you will begin to know it and understand it from the depth of your being.

COSMIC ACCORDION. The journey between the infinitely small and the infinitely great, back and forth, and back again. Expansion and contraction. The ebb and flow of the breath, the dance of balanced being

THE DOORS ARE ALWAYS OPEN.
When a door bangs shut, most people are attracted to the noise and get distracted by where all the attention is. However, the time when the door is shut is the **exact moment** when you should be looking for the next door that is now opened before you.

There is no need for "keys." But if you feel you need a "key," remember, YOU are the key. Use it and enter the door.

ELASTICIZING THE PRESENT.
Stretching the moment, elongating the moment. Being 100% present, breathing the Great Breath.

ELEPHANT IN THE DARK MENTALITY.
Seeing only the part, not the whole.

ENDARKENMENT. The exact opposite of enlightenment, meaning the unconscious state of sleep and slumber that most humans are always in, away from the essential self and especially from this present moment.

EXPERTS ARE THE ULTIMATE IGNORANTS.
"Intelligent" people who specialize only in one topic, that pretend to know, and speak nonsense based on supposition and guessing.

FIRST THOUGHT, LAST THOUGHT (FTLT).

Become aware of your first thought when you awake in the morning, and your last thought before you sleep. Before you sleep, do a **daily review** of your thoughts and experiences of the day, and resolve to sleep well with a clean conscience of having lived that day with awareness and honesty.

FROM ECSTASY TO LUNCH.

The ability to always return to the Artistic Zero from any state, at any moment. The ability to remain totally here while transiting from here to there, from sadness to joy, from inhaling to exhaling, etc. The state of "between."

GIVE IT FIRST.

If you want something in this life, give it first.

GRASPING THE VOID.

Working in the space between thought and action, between the yes and no. <u>The music happens between the piano keys</u>. To be always in the state of between, the state of transit, as all is passing and nothing is permanent.

THE GREAT SECRET OF THE UNIVERSE!

<u>Remember</u>! I asked you in every session— What is the greatest secret of the universe? It is so obvious that you may have difficulty to answer.

It is the breath. Notice this remarkable circulation of breath that allows us to live every moment. Always remember to breathe!

The reason we are not present and take our everyday movements for granted is because we forget to breathe. Movement with breath is alive. Movement without breath is dead.

HIDDEN OBVIOUS.

That which seems as if it is hidden from our awareness, but actually is very obvious. We do not notice the obvious, the state where "miracles" are occurring every breath of our life. Becoming aware of the obvious can reveal to us the "Miracle of life."

From Ecstasy to Lunch

THE IMPERMEABLE. This is a practical exercise for maintaining a mental state that does not allow outside events to affect one's balance and harmony. It cultivates the ability to be involved, yet remain detached and objective.

Visualize yourself wearing an invisible raincoat. Like a real raincoat that protects you from the drops of rain, this invisible one allows outside circumstances, events and energies, to simply slide off. The raindrops slide off, leaving the inside dry.
The rainwater does not affect the coat. Learn to become calmly detached, but not indifferent, to interacting with the world. Remember well: **Detached, but NOT indifferent**.

INHALE IMPORTANCE, EXHALE INSIGNIFICANCE.
This is a suggested practice, to balance between importance and insignificance. With it, you delete the pretense of being.

THE JOURNEY FROM THOUGHT TO ACTION.
Making the Invisible, Visible.
Jump into yourself. Un-block. Translate thoughts into words, and bright ideas into action. Transform the ordinary into the extraordinary. Make the abstract concrete. Improvise. Be spontaneous. Condense the time/space between thinking and doing. Tap your creative resources in a magical, entertaining, Body*Speak*™ learning event.

JUMP INTO THE FIRE. Do that which you are afraid of. Face your fears. Dare to experience the edge. **Envision yourself totally fearless**.

JUMP INTO YOURSELF. To dare to be yourself, awake and ready, being the real being you were meant to be. Live your purpose for being here at this time.

JUMPING FROM STREAM TO STREAM.
When one does not follow the path one has chosen to walk, instead going from one path to another, jumping from stream to stream, and thus getting nowhere.

"KEEP ME SANE IN THE MIDST OF MADNESS".

My motto is to say to myself always: **"Keep me sane in the midst of madness."** Reflect on this every second. With it, one can walk sanely and peacefully among the imbalance and perplexities around us.

The fear and negativities that we see broadcast from so many sources around us are meant to cause fear and weaken the human will. This is done by greedy and selfish people, who want to control people's will, to serve their own selfish ends.

"Keep me sane in the midst of madness" is a safety valve to protect one from those distorted thoughts. It is a reminder to keep the flame of sanity alive, by thinking objectively and maintaining common sense. Develop a keen sense of observation to identify irrationalities around you. Trust your own judgment, and practice honesty, even when people tell you it doesn't pay. Practice freedom of thought and action in all you do.

Doing this, one can stay alert and consciously awake, aware and ready to adapt to any winds of change. One stays armed with a healthy sense of life, with the determination to be creatively happy—and above all, to increase kindness to all beings.

Note: See the article Madness and Sanity on Broadway

MAKE NEW MISTAKES.

Mistakes are useful, because we can learn from them. After you are **perfect**, then you make mistakes again, so why wait? Enjoy your mistakes, and master the ability to correct them.

Do not be afraid of making mistakes. Please, I am just asking you to always be sure to **make NEW mistakes**, now that you know how to correct them creatively.

MENTAL CONTROL.

Observing reality **AS IT IS**, become aware of your thoughts as an observer, and the one who is being observed. Develop your mentality in a healthy, balanced way, using your faculties of thinking creatively, with no limitation. **SEEING THINGS AS THEY ARE** will become natural.

MINIMUM MOVEMENT, MAXIMUM EXPRESSION.

Small gestures can express greatness. Use the right energy and focus to create great results without less effort. Do more in less time. Leave the dramatics at the stage door and explore the expressiveness and power of simple movements.

NO BECAUSE.

"Whenever love depends upon something and it passes, then the love passes away too. But if love does not depend upon some ulterior interest, then the love will never pass away."

כָּל אַהֲבָה שֶׁהִיא תְלוּיָה בְדָבָר, בָּטֵל דָּבָר בְּטֵלָה אַהֲבָה, וְשֶׁאֵינָהּ תְּלוּיָה בְדָבָר, אֵינָהּ בְּטֵלָה לְעוֹלָם.
Sayings of the Fathers 5:19

I call this "BECAUSE." If love depends on some cause, it will not last. But if one loves and there is **NO BECAUSE**, that is a good sign that it will last.

NO UNNECCESARY MOVEMENTS.

This practice will lead one to a great state. One learns to move only when necessary, and not to do unnecessary movements. Economy of energy is attained through less movement.

ONE DAY OF SILENCE.

Fast from words and fast from food, in order to strengthen the immune system.

A suggestion: In a world full of noise, choose one day a week not to use words to communicate. Simply practice silence. Go about your everyday activities, and observe your essential presence at work. You can choose half a day instead, but do it regularly, the same day each week.

In addition, one of the great hidden secrets of longevity, as practiced by conscious kabbalists, is fasting from food. Done on a regular basis, one day every week, or every two weeks, this will prevent many diseases. It regenerates your digestive system, allowing it to rest. If possible, combine the day of silence and the day of fasting.

"PARADOX". "Paradox" is a deeply imposed conflict of intelligence, created by directing awareness only to one small aspect of one's being. In reality this is a tool in the hands of people who manipulate others to their own benefit. (See "Conscious Innocence.") Go ponder on this and you will find whatever you will find.

PERFORMER, PEFORMING, PERFORMANCE ARE ONE.
In a performance, there is the one who is doing it, and that which is being done. There is the experience of performing, and the ability to watch the performance. When all of these are experienced at the same time, all becomes one whole reality. Then performer, performing, and performance are all one.

PRESENCE. Charisma is the force of the personality. Presence is the life force of manifesting itself in the now. There is ONLY this moment, where all and everything is happening, right now.

THE PRESENCE ZONE: <u>The Posture of Enchantment, The Turnkey Posture</u>.
This Presence Zone practice is closely connected with the practice of the Artistic Zero. The idea is to integrate the two in order to sense the power within yourself.

For this practice you are free to choose any comfortable movement. You can sit, walk or stand, lean against a tree, etc. Notice your calm breathing. Just watch your thoughts passing through, like birds flying past. Observe them from this state. Let them go, and just be.

RELAXATION. A state of being conscious and ready to respond not react. A state of being totally here, ready to be active and creative. Consciously respond, rather that reacting from an emotional state.

RESPONSEABILITY. The ability to respond, creatively and appropriately to the immediate activity at that moment.

SLOW MOTION. To experience and do things slowly, slower that you think. This state of "Moving Meditation" can be done at any time. Move slowly, like a cloud — it moves so slowly if you are not watching, you do not even notice its motion.

STOP AND CONSIDER. In any activity you are doing, stop, and experience a moment of silence and stillness before continuing. This is the way to shift from reaction to responding. It can be done in conversation, in action, in planning, etc. Give yourself a moment to stop and consider any situation from a clear state.

THIS TOO SHALL PASS. גַּם זֶה יַעֲבוֹר

This well-known Hebrew proverb is a nugget of applicable wisdom. It suggests that nothing is permanent. When we are always present, we realize everything will pass. If you are sad or joyous it will pass, so enjoy the present moment of now.

THREE GATES BEFORE YOU SPEAK.

There is a proverb from the Kabbalistic tradition, which says that every word should pass through three gates before being uttered. At the first gate, the gatekeeper asks, "Is it true?" At the second gate, he asks. "Is it necessary?" At the third gate, he asks. "Is it kind? If you answer in the positive, go ahead and utter it.

UNKNOWN VERSUS NOT YET KNOWN.

"In the beginning was the word. Before the word, there was motion, vibration, movement—the source of all life."

Remember, the "unknown" is just that which "is not yet known." It has the potential to be known, if only you look for it, because it is there and always looking for you.

The artist is the one who steps into the "unknown" and acts as though it were just another day. That simple, ah!

"THE VIEW FROM THE HELICOPTER AND THE BOAT."

The ability to see things as they are from two levels: the objective (the helicopter-whole) and the subjective (the boat-details) to integrate and see the whole.

Observe any situation from your personal vantage point, the boat view. This boat view is personal, limited, with blinders. Then, take a few minutes to close your eyes, relax your body, and see your situation from high above, as if you are on the ceiling, or up in a helicopter. With this observer awareness, you can see the whole from different angles. Any time you need to make a decision, it is very beneficial to explore both of these ways of seeing.

Relax your body in any position you choose, while seeing yourself AS IF you are in the helicopter or the boat. Consciously do this 3 times a day, 5 minutes each time, until it is established as a consistent state of being.

WHO IS WRITING YOUR SCRIPT?

Be the Author and play the Lead Actor in your life, Now. This is a **Body***Speak*™ exercise to unleash the Fearless Creative Power Within You.

WORD HONESTY, BODY HONESTY.

You can twist the meaning of words and take them out of context, being dishonest. But you cannot do this with the body.

You can't turn your head 360 degrees, without **discovering** your spine. You do that by going to the edge of your limit in turning your head right or left. To go beyond that limit of turning, you discover the **pivot** of the whole body, and the rotation of the **spine**.

WORDER/WORKER.

One who <u>talks</u> (<u>words</u>) about doing, versus one who <u>does</u> (<u>works</u>). Develop the habit to speak less, preserve energy, and do more. Remember, the abuse of words can lead to verbal and physical terrorism.

YOU DO NOT HAVE THE RIGHT TO BE SICK.

This is a sane suggestion for my students that I emphasized over the years: The body is born to be totally healthy. Disease comes only according to the degree of our awareness, or lack of awareness, in how to nurture the body with healthy foods, healthy thoughts, healthy actions, and healthy behavior. When we interfere with our imaginary thoughts that have nothing to do with authentic reality, one gets a dis-ease either mentally or physically.

LAST WORD

A Letter for These Times

Last Word

Samuel Avital

A LETTER FOR THESE TIMES

As I write these last words for this book, the current self-created panic over this virus has been increasing. And with hype from the local and world media, it is doing its best to scare humanity. Yes, we must take care of this passing virus, acting practically and logically, but we also do not need to be swept up in the wave of mass hypnosis going on these days. In a calm way, we can use our intelligence to address what is, and not be swept by the general panic, or exposed to crooked thinking that plays on our emotional states.

Actually, I see this virus as a blessing, and also a warning for humans. It can teach us to slow down and stop abusing our energy and intelligence, those gifts that are naturally within every human being on this planet. It can be an opportunity to do a retreat to contemplate our true state of being, and get busy correcting our mistakes, and restoring our negative thoughts and actions into ones that are beneficial and productive.

Please consider the precious time we are given to isolate ourselves, and see the good that comes from it, versus the negative categorizations put on it by our intellect.

By slowing down, we may use the precious time of being present. We can learn to do just what we need, and not always what we want, and especially to curb our compulsive consuming. We can conserve our energy, overcome this wave of media frenzy, and consider this virus event as a good warning. It is an incentive to correct and restore our ways and characters. That way, we will not abuse the abundance of the energy given to us when we were born into this dual reality.

Our inner intelligence, when used properly, gives us the great faculty to choose what we need to live well and harmoniously with all life here.

One of the good ways to overcome this crazy wave of fear and brainwashing is to help others around us, to Increase Kindness, and to know for certain that <u>THIS TOO SHALL PASS</u>, and <u>THIS ALSO IS FOR THE GOOD</u>. Nothing is permanent. There is only this present moment to live and let live. Remember, nothing stays the same. Accept the rapid changes and adjust to the new way of being. And I am very confident we will pass through this wave, peacefully and safely, for ourselves, our environment, and all living beings. For those who know now, that Life is a mystery to live and NOT a problem to solve.

Bon courage and do DARE to be PRESENT and appreciate what is. I am confident that great results and goodness will come out of this dark cloud we are now passing through.

Samuel Avital, Friday, March 20, 2020

"LAST WORD"

"And further, by these, my son, be admonished:
Of making many books, there is no end,
and much study is a weariness of the flesh.
Let us hear the conclusion of the whole matter:
Be in awe of God, and keep His instructions,
for this is the whole duty of a human."
Ecclesiastics 12.12.

The Neshama - נשמה, the Soul, lands in the physical body at that precious moment when we are born, to experience the duality of matter—and at that moment, the process of life and death begins to occur. (In truth, one lives and dies every moment, with some cells dying, and some being created anew at every time.) This is something we can come to understand by practicing conscious sleep, and by being awake while we sleep.

While the soul experiences this great challenge, and begins to activate the function of the marvelous gift of life of this body, she begins to experience duality. And the soul has within her the ability to restore that duality.

The duality is in our bodies: Two sides, two hands, two legs, two eyes, two nostrils, two ears, two inclinations, etc. Now, according to the great gift of choice, we go here and there, right to left, good and bad, bouncing against both sides of the walls of life. One's choices result in a certain quality of life, positive or negative. And so, the gate of duality is on.

Please consider this simple fact: We have five fingers but only one hand, many organs and billions of cells but Only One body, many petals of a rose, but Only One rose. And there are so many similar examples surrounding us, but we do not notice them.

The body is dual, the Soul is ONE, and the purpose of life is to balance the two into one. The essence of being is one, formless and passing. The oneness of our being is always one, and the one who realizes this will see that, in fact, life does not die. Life lives.

The way to realize this oneness is available to any human being. But our own choices cause us to stumble in our ways, and then, we categorize everything as good or bad. The constant "paradox" perplexes us - all because of the illusion of separation, which we wrongly perceive. Meanwhile, we do not see the source of all of this: It is caused by our own ignorance in the choices we make all the time, without being conscious of them.

There is a simple way to realize this oneness, that is accessible to any human being. I call it the **"Center of Silence and Stillness."** Simply be here totally, noticing, in this very moment, the presence within stillness and inner silence. It is so simple, but most of us are too lazy to "stop and consider" this constant present moment of breathing and being.

The **"Center of Silence and Stillness,"** which is also called the **"Hidden Obvious,"** and **"Conscious Innocence,"** is a powerful way to begin to realize our oneness. It gives us a glimpse into being beyond the form. Our Kabbalistic tradition calls this "The empty space," in which we merge with the formless and the (אֵין סוֹף) Ein Sof, the Infinite.

So, you see that through our choices, we can realize the oneness easily. But the great obstacle we face, is what is called "Laziness." Actually, with every breath, we experience the continuous and constant renewal of life - we just do not notice it. But, with the practice of conscious and increased awareness, we can activate and assist this renewal of life within us. This is truly a good thing to do.

I wrote these words, to say that in life, we bounce from here to there, and we think that we are manipulated by this world. Instead, we could use our own choice of will to guide this form to the formless. It is possible to do this during one's life, while the Soul (Neshama) inhabits this body form*.

I called this book "From Ecstasy to Lunch," in order to illustrate this duality illusion, as expressed through various writings from different times in my life. This is to share the mosaic of infinite possibilities that give us glimpses into that state of oneness. In this, we find that state of just being and becoming, until… we realize that we are actually becoming that nothing.

The following verse illustrates beautifully that this oneness is in the vicinity of our being. It is very near to us and we can be it.

"כִּי־קָרוֹב אֵלֶיךָ הַדָּבָר מְאֹד בְּפִיךָ וּבִלְבָבְךָ לַעֲשֹׂתוֹ" דברים ל. ד.
"And the word is very near to you, it is in your mouth,
and in your heart that you can do it," Deuteronomy 30. 14.

So dear reader, please enjoy all these journeys, which are actually only one journey.

Samuel Avital

*(See *The Three Partners in Creation*, at the end of the article *Spiritual Archaeology*)

Samuel Avital